BSG

HOMELESSNESS IN AMERICA:

A Forced March To Nowhere

by Mary Ellen Hombs and Mitch Snyder

with a foreword by Daniel Berrigan, S.J.

Published by the Community for Creative Non-Violence

Washington, D.C.

Copyright© 1982, 1983, 1986 by the Community for Creative
Non-Violence, Washington, D.C.

All rights reserved, which include the right to
reproduce this book or portions thereof in any form
whatsoever. For information, contact:
Community for Creative Non-Violence
1345 Euclid Street, N.W.
Washington, D.C. 20009
(202) 332-4332

First edition published December 1982.
Second edition published September 1983.
Third edition published April 1986.

Cover by Patrice Gallagher

Photo by Michael Hoyt

Faith as Art, or How to Remain Standing in Gale Force Winds

a foreword

by Daniel Berrigan, S.J.

Sometime in your life,
hope that you might see one
starved man,
the look on his face
when the bread finally arrives.
Hope that you might have
baked it or bought it
or even needed it for yourself.
For that look on his face,
for your hands meeting his
across a piece of bread,
you might be willing
to lose a lot,
or suffer a lot,
or die a little,
even.

Theologians tell us that faith properly understood sets up resonances, contradictions, ironies. I agree. And so does art, properly understood.

This book is, among other things, a work of faith. It grows from the story of how many communities, with simplicity and patience and so large a store of courage as to seem positively unreal, set about mitigating an unspeakable injustice. Its roots are faith in action, about which we hear much from theologians and divines - and see so little.

These faithful communities are also artful. Not merely as a matter of tactic (though resourcefulness in the face of faceless bureaucracy sets one hurrahing); but as a matter of soul, principle. Their faith is an art. Which is to say, the members endure, enter upon successive stages and steps of human life, steps taken by those serving as well as those served. No exceptions sought; high points and low, good humor and tenacity, yelling and silence, beautifully cogent convictions, street savvy and wide-eyed presumption of human goodness. All of it is here. All is genuine, modest, patient, good humored. Faith is an art.

And what of the *work* of art? It is literally a life-saving task these communities have set themselves. In the winter, homeless people are dying in the cold. Every winter, people die. Their deaths (they being poor and therefore of little moment) are taken for granted. Built-in deaths, systemic, a phenomenon of nature.

These communities would have no part in this monstrous *laissez-mourir*. Something has to be done; such deaths are criminal, a capital punishment inflicted on the helpless and innocent. People must cry out, lives must be saved. It is as simple as that; the logic leaps the cracks in the public pavement (the cracks in our souls) and lands on the other side, on its feet. On the side of salvation; and in the nature of things, sharing in setback, public conflict, deep communion with suffering.

There is no need to recount details here, they are told quite capably and dispassionately in the text. Let me say only that the story of these communities and their struggle touches the wellsprings of life, faith, art. That it touched these springs in me. And that releasing the springs, these communities also put me gently in touch with gospels, modern and ancient. With Gandhi's long trek to immortality, and King's ineluctable truth and consequence, and the Beatitudes and the Buddhist vow of compassion. Faithful art, a faith that is artful. We have here tactics, action, self-testing, social thrust, and recoil.

And something deeper. A question of soul, resources. The question arises: What keeps a community going in bad times, when "bad" means the nuclearizing of human relationships, attitudes, breakup of symbols, loss of a common language, to the point where some grow mute and learn only to shout?

The faithful community endures. Faithful, they know how bad the times are. But by no means do they allow such times free play. They salvage what they can, they cherish and foster life. They know that a loss of this sense of the preciousness of life inducts everyone into the common madness, anomie, despair. No, they assert the power of a common life, they live it out, explore it, submit before its discipline, follow through on its task in the world. They never give up. Never give up on prayer, never give up on one another, never give up on those who have given up on themselves - whether these latter are the down and out, or the despairing, incoherent public authority.

The faithful know something more. They know that evil is no flash in the pan, no deviant occasional fall from grace. The Vietnam war was no random embolism stuck in the bloodstream, skillfully removed, health reasserting itself. The poor who die in the streets of American cities, do not die by happenstance. There is a system of evil, a self-renewing web of selfishness and cruelty, whose true character is revealed only in the Bible. Sin. The demonic historical persistence of the Fall. That web as intricate as a spider's airy parlor, strong as cabled adamant.

In it we are stuck. Or more precisely, to come to the subject of this book, in the web are stuck the resourceless, unhoused, ill-clothed, and ill-fed poor. Therefore they die, out of due time, after much suffering and self-defeat. They are people who by every canon of decency should not die. Their death being as ethically outrageous as the death of children by nuclear blast.

And in this sticky web, let me add with all haste, we also are stuck. One has only to encounter American structures to understand this. Or to encounter any of a great number of "counter" folk: communes, individuals, those making it with "simple living," the noxious Bloomingdale cliches, the psychology ripoffs, the airlifted gurus, and so on.

A thousand ways of falling, only one way of standing up. Systemic evil, immensely inventive and persistent; goodness, a flash in the pan. Goodness that is, so to speak, good at giving up. American goodness that partakes of the tricky time-sense of the culture itself, now stalled, now feverishly hyped, now up, now down. But seldom consistent, reasoned, patient, humanly reliable, imaginative, submissive to the long haul.

Injustice, as Peguy reminds us, is eternally self-renewing. It is reborn, it has its seductions, its epiphanies, this anti-savior, this savior of the few and executioner of the many, this demon infesting the makers and breakers of history, infesting revolutionaries gone sour, possessing the nukes and their engineers, seated in the "high places," thumbs down on our human chances.

If goodness gives up, it is not goodness at all. It is usual American conduct, good in fits and starts, good now and then. But not, as the old theology would have it, a virtue of the soul, a constant energy, a way of seeing and responding and risking.

Is typical American "goodness" enough? Let the poor judge. The one who is starving today can be fed today. But what of tomorrow, when he will starve all over again? And the woman who is battered, cast out today; one night's shelter is indeed something - but what of tomorrow?

These are questions that grow, that distress. What of the system, the web? The system does not strike at random, strike merely once; it is a triphammer, nicely calibrated to deliver repeated blows, death on the hour, the day, the lifetime. But what fuels so horrid an engine, who devised it? And how dismantle it? And finally, what to put in its place?

The persistence of evil; that is the first understanding. And then, to counter with a persistent goodness, a life of active virtue, a community in which it is less difficult to be holy; as a sign of a holy future, available to all.

Meantime, a faith that does not give up. This, I take it, is nearly the best we can do in a time when almost everyone, in one way or another, gives up.

"It is not allowed to give up." If I could read the silence of Jesus as he makes his dolorous way toward his execution, that is the look he turns on us. We are not allowed to give up. I read the look in spite of myself, I cannot not understand.

Not giving up; no great message for sophisticated Christians in an advanced culture. Everything, every ad, every political pronunciamento, every hype, flash bulb, successful face (they are growing rarer) - all assure us, we've made it, we have a better evangel than that, a more refined "spirituality," a gospel in tune with our intellects, our egos, our gross (*sic*) products, a gospel less abrasive, edgy, primitive.

(But then again, in this case too, the medium is one with the message; and the Medium here is by no means one to engage hearts and minds. No; but a dying criminal trudging toward a just fate, solemnly enacted, agreed on by church and state. And who can stomach that?)

Do not give up. Not much of a command. Nothing attractive, negative, a burden, a pain. Hardly calculated to make a noise in the great world, or bring disciples or a cash flow.

Still, given the times, given the nukes, given the waste of talent and brains in slavery to extinction, given the dying poor and the tottering social system, given Reaganmadness, given all this (and more to come) - not such a bad gospel after all.

Thank you, CCNV. My thanks, dear friends, to all who reach out in faith and in compassion. Please do not give up. Or to put the matter another way (but the same way), please allow that Thy Kingdom Come.

Daniel Berrigan, S.J.
New York City

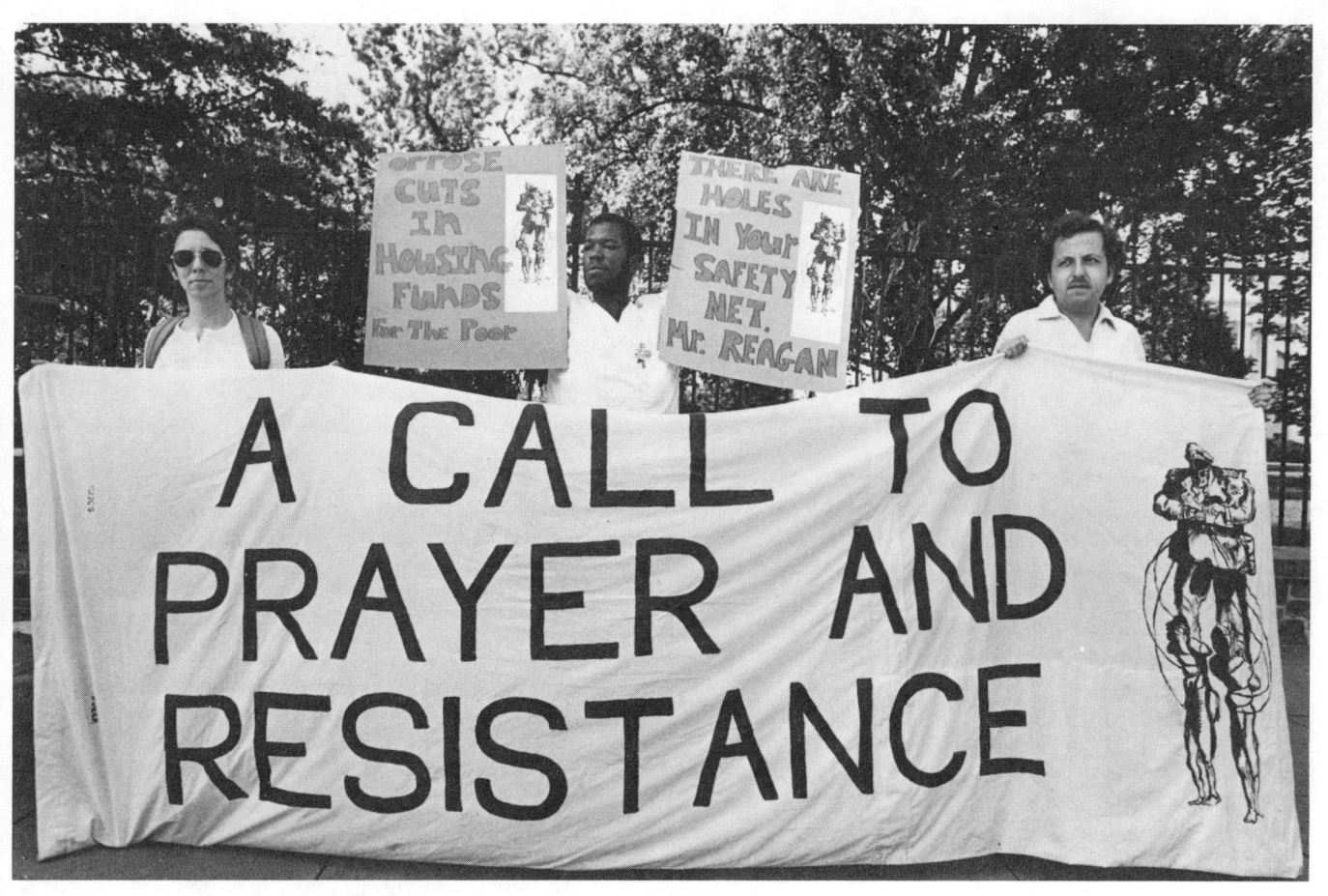

Part of the month-longth June 1981 presence at the White House in response to the Reagan budget.

Homelessness and the Hundredth Monkey: A Preface

*The Japanese monkey, **Macaca fuscata**, has been observed in the wild for a period of over 30 years. In 1952, on the island of Koshima, scientists were providing monkeys with sweet potatoes dropped in the sand. The monkeys liked the taste of the raw sweet potatoes, but they found the dirt unpleasant.*

An 18-month-old female named Imo found she could solve the problem by washing the potatoes in a nearby stream. She taught this trick to her mother. Her playmates also learned this new way, and they taught their mothers, too.

This cultural innovation was gradually picked up by various monkeys before the eyes of the scientists. Between 1952 and 1958, all the young monkeys learned to wash the sandy sweet potatoes to make them more palatable. Only the adults who imitated their children learned this social improvement. Other adults kept eating the dirty sweet potatoes.

Then something startling took place. In the autumn of 1958, a certain number of Koshima monkeys were washing sweet potatoes - the exact number of monkeys is not known. Let us suppose that when the sun rose one morning, there were 99 monkeys on Koshima Island who had learned to wash their sweet potatoes. Let us further suppose that later that morning, the hundredth monkey learned to wash sweet potatoes.

Then it happened. By that evening, almost everyone in the tribe was washing sweet potatoes before eating them. The added energy of this hundredth monkey somehow created a breakthrough.

But notice. The most surprising thing observed by these scientists was that the habit of washing sweet potatoes then spontaneously jumped over the sea. Colonies of monkeys on other islands and the mainland troop of monkeys at Takasakiyama began washing their sweet potatoes.

Thus, when a certain critical number achieve an awareness, this new awareness may be communicated from mind to mind. Although the exact number may vary, the Hundredth Monkey Phenomenon means that when only a limited number of people know of a new way, it may remain the consciousness property of these people. But there is a point at which if only one more person reaches a new awareness, a field is strengthened so that this awareness reaches almost everyone.

So it is with the problem of homelessness in America. We see this book as part of a process to propagate and deepen awareness, an awareness which, when carried to its inevitable conclusion, will result in the elimination of homelessness. Our ultimate enemy is evil born of ignorance, itself a product of distance from suffering's reality and source. In the following examination, much will be said about homelessness, but here our job is as much to tell "why" we have written as it is to tell "what."

There was a time when we did not see the homeless around us, even though their broken bodies littered our city's streets. There was a time when we did not make an effort to understand what we did see. We coasted, accepting the imprints that others put on what we witnessed.

Somehow we have come beyond that, each by our own route. We have moved closer to the people on the street, and we have been able to discern some of what their lives are about; some of us have lived that life ourselves. On the journey we have taken, we have learned a basic truth: we cannot change what we do not understand, nor, in turn, can we begin to comprehend what we have never seen. True power, it has been said, flows out of true knowledge. It is where and with whom we stand that largely determines what we see and, therefore, what we know.

Where has this brought us? In the following pages we try to report what we have seen. But it is not enough to recount our own experiences or recite the sad vignettes or heroic details that describe the homeless people that we know. We cannot assign their plight to individual accidents, sponge their wounds, and hope for a better day. We must look beyond what finally pushed each of them onto the street; we must give a searching examination to the policies and indifference that sustain such cruelty. Only when we put these diverse understandings together can we take whatever simplicity, patience, and courage we have and begin to alleviate the unspeakable injustice that is homelessness.

We offer first the basis for our own belief that the pain and misery of those on the street is more than the product of personal circumstance: both the roots and the branches tightly grip all that can be described as "American Life."

The forces, systemic as well as superficial, that have had long and short histories in the building of the army of the homeless - mental health policies, the Reagan budget, a deteriorating economy, a national history that has not always meant "liberty and justice for all" - can be seen as predecessors and determinants. This foundation is established with facts and personal stories that focus on the economic, political, and social sea-swells of our time.

Quite a few words are devoted to deinstitutionalization/mental health and Reaganomics. That is because both factors have had a profound effect on the size and composition of the homeless population.

The world around us shapes us, forming our perceptions and our responses. Having once established such an understanding of the framework that regulates personal circumstance - despite our desire to believe otherwise - we look at five cities where awareness has begun to take hold. In each of these places, some people have rejected a punitive or passive relationship to the homeless. Anxiously, cautiously, with fear and apprehension, the haves and the have-nots inch their way toward one another. As that space is reduced, hope and understanding grow.

Each of the cities represents a somewhat different approach. In New York City, for example, litigation has been successful; in Atlanta, the religious community hás carried the standard. Richmond and Chicago represent an earlier stage of development, while Washington, D.C.'s story is unique. In addition, we take a brief look at nearly 30 other cities from coast to coast, where a massive upsurge in the street population has elicited both positive and negative responses.

Problems and possibilities are spelled out in this way. The picture is grim, yet we cannot, need not, must not give up. We offer what we have found in the hope that it will carry each of you over that edge of understanding that will change life for you - and the homeless.

Mary Ellen Hombs
Mitch Snyder
November 1982

Acknowledgements

Many people graciously helped to make this book possible; others inadvertently contributed to it by their words and actions. To all, we are grateful. Help with sources, critical expertise, moral support, and constructive commentary have pulled us through the months of work. We could not possibly mention everyone who has helped; others we cannot fail to name with thanks:

* Kim Hopper, Ellen Baxter, and Bob Hayes, for their unfailing willingness to be with us spiritually and physically.

* For their assistance in preparing the special local sections, Peggy Hombs and Valerie Marsh of Richmond, Virginia, Elaine Lamy of Chicago, and the Reverend Eduard Loring of Atlanta.

* Mark Lee, who tirelessly read and critiqued several versions of the manuscript, with special thanks for his attention to detail and quality.

* Richard Miller, who was unfailingly cheerful through days and nights of typesetting and proofreading. He is our silent third author.

* Edythe Fried, who appeared at the right moment to lend her expertise with layout.

* Bob Weeks, for his generous help with typesetting.

* Barbara Koeppel, for her helpful editorial comments.

* Beth Goodell, for her invaluable help with typesetting.

* B Wardlaw, for his patience, dedication, and careful attention with proofreading.

* Most of all, we humbly thank all the past and present members of our own community, whose willingness to pick up our share of the load made this book possible, and without whose individual and collective pursuit of justice this story would not have come about.

We dedicate this book to all the John Does and Rebecca Smiths of the world. May our blindness to you end here.

About the Photographs

The Community for Creative Non-Violence has maintained a firm policy in regard to photographs of our homeless friends. We do not permit the intrusion of cameras into places where we offer food, shelter, or friendship, for these places offer some of the only refuge available. Nor have we ever encouraged photographers to use homeless people as subjects; the need is for more than photos.

Till Bartels
xviii, 5, 12, 35, 52,
54, 55, 121, 128, 133

Justin Brown
118

Cleveland Plain Dealer
26

Don Harris
101

Mary Ellen Hombs
6, 94

Michael Hoyt
42, 113, 146

Rick Janisch
11

Ken King
35, 53, 55, 89

Rick Reinhard
vi, vii

Religious News Service
30, 62

Dagmar Schroeder-Hildebrandt
17, 127

Shia
xvii

Jon Siverts
vii

Ed Spivey
114

All of the pictures of men and women on the street were taken by Rufus Wysong - "Pepper" to his friends. He has himself spent time on the street, come to know the people whose lives he depicts in pictures, and photographed no one who did not wish to be photographed. In spite of that, it is with extreme hesitation and a nagging sense of infidelity that we share these photos with you.

Lisa Turkfeld
99, 110, 111, 120

B Wardlaw
15, 35, 36, 53

Rufus Wysong
i, ix, 1, 19, 46, 50,
57, 60, 65, 69, 76, 79,
83, 85, 86, 87, 88, 98,
107, 109, 119

Table of Contents

* Faith as Art, or How to Remain Standing in Gale
  Force Winds, *a foreword by Daniel Berrigan, S.J.* iv
* Homelessness and the Hundredth Monkey:
  A Preface viii
* Acknowledgements x
* Introduction xvi
* Thoughts *by Robert M. Hayes* 1
* A Basis for Understanding 4
* National Questions: Who and How Many? 8
* Policies that Kill 18
* Mental Health, Mental Hospitals, and the Homeless 43
* The Woman Who Died in a Box 56
* A Quiet Violence: The Homeless Poor in
  New York City, 1982 *by Kim Hopper* 61
* Richmond: Southern Hospitality for All? 69
* Atlanta: I Was Homeless and
  You Offered Me Shelter 75
* Chicago: Does It Work for the Homeless? 79
* Washington, D.C.: City of Magnificent Distances 90
* Life on the Streets 107
* Signs and Symptoms: A Look at 29 Cities 121
* Oral Testimony 128
* Appendices 134
    * A Proposed Policy Toward the Elimination of
      Homelessness in the District of Columbia 135
    * Directory 138
    * Some Important Resources 144

Homelessness in America: One Year Later

Nearly a year has passed since we first released "*Homelessness in America: A Forced March to Nowhere.*" During that time, $50 million was appropriated in the Jobs Bill for the provision of overnight emergency shelter. Those funds "bought" 2.2 million nights of shelter - one night for each American estimated to be homeless.

In February 1983, the White House announced that federal buildings under the control of the Department of Defense, the General Services Administration, and the Department of Housing and Urban Development would be made available for use as emergency shelters. To the best of our knowledge, only one building has been put into service under this plan.

From every indication, there are more people on the streets now than there were a year ago, when this book was released on December 15 in conjunction with the first Congressional hearings on homelessness in 50 years. What has decreased, as a result of the emphasis placed on economic recovery, is the awareness of the urgency and magnitude of the problem. Thus, Congressional hearings entitled "Homelessness in America: One Year Later" are scheduled for December 1983.

While these events and developments might be construed as devastating blows to the effort to shelter the homeless, there is, in fact, cause for hope, and it springs from its customary source: the reduction of distance between human beings. Lives - both of the homeless and those who care for them - have been changed. We see and hear, in all corners of the nation, a modest increase in bed space, warmth, and compassion. In times such as these, it is absolutely necessary that we maintain a sense of proportionality and humility. There *have* been positive signs. They are a beginning.

Mary Ellen Hombs
Mitch Snyder

*I am done
with great things
and big plans,
great institutions
and big success.
And I am for those tiny invisible loving human forces that work from individual to individual, creeping through the crannies of the world like so many rootlets, or like the capillary oozing of water, yet which, if given time, will rend the hardest monuments of human pride.*

William James

> *I have encountered nothing in 15,000 miles of travel that disgusted and appalled me so much as this American addiction to make-believe. Apparently, not even empty bellies can cure it. Of all the facts I dug up, none seemed so significant or so dangerous as the overwhelming fact of our lazy, irresponsible, adolescent inability to face the truth or tell it. . . .If we, as a people, are to go down helplessly in a fatuous and seemingly unnecessary chaos, it will be this where-life-is-better daydream that ensnared and tripped us. . . .*
>
> James Rorty
> *Where Life is Better*
> 1936

Introduction

Americans, more than many people, are severely addicted to some very dangerous myths. Yet, we cannot address reality, or hope to change it, until we free ourselves from the fables that entrap us. Perhaps nowhere is this more true than in regard to homeless people. To see them clearly, to understand what their existence says about us personally and collectively, and to comprehend what their needs are requires this: we must face facts as they are, peel away stereotypical prejudices and delusions, boil off foggy thinking, and listen to the voices of those who have known and seen.

We must work from a single point: this is America, 1982. Homelessness is a national problem of massive and increasing proportions, affecting at least 2 million people.* As a fabric, it is made up of the consequences of a number of elements and conditions basic to the way our nation and our society function. We do not always choose to see these clearly, but we will examine them here in as current, authentic, and non-academic a fashion as we can.

It is significant that only two years have elapsed since we prepared the report for Congress. In that time, homelessness has begun to smolder and then ignite as a national issue. The signs of our time can be read in a few events.

---

*No one can say with certainty how many people in this nation are homeless. Not until they come inside will we know for certain how many there are. However, in 1980, we prepared a report, for a Congressional committee, on the national dimensions of the problem. At that time, we concluded that approximately 1 percent of the population, or 2.2 million people, lacked shelter. We arrived at that conclusion on the basis of information received from more than 100 agencies and organizations in 25 cities and states. That figure has since been widely used by the media, politicos, and organizers. It is as accurate an estimate as anyone in the country could offer, yet it lacks absolute statistical certainty.

In gathering information for this book, we have learned nothing that would cause us to lower our original estimate. In fact, we would increase it, since we are convinced that the number of homeless people in the United States could reach 3 million or more during 1983.*

Big Red used to be a professional country and western guitarist. Now he is middle-aged and an alcoholic. After eight years of living on Washington's outdoor heat grates, Red's hands are so badly burned that his fingers make crackling sounds when he moves them. His usual place of residence is the grate at the Corcoran Art Gallery. Surrounded by billowing clouds of steam, in a scene reminiscent of Dante's "Inferno," Red needs only look up to see the home of his nearest neighbor: the President of the United States.

In March 1982, a photo of Red on his grate ran in a two-page story on the homeless in *U.S. News and World Report*. The story was one of several similarly-timed media accounts. Among others, "60 Minutes," *Newsweek*, "The McNeil-Lehrer Report," and *The Christian Science Monitor* have carried feature pieces. If the winter of 1981-82 represented anything, it was an incalculable multiplication of media focus on the homeless. Most stories served the useful purpose of throwing a rope into the quicksand of our illusions, offering us a first step out of our ignorance. If we listened and read carefully, we could know that the traditional and persistent picture of street people as "dirty, lazy, drunken bums" bears scant resemblance to today's chronically homeless person. Wino, tramp, hobo: these are images from another era.

Homeless people are a complex group; their identities and the circumstances of their "previous" lives frequently do not match conventional stereotypes. Thus, shock meets the announcement of the opening of a free soupline for destitute children under age 12 in Washington, D.C. Among the first guests was a 3-year-old boy accompanying a 17-month-old. Within three weeks, "Martha's Table" was serving 30 children a day in a neighborhood that, not surprisingly and not untypically, has seen little change since it hosted the 1968 riots.

If these events awaken us to reality and to action, we must remember that others have paid with their lives to make it so.

Big Red

There may be a message in the 34-year-old Chicago man who was killed recently when the out-of-order trash compactor in which he had been sleeping for weeks was mended without his knowing it and the man, having conceived of himself as an ally of refuse and having been for all practical purposes refuse, finally became refuse and was compacted. But if there is a message, I'm not sure that I want to know what it is.

Ebenezer Hob
"Confessions"
Washingtonian
July 1978

There is indeed a message contained in the life and death of the man from Chicago, just as there is in the story of Big Red and Martha's Table. And, as Ebenezer Hob confesses, most people are not quite certain that they want to know what it is. The discussion, documentation, and reflections on homelessness offered here are for those who realize that they must decipher that message, regardless of where it may lead.

THOUGHTS

by Robert M. Hayes

In Pittsburgh, homeless men sleep in caves above the Allegheny River. In Los Angeles, homeless men and women go door-to-door in suburban neighborhoods peddling fruit. In Washington, D.C., homeless women sleep on Pennsylvania Avenue, in front of the White House. In Houston, the state director of the AFL-CIO tells the jobless to stay out of Texas: there are no jobs here, he says, and there are no beds.

From coast to coast, signs of the 1930's reverberate. Grapes of wrath, more bitter than ever, are being harvested in cities large and small alike. The crop of wretchedness is fertilized by a federal administration whose policies toward the poor are increasingly characterized by their heartlessness, a heartlessness symbolized by human beings living and dying in cardboard boxes.

For those under 50 years of age, these are - without question - the worst of times for the very poor of this nation. So, at the risk of playing the fool, I want to suggest that, with vision and with struggle, we can transform these times.

There are many causes of homelessness, causes which have been identified and analyzed here and elsewhere. We know that the homeless do not voluntarily choose life on the rough. They are not out in the cold because they reject offers of assistance, or because the homeless have a peculiar predilection for hypothermia. No, the homeless poor live and die on our city streets for reasons less related to personal pathology than to societal failure.

The roots of homelessness are as obvious as they are ruthless: a housing policy that is bankrupt on both national and local levels; an economy characterized by rank inequality and brutalization of the weakest; an incompetent, if not reckless, system of care for the mentally ill; a social service system so rigid as to disqualify the poorest of the poor - indeed a safety net replete with holes.

So the soup lines grow. The flophouses fill to overflowing. The park benches become crowded at night, as well as during the day. The newest token of a failed American dream is a cardboard box.

We must be frank about what we can do collectively. For now, and perhaps for the forseeable future, we can be but a salvage operation. We try to provide warmth from the cold, food for the hungry. Indeed, we shame both the homeless and ourselves with how little we ask.

Despite our shame, it is important to recognize what has been achieved - and what will be achieved - for the homeless, however much remains to be done. All of us who care for the homeless are besieged by adversaries, so we must be prudent and cleave to a goal that is modest, if difficult: shelter for the homeless.

Then let the most reactionary of our adversaries call us idealists. Let them call us utopians. Let the most heartless fiscal conservative claim we seek too much. For when we dare to ask so little - and when we merely ask for enough to preserve human life - our adversaries will be seen for what they are. Then room inside will be found for the homeless.

A call to action for a modest salvage operation is not an excuse to ignore the causes of homelessness. If we fight for the homeless, we of course will demand affordable housing for all Americans. If we fight for the homeless, we of course will reject economic and monetary policies that create and promote joblessness. If we fight for the homeless, we of course will seek to secure decent community services for the mentally ill. If we fight for the homeless, we of course will denounce a diversion of public resources from the needy to the greedy.

But the immediate job, the job that for many of us defines our day-to-day work, is the most basic. It is the fight to shelter the homeless. To feed the hungry. To preserve life. That isn't much to ask.

Or is it? In my gloomiest moments, I am shaken by the realization of how difficult even this modest goal may be to attain. Our battle to provide mere shelter for the homeless will be waged against forces of ignorance, apathy, bigotry, and in some cases, petty-minded meanness.

Some examples follow:

> *In Eugene, Oregon, the city manager, under pressure from business interests, is using the area's zoning laws to attempt to close the principal shelter for the homeless.*
>
> *In Fort Lauderdale, Florida, a city council member proposed spraying public trash cans with rat poison because he found offensive the sight of the homeless picking through garbage for food.*
>
> *In Phoenix, Arizona, the city - fearful that the homeless in the downtown area would stifle urban renewal - decided to terminate services to them in the belief that they would then go away.*
>
> *In Washington, D.C., with only 72-hours notice, two volunteer attorneys stopped the mayor from shutting down all municipal shelters for men in a city where thousands of people live on the street.*
>
> *On New York's Long Island, Nassau County continues to deny emergency housing to the homeless even in the face of public reprimands from the courts and the state social service agency.*

Robert M. Hayes is counsel to the Coalition for the Homeless in New York City. As an attorney in a Wall Street firm, he was responsible for several landmark suits on behalf of homeless people.

New York City - the one municipality doing more for the homeless than any other in the country - has adopted a public policy that shelter will be provided only in large human warehouses, preferably far removed from public view. A leading social service official suggests that some of the poor seeking shelter from the city do not deserve shelter at all, that they are not "truly homeless."

These are some of the adversaries we face. With the causes of homelessness intensifying, and with feeble responses abounding throughout the country, you will understand my fear of playing the fool in proposing that we can turn this around. I can't marshal the evidence to prove that we *can*, but things are stirring that lead me to believe that it is possible.

In the first place, while the homeless have not broken out of their anonymity, they are shedding their invisibility. This may well be the key. Once the myths surrounding homelessness fall away, I believe that very few Americans will tolerate other human beings living and dying on the streets of this country.

In Denver - a city without public shelter - a single parish opened its church doors to the destitute. Within days, 500 homeless men and women found refuge in the church's pews. Contributions to the church skyrocketed.

In one New York neighborhood, when a church asked for volunteers to help run an emergency shelter, more than 150 people signed up.

In Minneapolis-St. Paul, church after church joined in a crusade this past winter to shelter the homeless of those cities.

On an even larger scale, in New York City, under a mayor not universally recognized for his sensitivity to the plight of the poor, public sentiment forced a dramatic expansion and improvement of that city's shelter facilities. The city government was asked to open shelters in many neighborhoods.

Indeed, throughout the country, public attention is focusing on the lives of these poorest of poor people. Popular support to shelter the homeless invariably follows this attention.

It is this insistence that the homeless not be allowed to live and die on our streets that is creating a climate that will enable us to develop what the homeless so desperately need: beds. It is that climate which we must utilize. Now.

Dorothy Day wrote that those of us who labor on behalf of the poor need not see results. "Our work is to sow," she said. "Another generation will be reaping the harvest." That, in large measure, must be the credo of those of us working for and with the homeless.

But I believe that we - our generation - can reap not only a harvest of bitterness but one of caring and comfort for the homeless.

Our work, like the work of Sisyphus, is work which will never be finally done. But it is work where each incremental step forward, however small, is a significant one.

For each step eases human pain. Each step preserves human life.

The homeless are indeed the most egregious symbol of a cruel economy, an unresponsive government, a festering value system. The homeless are human beings: hurting, crying, bleeding, sweating, freezing human beings.

To rage against such visible human suffering is the right course; it is the moral course; it is the true course.

So we must rage, and we must reason, and we must work, and we must build.

And we must - and we shall - shelter the homeless.

Man has places in his heart which do not yet exist, and into them enters suffering, in order that they may have existence.

Leon Bloy (1846-1917)
French author and social critic

A Basis for Understanding

The poorest of the poor - the homeless - are literally on the streets, without resources and absent any choices save those that promise survival. Statistically non-existent, they simply slide off the charts and graphs that fail to tell the story of their lives.

They are our nation's untouchables, those for whom the binding threads of emotional and material well-being have continuously frayed until, finally, they live, barely surviving, on the very fringe of life, often sacrificing everything else in the quest for physical necessities.

We live in a disposable society, a throwaway culture. The homeless are our human refuse, remnants of a culture that assigns a pathologically high value to independence and productivity. America is a land where you *are* what you consume and produce. The homeless are simply surplus souls in a system firmly rooted in competition and self-interest, in which only the "strongest" (i.e., those who fit most snugly within the confines of a purely arbitrary norm) will survive.

Who lives on our streets and in our back alleys? Those who, for a myriad of reasons, silently plummet through changes of circumstance, with no hand to grab, until they finally - and quickly - hit bottom. Some are senile, others alcoholic. Many are unemployed, victims of harsh economic realities and congenital poverty: the last to be hired, the first to be fired. There are the physically disabled and the mentally incapacitated; there are victims of urban renewal and the brutal scythe that is Reaganomics. All share equally in the democracy that is poverty: bodies broken, spirits equally disfigured.

The combination of factors that gives one substance and worth in one's own eyes and in the eyes of others, melts away with the advent of homelessness, leaving the person physically tattered and emotionally out of control. We simply cannot focus on the homeless as people, though we may pass them daily. We see only beyond or through them.

When, in spite of our own best efforts, our eyes do focus, what we "see" is a reflection, not of reality, but of a persisting mentality of another era. Beset by stereotypes and old, outworn images, we ignore the facts and conditions of 1982, while nurturing increasingly questionable self-images of moral superiority and invulnerability.

Seeing and understanding "why" people are homeless explains a great deal about "who" is homeless. Personalized into names and faces, ravaged by time, anxiety, and the elements, old images lose their credibility. We can then begin to glimpse identities and origins. We quickly learn that, in reality, it is the old, the sick, the mentally ill, the unemployed, the disabled, the displaced, and the disenfranchised who populate our cities' streets.

"Why are people on the streets?" A list of structural causes, calculable on charts and graphs, comes easily to anyone who has examined urban and economic problems. Such a recital bears a striking resemblance to the one we wrote for a Congressional committee almost two years ago, but with an unnerving difference. The pressures in virtually every group of causes have multiplied under the Reagan Administration and have reached up from below to include working people who never foresaw such possibilities, and members of the middle class. The situation is deteriorating, and it is alarming: rather than holding out hope for relief and the promise of better days ahead, the times augur only increasing pain and frustration.

* * *

1. **Inflation**, especially as it impacts on fixed incomes, and the already marginal. Perhaps nothing makes more clear the kinds of choices forced on pensioners, old people and the retired than the fatalities of 1981-82. In virtually every major metropolitan area in the United States, people were found dead in their homes, victims of exposure to cold in the winter and extreme heat in the summer. People who rely on often modest monthly checks have had to spin a roulette wheel on which their very lives are up for grabs. "To heat or to eat," has become the question. They could pay for housing (whether room, apartment, or home); they could heat it; they could eat; or, they could pay for medicine, clothing, or other personal needs. But the chances were and are very great that they could not do more than two of these adequately. Thus, scores of people froze to death in unheated apartments, or huddled in heated ones, barely subsisting on what little nourishment they could afford. Some didn't make it: they lost their homes or their lives. If there was this much risk and uncertainty for those already housed, how much more suffering was there for those living on the streets?

Below:
October 1982 demonstration at U.S. Labor Department in response to first double-digit unemployment rate since 1940.

2. **The shortage of affordable housing**. Urban housing markets have been extremely tight, with high interest rates and very low rental vacancy figures. The "urban pioneers" are not marching as they were a few years ago, but those who live in the center city by choice are still taking a toll on those held there by economics or by race. Renters and home buyers continue to make incursions into neighborhoods once considered dangerous to live in. The price is paid by those who had no choice but to reside in the already abandoned and "worthless" sections of the city, and who will, as a result of ongoing development, be forced into the next devastated slum area, or onto the streets. Many newly-constructed condominiums are being rented out as a last resort by their hard-pressed developers; the low-cost and no-cost housing that came down in the builders' path (including abandoned buildings offering a refuge from the street) has never been replaced. Single-room occupancy hotels in New York City and elsewhere have contracted the terminal profit-making disease of conversion; they will soon be rendered anachronisms. Rooming houses and by-the-week hotels almost everywhere are receiving the minimal refurbishing that makes them appealing to budget-conscious travellers, tourists, and students and financially untenable for single poor people.

3. **The failure of deinstitutionalization.** This factor will elsewhere receive the more complete treatment it deserves. The deinstitutionalization of the American mental health system has contributed heavily to the number of people on the street; it is believed that mental patients comprise one-third to one-half of the homeless people in this country. Over the last two decades, the wholesale and careless depopulation of mental institutions has perverted the implementation of the judicially-mandated right not to be confined if one is not a danger to oneself or others. By the hundreds of thousands, mental patients who have been aided by legal precedent and the advent of therapeutic drugs have been released to the streets, often with no more than a bus token.

   This explosion of mentally fragile people returning to society occurs without the assistance and community support services that were ordered for them. The criminal lack of aftercare for such people has meant that their lives are often on display for the rest of us, contributing to one of the more popular images of the homeless: the woman or man, aimlessly wandering and animatedly talking, perhaps to an unseen companion. History will assign responsibility for these handicapped and helpless people. That answer will tell us who is truly mad.

4. **The burden of history.** At first glance, this might seem an overly-broad rationale for pain and suffering. Again, there are addictions to the make-believe that we studiously choose to ignore. Ours is a racist society. All people of color endure this evil. Black people endure it in the greatest numbers. It is a physical and emotional battle to grow to an adulthood that holds out little to many. Suicide, itself the product of hopelessness, is the leading cause of death among young blacks. There is a grim irony for the young black man who scrapes his way to voting and draft age, only to find that he must seek shelter in a city-run refuge that is housed in his former elementary school. Such is the case in Washington, D.C., but deep-seated racist manifestations and practices everywhere push the haves and the have-nots further and further apart.

*   *   *

'Concomitant with virtually total disenfranchisement is the reality of more specific historical events. The "War on Poverty," a noble undertaking, was, in fact, an abject failure. Similarly, we as a nation refuse to come to grips with the disproportionate suffering, injury, and death inflicted on black people by the Vietnam war. In nearly every American city, downtown streets are filled with knots of black men who fought our war and have only scars, stumps, night-

One of D.C.'s many evictions.

mares, and bad discharges to show for it. They have no grip on the system as it is, and they knew there was no "safety net" before anyone thought of naming it.

Our prisons, mental hospitals, and death rows are filled with a hugely disproportionate number of men and women of color. So are our streets.

5. **Reaganomics.** The pre-existing effects of the economic cycle of inflation, recession, and depression have been turned into a cumulative knock-out punch with the added factor of devastated social service programs. The Reagan Administration and rising unemployment have gone hand-in-hand; the exact numbers are of little importance because they rarely reflect the truth.

   What does count are the accompanying slashes in federal benefits. They spell disaster for anyone already at the bottom of the ladder and hard times for all those who are being forced inexorably down - rung by rung - by those at the economic peak. The cuts are familiar - food stamps, welfare benefits, school lunches, public service jobs, housing subsidies, unemployment assistance, heating fuel aid. What is not so well known, what we try hardest to stave off, is the acknowledgement of the eventuality of all resources crumbling or running out. The floor of the economic style of life we are used to leading gives way, the benefits run out, there is no way to make the rent, no job in sight, no one to take us in. Some very surprised people are finding themselves eating on soup lines, selling their blood, looking for shelter.

6. **Unemployment**. More than 11 million people are "officially" unemployed, and at least 1.6 million more have exhausted their benefits, given up looking, and been dropped from the rolls. In sum, nearly 20 million Americans are unemployed or underemployed. Not surprisingly, black youths have been hardest hit, with 50 percent or more out of work. Soup lines and shelters across the country are reporting the same phenomenon: the median age of users is rapidly dropping, and unemployment has become one of the most frequently given reasons for their condition. Not since the Great Depression have so many people been unemployed or homeless as a result of their joblessness.

7. **The breakdown of traditional social structures, relationships, and responsibilities** has meant drastic changes and deviations from time-honored ways of addressing all of the other problems. We no longer offer charity to the "village idiot," take our mother or uncle into our home with much frequency, or maintain relationships that are not "working." While this is the one category with the immediate potential to keep a person off the streets, it just doesn't happen very often.

The conditions and problems discussed so far are all symptoms and expressions of a deeper malaise, which, in reality, reflects deep-seated changes that are a product of profound contradictions and systemic inadequacies in our culture. We have built our nation on an economic value system that is rooted in the false assumption that through competition and isolation, rather than cooperation, compassion, and community, we can build a sane and livable world. We are figuratively and literally exploding, moving away from one another and our own inner center. Is it any wonder that we are increasingly isolated, insulated, and separated?

* * *

In the following pages, we will explore the problem of homelessness, and the identities of those who inhabit our cities' streets.

National Questions: Who and How Many?

No one would seriously question the existence of homeless people in America, yet many believe that the homeless are not to be found in *their* neighborhood, town, or city. Guided by outmoded stereotypes, these people believe that, if the homeless *were* in the area, surely they could easily be spotted - dressed in rags and lying in the gutter. They have seen few, if any, such people.

When we use old images of the homeless as a test of their presence, we miss the mark. Because most of them don't fit into this mold, we overlook them. We just don't recognize their presence among us. There are, in fact, many homeless and destitute families and single men and women in these areas, but they are often so ordinary in appearance and conduct as to be invisible - except to those who know exactly where, and for what and whom, to look.

A tattered appearance, bizarre behavior, belongings carried in plastic bags or cardboard boxes tied with string, swollen ulcerated legs or apparent aimlessness: these are the obvious features which distinguish the homeless from other pedestrians and travelers. But there are also those who have been able to maintain a reasonably good personal appearance and whose behavior betrays no apparent sign of disorder, and they are often overlooked by casual observation. Their presence during late night hours when commuters have gone home and stores have closed, and especially their repeated presence in the same sites days or weeks later, is the only telling sign. After midnight, a prime time for research, the homeless become the majority in the waiting rooms of stations and terminals.[1]

Thus, the older woman next to you on the bus may be going nowhere in particular, riding only to keep warm or dry or seated. Thousands of people live in the subway systems of American cities. The well-dressed man nursing a cup of coffee at the lunch counter is not necessarily an executive mulling over a tough business decision, nor is the family at the local campground necessarily on vacation. The homeless are, in fact, all around us, disguising themselves as best they can.

In the world of the streets, invisibility equals access, and those who can pass unnoticed into public places also suffer less abuse and harassment. Many daily activities, such as maintaining a clean and presentable appearance, changing clothes, scavenging for food, resting, or using the bathroom, are dependent on the ability to "blend," to remain undetected. Consequently, one can find homeless people who sleep sitting up to prevent their clothing from being wrinkled, and others who spend many hours and walk great distances to maintain a "normal" appearance.

- a button that is popular in Fargo, North Dakota.

That our expectations of the homeless can make us unaware of their presence all around us is well-illustrated by the following story. A reporter, standing in the center of Lafayette Park across from the White House, wondered aloud about the many homeless people he had heard were living there day and night: where were they? Had they been frightened off by tourists and office workers having lunch? In fact, at the moment that he voiced these questions, some 20 to 25 chronically homeless people were literally surrounding him.

With invisibility established as a necessary protective cover, and an infinite number of places to hide at night, the only reasonable and honest answer to the question of how many homeless people there are in the United States is this: there is no one who knows for sure, and only a handful can venture an intelligent estimate.

Numbers are fierce opponents; they pull us into an undertow of debate, or they generate a life of their own and become a self-sustaining center of attention. Those who work with and serve the homeless must try to convey a sense of dimensions, while those who fear that an accurate portrayal of the problem will result in untenable demands must minimize and trivialize the situation.

Through experience, we have learned that, since perceptions of homeless people are faulty, inadequate, or determined by economics, "counts" or estimates of them tend to display the same characteristics. The procedures for enumeration bear withered fruits because they do not reflect a real desire to gauge accurately the dimensions of the problem. While the intention of a census may be the best, what is absent is an understanding of the reality of homelessness.

Thus, the underlying dictum in counting the homeless is this: we will know how many there are only after we have brought them inside. That, in turn, will only happen when there is adequate and accessible shelter space, offered in an atmosphere of reasonable dignity. For all of the individual reasons that keep people homeless and hidden, efforts to find them where they are - whether through a police count, a national census, or a poll of welfare agencies - will be flawed and deficient. A look at some previous (misguided) efforts will elaborate on this point.

In early 1982, the Baltimore City Planning Department conducted a street census of the homeless, using police officers as enumerators. The result during a 24-hour count: 29 homeless people were located. Even if such a direct approach could yield accurate results, it seems a clear defect in method to implement a program with people whose jobs are usually at odds with the lives and ways of the homeless.

The person who lacks shelter is constantly occupied with meeting daily and basic needs - eating, sleeping, washing, urinating, defecating - that are often illegal when performed in public. These are "status offenses" which inevitably result from the very existence of the homeless. Police officers are the enforcers of these laws, and most street people, knowing this, endeavor to avoid their purview. Few - for reasons of survival and dignity - would answer a direct inquiry about their situation.

At the same time, painting a picture of police officers as totally unsympathetic is inaccurate. Many do express concern about the people they see day after day; many are personally grateful to have shelters to which they can take people, now that vagrancy laws are history.

Another familiar effect is seen when homeless people, desperate for "three hots and a cot," commit a minor criminal offense in full view of the police, simply for the material and physical benefits provided by arrest and incarceration. But a homeless person approached by a police officer and asked about his or her situation is less than likely to know whether jail, shelter, brutality, or nothing will result from the answer.

The 1980 national census was another case of poorly conceived and executed tactics. "On April 4 and 5, [1980,] some 80 census takers will fan out across the District to count the homeless in missions, flophouses, and all night movies . . ." They also planned to seek out those sleeping in abandoned buildings across the country; six million forms were sent to vacant buildings just in case. "There may be people living in these abandoned places the mailman doesn't know about," according to a Census Bureau spokesperson.

A D.C. church social worker recently visited a couple he was aiding in finding work. He had good news to deliver, and, since the couple had no phone, he went to the address they had given. The house, with curtains at the windows, seemed an ordinary one on first inspection, but he soon realized that it was abandoned. One entire floor substituted for the lack of plumbing. A census form was probably mailed there and to several other buildings he knows of where the needy have simply taken the barest shelter available.

Destitute, homeless people are not transient in the same way as students or patients, and therefore they cannot be counted in the same way. For instance, results of a one-night count at missions and municipal shelters did not reflect the fact that most of those institutions limit their use in some very real way, such as allowing people one or two free nights a month. Such an understanding would seem fundamental to constructing an accurate count.

The 1970 national census counted 18,731 men and 2,225 women who were homeless, about half of the lowest number estimated to live in Manhattan alone. Census figures for 1980 - whether from the two-week "casual count," the "M-Night" for missions, or the 6 million forms - are not yet available. But realistically we cannot expect accuracy from procedures that do not account for the living patterns of people on the street. Nor is it likely that people illegally squatting in vacant buildings received the census forms, answered questions about their plumbing facilities and income, and returned them to the Census Bureau.

When it was already too late, census officials requested, then ignored, the advice of people who work daily with the homeless. Specifically, the Census Bureau designed two special procedures for counting the homeless in 1980. The first of these was "M-Night," specified for one night and the following morning. Target areas were flophouses, low-cost hotels, motels, tourist homes, missions, train and bus stations, all-night movies, and short-term jails.

The selection of the enumeration dates (April 8-9) did not reflect the fact that the use of low-cost and free housing varies greatly according to the time of the month. Since some homeless people receive benefits of one kind or another, it is possible to afford cheap housing in the first part of the month. Thus, by selecting only one date for counting and by choosing a date that runs counter to this pattern, much potentially valuable information was sacrificed.

The second operation, the "casual count," was aimed at the following places where "highly transient" individuals might be found: employment and welfare offices, food stamp centers, pool halls, street corners, and bus and train stations not counted on M-Night. Procedures for this effort specifically stated: "[Such] individuals often have no permanent place of residence or live at several places and must, therefore, be enumerated wherever they are located." The choice of sites was wide-ranging, but there was no provision, as recommended, for using the homeless to find the homeless. Only those who have traveled the road of invisibility could help to transmit the vital information that would locate the homeless and encourage them to cooperate. Hiring homeless people as enumerators would also have provided them with a few days' work and some badly needed money.

While the enumeration itself has certain alienating aspects, some surfacing of current figures might have awakened the public to the size of the problem, but census officials did not take seriously such suggestions as the use of homeless people to aid in locating others and the waiver of certain personal identification questions. Again, the homeless person's motivation for unobtrusiveness and antipathy for prying questions work against accuracy.

A serious effort to count the homeless could have begun with the single act of opening adequate space. Admittedly, this is an extreme and unusual measure, relative to other census procedures, but it must be remembered that *every* American - homeless or not - has a legally protected right to be counted. As a group, the homeless are no more or less unusual than the procedures needed to enumerate them. But, in truth, in the 1980 census, only the appearance of a count was sought.

In February 1981, the Community Service Society of New York released *Private Lives/Public Spaces: Homeless Adults on the Streets of New York City*, a report estimating that 36,000 adults in the city were homeless. A sub-total of 30,000 men was drawn from an internal memo of the New York State Office of Mental Health, dated October 1979. The estimate of 6,000 to 6,500 women was based on information supplied by the Manhattan Bowery Corporation. The combined 36,000 figure became a cause unto itself.

The facts surrounding these estimates are readily available: 1) there has been a three-fold increase in New York's available shelter space in the past 2½ years, and each new shelter has quickly filled; 2) the same state office proffering the 30,000 figure acknowledges a state-wide shortfall of 10,000 beds; and, 3) there is an obvious presence of large numbers of people sleeping in New York's streets.

Nevertheless, Human Resources Administration Deputy Commissioner Robert Trobe had the following response to the estimate: it "irritated us severely." Initially, the city not only questioned the figure but announced in December 1981 that it would pay private consultants over $100,000 to conduct a count. In August 1982, the city retreated from this plan, but Trobe added that, while the city does not have its own figure for the number of homeless, it also disavows an estimate of 12,000 attributed to it in the *New York Times*.[2]

A local study of homelessness was conducted by the Interfaith Conference of Metropolitan Washington (D.C.), in June 1980. Information was provided by 30 public and private agencies. About one-quarter of the agencies surveyed were government facilities, including benefits offices, outpatient centers, and detoxification units.

The findings themselves are outdated, but certain conclusions are worth repeating. Estimates of the number of homeless people ranged from 300 to 15,000. The report concluded that, while no one had a definite answer to the question of numbers, there was one area of general agreement: 90 percent of the agencies surveyed said that the number of homeless people in Washington was on the rise.

In September 1980, the Community for Creative Non-Violence prepared a report, at the request of the House District Committee, that examined homelessness as a national problem. The study looked at more than 25 American cities, towns, counties, and states. Just as in the D.C. study, the nature of the findings, rather than the findings themselves, are useful. The CCNV report also looked at the role of the federal government in dealing with homelessness.

While there had been discussion within the Department of Health, Education and Welfare (now the Department of Health and Human Services (HHS)) and other federal agencies, of the need for a statistical analysis of homelessness, there were no statistics, nor were studies underway or planned which would attempt to gather that information. No federal agency bore responsibility for the homeless. This report found that, just as in the case of the District of Columbia, there are widely differing assessments of other local situations and a politicization of the information provided: "official" sources invariably ignored requests for information or minimized the magnitude of the problem. For instance:

> *On Los Angeles, California's Skid Row, estimates of the homeless population ranged from 1,000 to 8,500;*
>
> *From 320 to 8,000 were estimated to be homeless in Baltimore, Maryland;*
>
> *Although there were more than 900 requests monthly for emergency shelter, estimates of Dayton, Ohio's homeless population began at 150;*
>
> *Between 10,000 and 75,000 are said to be homeless in New York City;*
>
> *In Chicago, Illinois, the range of estimates is a mind-boggling 1,000 to nearly 250,000.*[3]

Figures in most locales are similarly unreliable. Local officials are constantly thinking of new ways to declare more people "not homeless" and send them away unserved. It is also common bureaucratic practice to define away the needs of those who do not fall under a particular agency's jurisdiction.

When confronted, government officials initially deny the existence of the homeless, and then point with pride to the services they have been forced to provide. Simultaneously, they look for new ways to avoid providing the services.

A case in point is Washington, D.C., where public pressure and federal court orders have forced the creation and continued operation of municipal shelters for men. Audrey Rowe of the D.C. Commission on Social Services, a component of the Department of Human Services (DHS), has stated that her agencies are not statutorily mandated to serve single people. Most, however, are grudgingly referred to Adult Protective Services as a route into the city's already-bursting shelters. However, as a result of research done for the appeal of the federal court ruling on the attempted closing of the District of Columbia's men's shelters (*Williams* v. *Barry*), it was found that a 1970 DHS regulation states that the social services branch "shall provide, on a contract basis, temporary shelter and social services to homeless, unattached adult males; homeless, unattached adult females; and homeless couples without children." Experience has shown that statutes and regulations are far less meaningful in determining the level and quality of services delivered than are the perceptions of the officials in charge of the implementation of such policies.

CCNV members testify in 1980, before the House District Committee, on homelessness as a national problem. Cremated remains of "John Doe" are in box on table.

When commissioner Rowe, Protective Services, and a number of other critical assistance offices changed their phone numbers in 1982, callers were still not receiving any referral numbers months later. How many concerned citizens or people in need called to find out what the city had available and simply gave up trying? DHS did not take any measures to insure continuity of service, because it is the reduction of services that most appeals to DHS officials who are starved for revenue and creativity.

People are not on the streets because they freely choose to be. Those who abandon the search for help are an important and overlooked source of information and direction. Obviously they are difficult to trace. Once found, they may be people with whom communication is arduous - victims of the long-term effects of alienation and oppression. But, just as the chronically ill tell us something about the efficacy of medical institutions, the still-homeless are a statement about the adequacy and accessibility of existing shelters. The simple implications of their existence tell us something we need to know and put disputes over estimates in their proper perspective. Consider the following:

> *In Washington, the homeless figure varies from 3,000 to 5,000. Washington's officials claim the estimate is too high, but they do admit that more than 12,000 homeless men have passed through city-operated and city-funded shelters in 26 months.*[4]

Certainly one thing the city affirms - the 12,000 figure - also indicates something about the other estimate. Each is a different side of the same coin. If the city's estimate and the available information seem a direct contradiction of one another, it is a situation which advocates for the homeless constantly encounter. What is even more amazing is the apparent unwillingness of the media and the public to acknowledge and explore those contradictions.

The 12,000 counted by the city were lucky; they made it to the shelters and found beds. What about those who didn't? No transportation is provided, so a homeless person must either be able to walk or get bus fare, follow directions, and arrive early. Those who can't or don't are surely lost, as are those who are unfamiliar with the city. There are no provisions for the physically disabled at the municipal shelters, and so they are turned away. Certainly among those who have given up and are not counted are those who are repelled by the prison-like atmosphere in the shelters and those who have been turned away so many times that they no longer make the effort. Which group is the majority? Those most familiar with the challenge of daily survival know that it is those who remain on the street.

In the few cities where such measures have been tried, the work of outreach teams and decentralized shelter pick-up locations has helped all those involved: the homeless have greater access to shelters, and the volunteers are exposed to more aspects of homelessness than are visible from inside the facilities. In addition, the work of personally committed individuals who help the homeless - wherever they find them - has added significantly and meaningfully to the body of available information.

As more and more families face economic dislocation and devastation, they, too, seek shelter in ways not easily discerned by institutions. It is in the interests of local governments to maintain the invisibility of homeless families, for the same reasons that they obscure the true dimensions of homelessness among single persons. Many of the families live in cars, abandoned buildings, campsites, and with relatives. Traditionally, poor families have doubled up (and more) during times of crisis, but for others it is a new and traumatic way to keep the family together. Safely situating the children is often a priority, but, just as often, men are forced to leave home to enable their families to obtain more public assistance benefits

In the face of severe and growing economic pressures on poor people, the D.C. government may have set a record for successful shelter closings, eliminating three in less than two years. Yet families continue to seek relief from city agencies. They have no choice. In a city where some 7,000 families are on the waiting list for public housing - usually for five to seven years, depending on their size - it is well known among the poor that this route does not offer immediate help.

Although conditions in the family shelters are predictably regimented and dehumanizing - calls are monitored, cooking is prohibited, no food is allowed, and beds are shared - many more people are eligible and seeking that space than can be accommodated. Most are forced to double up with willing and generous friends or relatives, although quite often it means family members must separate, with one or two going here and one or two going there. If space is unavailable in the family shelter, as it almost always is, DHS is willing to take the children, place them in foster homes, and send the parents to the men's or women's shelter. Not surprisingly, few families are willing to see this happen. Parents, even when they are deemed to be unfit for failing to provide a home, are understandably unwilling to give up their children. Once the children are taken, assistance checks are cut off, and obtaining housing becomes impossible.

While there is no way of knowing how many single homeless men and women were initially members of the increasing number of families shattered by crisis, it is important to remember that - somewhere - many homeless people have "somebody," be it spouse, parent, cousin, or child.

> *It makes it easier to accept [their existence] if you believe that they have no families, no relatives, no friends. Why else would they be allowed to live in a manner that some animals wouldn't survive in? Unfortunately, that is usually not the case....*
>
> *"It's less difficult to imagine [them] without anybody," says Tess Sneesby, a staff worker at Abby's House. "When you find out they do have people who don't want them, it's worse. No wonder they are incoherent. It hurts too much to face reality."*[5]

Even with so many disincentives at work, record numbers of families are applying for emergency relief. Despite the flaws represented by the numbers themselves, we can glean some insights from them. In Washington, D.C., for instance, the city records that it sheltered 406 families in 1981, but expects the figure to top 700 in 1982. The number of families who sought emergency shelter in Washington, D.C. in July 1982 doubled to 96 - the biggest monthly increase in memory - and the rate was accelerating even more rapidly in August, according to city officials:

> *"We were very surprised," said Patricia Yates, chief of the D.C. Department of Human Services, who blamed the deterioration of the economy and the lack of affordable rental housing for the increase.*[6]

According to published reports, about 4,000 evictions occur in the District of Columbia each year, and observers believe that the record wave now seeking city aid actually represent housing "casualties" from the most recent winter. Welfare and food stamp cuts that affected people in late 1981, causing them to fall behind in their rent, might only now be maturing within the legal system, resulting in eviction. Until July 1982, an average of 40 to 50 families per month had been seeking help. A motel that houses families under a city contract was told to expect the use of 40 rooms, but, by August 23, there were 111 in use. Said the motel's manager, "I was shocked. I didn't realize that there were that many homeless people."[7] Similarly, a D.C. Catholic Charities worker in an inner-city parish reports that she is seeing twice the number of people she saw in 1981 and has simply given up counting. In city after city, from one end of the country to the other, the same phenomenon is occurring.

In much the same way that photographs of the homeless can be a diversion and an objectification, so, too, can be statistics. Numbers can never be material for complete agreement, and they keep us a safe distance from those in need. Yet, statistics can be useful if we acknowledge their flaws and keep them from becoming an end in themselves, for they do yield an image of unmet need.

To this point, our focus has been on the role of numbers in helping to discern the dimensions of the problem we face. It should be well established by now that numbers are very political creatures. They can be interpreted much as the three blind men feeling the elephant and describing what they found: the picture you get depends entirely on where you stand.

As familiarity with the problem grows, and as more layers of the reality of homelessness are peeled back, there is another, more tragic side added: the injuries, illnesses, and deaths of those we know or have seen.

In sickness and in death, the homeless are no easier to count than they are at any other time. As interest and awareness have grown, injuries and fatalities have become a very sensitive and political subject. Even in the mildest weather, many homeless people are injured or die, because they are not only exposed to the extreme temperatures of summer and winter, but also to illness and acts of violence and abuse. In addition, the ravages of time and neglect, indeed, death from homelessness itself, take a toll.

In most locales, mental health and hospital patients cannot be released to the street, so a fictitious address or the address of a local shelter is listed. The effect is to obscure official hospital records and make it impossible to determine with any degree of accuracy the nature and severity of health problems resulting directly or indirectly from homelessness.

Mayors and medical examiners recognize the potential of an accurate portrayal of the ultimate cost of homelessness in lives lost, and so numbers are increasingly manipulated, falsified, and difficult to acquire. These are not statistics to which anyone can point with pride, though even one such death or injury would be ample cause for shame. But limbs lost and lives quietly squandered are a continuous, although well-hidden, year-round reality.

Deaths among the homeless are generally of two sorts: those that occur on the streets and those that occur in hospitals. In either group, there are frequently seen causes: violence (shootings, stabbings, beatings, fires, assaults), exposure to extreme temperatures (hot or cold), weather-related illnesses (including pneumonia, frostbite, gangrene, stroke, and heart failure), alcohol-induced (cirrhosis, cerebral hemorrhage, stroke) and a combination of any of these.

When death occurs on the street, the victim is taken to a morgue or medical examiner's office, where a cause of death is established. A primary and a contributing cause are usually determined. To facilitate record-keeping, every cause of death has been given a universal numerical designation. For exposure to heat and cold, the codes are E901 and E904, for example.

Determining the cause of death can be a highly subjective process, particularly in exposure cases, where the core body temperature is important and difficult to determine accurately. That, in turn, makes the process somewhat less difficult for medical examiners who are already reluctant to arrive at exposure as a primary cause of death.

At the same time, and usually in conjunction with the police department, an effort is made to locate the victim's next-of-kin. When someone is located, the next-of-kin's address will often be used for the victim, regardless of how distant the two may have been. Once an identity is established and someone comes forward to claim the body, the case is closed. If, however, no identity is established or no one comes forward with a claim, the body is either given to medical research, cremated (and the remains stored), or buried in a potter's field.

On December 28, 1981, the Christian Feast of the Holy Innocents, 539 small white crosses were planted in Lafayette Park, across the street from the White House. The crosses were arranged in 13 plots, representing deaths of homeless people in 13 cities or states in recent winters.

Weeks of research and investigation led to the synthesizing of the figures, and several things became clear. Perhaps we have difficulty enumerating truths we would rather not see; the very number of deaths and injuries are an indictment - and so we choose to look away, to postpone the inevitable. In Connecticut, Atlanta, New York City, Dayton, and Louisville, the information that ultimately was accumulated was obtained without the help of city officials, and, in a few instances, in spite of them.

There were wide discrepancies in statistical information that reflect local situations, politics, and the lack of context for tracking exposure deaths. In New York City, for instance, with a population of nearly eight million, 52 people froze to death in the same five-year period that Washington, D.C., with a population less than one-tenth that of New York's and a warmer climate, reported 45 exposure deaths. In

Richmond, Virginia, 23 people died of exposure and 30 others had exposure listed as a contributing factor during the winter of 1979-80, while the state of Connecticut, with a population of 3.15 million, reported that only 10 men and women froze to death during a recent two-year period.

Finding - in some cases amalgamating or extrapolating - these figures was an adversary process. Only occasionally were advocates actually assisted by sympathetic public employees, and by the time more crosses were added on March 21, to reflect the deaths of the past winter, the absence of help was even more noticeable. "There is nothing to be gained by your knowing, and everything to be lost," was the not-so-subtle message.

For some, the answer has been methodical scouring of old newspapers in search of statements and information from sources that later dried up. For others, the introduction of media inquiries has loosened up a few facts. In a few cases, "deep throat" sources were very helpful.

At the state level, where many kinds of health, mortality, and morbidity figures are routinely reported, there is less of a vested interest at work. Numbers are more readily available, though that is slowly changing, too. Unfortunately, while there is less reticence on the part of state officials, their figures are rarely compiled to reflect both homelessness and exposure as conditions and causes of illness or death; when patients are admitted to a hospital there is no way to differentiate between the homeless and the housed. Therefore, it is impossible to determine if death is the result of the absence of shelter.

While the homeless continue to live, suffer, and die in vitreous misery, slowly but surely, their pain and the injustice of their condition is eroding the wall of invisibility which, for so long, has kept them out of sight and out of mind.

Footnotes

[1] Kim Hopper and Ellen Baxter, *Private Lives/Public Spaces: Homeless Adults on the Streets of New York City* (New York City: Community Service Society, 1981), p. 22.

[2] "Homeless Census" in *Safety Network*; the newsletter of the Coalition for the Homeless (New York City), Volume 1:5, August 1982.

[3] The estimate of 250,000 was provided by the Pacific Garden Mission, the city's largest shelter, where 104,255 persons were housed in 1979. Traditionally, Chicago's homeless population has been enormous, fed by Appalachian and Southern poverty and unemployment. During times of economic crisis, the street population rises even higher.

[4] Anne Allen, "Who Killed Rebecca Smith?" in *Foundation News*, May/June 1982, p. 16.

[5] Carolyn Boulger, "Bag Ladies: The Plight of the City's Homeless Street Women," *Worcester Magazine*, August 25, 1982.

[6] "Shelter Requests Increase," by Peter Perl, *Washington Post*, August 24, 1982, p. B1.

[7] Ibid.

I don't think people are entitled to services. I don't believe that there is any entitlement, any basic right to legal services or any other kind of services... I don't accept that equality is a moral principle.

David Stockman
Director of the Office of Management and Budget

Policies That Kill

All of us ... together must bear the burden. The solution we seek must be equitable with no one group singled out to pay a higher price.

President Reagan,
in his Inaugural Address
January 20, 1981

Now you're hearing all kinds of horror stories about the people that are going to be thrown out in the snow to hunger and die of cold and so forth. ...
We haven't cut a single budget... We have been reducing the rate of increase that has been built in and that has been submitted to us for consideration in these budgets.

President Reagan,
in a speech in Bloomington, Minnesota
February 8, 1982

There have been no budget cuts. ...

President Reagan
at a $1,000-a-plate Houston fundraiser
June 15, 1982

Repeatedly, in performances that are soothing, reassuring, and highly professional, you have affirmed your Administration's commitment to across-the-board budget cuts - fair, evenhanded, and sparing of the truly needy.
Even as there is celebration, joy, and frivolity among the mink coat and limousine set, there is fear and tension in the ghettoes and barrios, among most Americans of color, among the poor of every hue and shade.
Your proposed budget and tax cuts are neither fair nor proportionate nor just. In fact what you have proposed is the legalized assault and rape of our nation's most vulnerable and defenseless citizens.

Statement of seven CCNV protesters, arrested for blocking traffic on Pennsylvania Avenue and pouring blood on the White House gates, in response to the President's state of the economy message delivered to a Joint Session of Congress the previous day.
February 19, 1981

February 19, 1981, in response to Reagan's State of the Economy message delivered to a Joint Session of Congress the previous evening.

The President is, in fact, accurate. "Budget cut" is a misnomer. The federal budget has increased. What has occurred, though, is a realignment of priorities, and the most radical redefinition of the role and responsibility of government in our nation's peacetime history. While billions more are to be pumped into an already bloated "Defense" Department, those for whom sacrifice means survival have been called on to give up what little they have.

According to the Reagan Administration, it is the protection of wealth and power, the subsidy of corporate America, and the maintenance of the military capacity to protect and defend our unfair advantage and disproportionate consumption of the world's wealth that are the legitimate functions and concerns of government - not the guarantee of the sustenance or well-being of America's economically, educationally, racially, physically, psychologically, or culturally disadvantaged citizens.

That the number of homeless people in America has grown astronomically in the past year is not mere coincidence. Increasingly, people have been driven into destitution by the policies and priorities that are Reaganomics. With frightening regularity, new layers of struggling and marginal Americans are pushed over the brink, slipping into the abyss that is utter and absolute impoverishment: homelessness.

Official policies that threaten, injure, and kill the powerless are nothing new. Indeed, they have probably been around as long as power itself. Certainly they have been with us since greed and might first obliterated need. Accurately written, history holds many examples.

The times have made the precepts of economic and social policy - as defined by the presidential candidate Ronald Reagan - acceptable to enough voters to put him into power. With his very candidacy, war was declared on the poor, both in the form of sins of commission (cuts to life-supporting social service programs) and sins of omission (massive transfers to a military buildup and tax breaks for the wealthy). With his inauguration and the acceptance of his budget, the casualties began to rise. A 1982 Congressional Budget Office study of the effects of tax and benefit reductions on households of varying income upheld this conclusion on three grounds: 1) gains from federal tax reductions increase significantly as household income rises; 2) decreasing federal benefits payments for individuals will hit hardest those who have incomes below $10,000; and, 3) programs that serve poor or near-poor people will contribute 60 percent of the savings resulting from decreased federal grants to state and local governments.

The tax cuts and transfers to the military budget obviously take away resources that might otherwise help those in need of the basic necessities and sustainers of life: food, clothing, shelter, and health care. For reasons of space, the study here will focus only on the reductions in programs that might otherwise meet these needs.[1]

> *[In 1982, there was]* a one-third cut in Title I and WIC; a one-fifth cut in child welfare; and a one-fourth cut in job corps and youth employment programs; and almost $5 billion in AFDC, food stamps and Medicaid. If we look at a broader range of programs that affect poor, handicapped, and homeless children and their families, proposed reductions total a massive $27 billion in FY 1983 alone. This includes $22 billion in new FY 1983 cuts and a proposed $5 billion in recissions from enacted FY 1982 budget levels.
>
> Children's Defense Budget, p. 3

What have been some of the results of the Reagan budget?

> *1,500,000 Americans lost their jobs in 1981.*
>
> *In September 1982, unemployment reached 10.1 percent, double-digit for the first time since 1940.*
>
> *An additional 3,500,000 Americans fell below the poverty line in 1981. One million of them were children. The Census Bureau estimates that 4 million more will join them in 1982.*
>
> *Publicly-supported child welfare services go to at least 1.8 million minors. Over 500,000 of these children are homeless, separated from their families and residents of foster homes and child care institutions. The children are often placed in these settings when the family needs or loses necessary support services. The average annual cost for most large cities to keep a child in a foster home is $5,000; the cost for institutional care is over $14,000. Yet for a child to remain in the family with special services averages only $2,300 per year.*

Additional hundreds of thousands of people have sought welfare benefits and food stamps, as a direct result of Administration policies affecting jobs, child care cuts, and work disincentives.

Changes in Aid to Families with Dependent Children (AFDC) will force many mothers with jobs to quit and go on welfare. Otherwise, they would lose vital AFDC benefits simply because of their employment. Medicaid for children is among the most prominent of these lost benefits. From FY 1982 cuts alone, 800,000 children of working mothers are expected to be dropped from AFDC.

A basic tenet of the Reagan program is the "New Federalism," a plan whereby the federal government takes over the expense of Medicaid in exchange for the states paying all the costs of AFDC and food stamps. Further, the federal government would "turn back" to the states more than 40 federal programs. Massive funding losses would, in turn, cause sharp cutbacks in public services and increase various state taxes. The cost to the programs of this "turn back" has been estimated at $43.5 billion for 1984, given the toll of inflation and the prospects for continuing budget cuts. This figure, computed by the American Federation of State, County and Municipal Employees (AFSCME), contrasts with the Administration's proffer of $30.2 billion, which omits the two factors of inflation and further budget cuts. Almost half the total - $20.2 billion - would fall on AFDC and food stamps.

The Entitlement and Benefit Programs

A question of considerable debate in the Reagan budget process has been the magnitude and vulnerability of federal benefit and entitlement programs. How much of the budget do they comprise, and are they being disproportionately cut?

Within that category of funding, the federal government operates two types of programs:

* *those available without regard to income, such as Social Security, Medicare, pensions;*

* *those for which there is an income test to determine need, such as food stamps, AFDC, Medicaid, housing assistance.*

Programs that have no income test primarily serve people whose earnings are above the poverty line ($7,070 for a non-farming family of three). About 85 percent of all recipients fit this description. In income test programs, in contrast, 90 percent of the recipients have incomes below the poverty line, and 50 percent of the families on food stamps make less than $300 per month ($3,600 annually).

Entitlement and benefit programs account for 40 to 50 percent of the federal budget. The income test programs receive less than 10 percent of the budget. Consider this contrast:

Budget for:

Food stamps
AFDC
Medicaid
WIC
Title I education
Employment and training programs
Free and low-cost meals
Legal services
Social services and community
    services block grants
Low-income energy aid
Low-income housing assistance

is
less
than

Budget for:

Medicare
Military retirement

The idea of a "safety net" for the "truly needy" has received much attention under the Reagan Administration. Three of the safety net programs - Social Security, Medicare, and veterans' benefits - accounted for 95 percent of the funds so designated. The deepest cuts were, of course, made from the remaining programs.

It is no secret that the non-income test programs are sacrosanct because their recipients have political clout and are not at all hesitant to use it. Recipients of income test programs, on the other hand, lack any semblance of political power; they are truly defenseless. Politics being what it is, it is the second group which bears a hugely disproportionate share of the economic burden.

It is that tiny portion of the budget that makes up the real safety net. Yet, O.M.B. Director David Stockman has referred to the federal budget as a "coast to coast soupline," a statement that is neither accurate nor just, but one which reinforces an image constantly projected by the Reagan Administration. For two years, the president has heaped reductions on the income-test programs, decimating the welfare of millions of already highly vulnerable Americans. A summary of these cuts makes the situation clear:

PERCENTAGE REDUCTIONS PROPOSED BY ADMINISTRATION FOR FY 1983 IN INCOME-TESTED AND NON INCOME-TESTED PROGRAMS[2]

Entitlement and Benefit Programs that are Primarily Middle Class and are not Income-Tested[1]

Social Security	0
Medicare	4.3%
Veterans disability compensation	1.4%
Military retirement	0.5%
Civil service retirement	2.3%
Railroad retirement	4.3%
Guaranteed student loans	23.0%[2]
Total Percentage Reduction	1.5%

Programs that are Entirely or Primarily Income-Tested

Entitlement[1]

AFDC	17.5%
Food stamps	19.1%
Medicaid	10.4%
SSI	3.1%
School breakfast and childcare food program[3]	34.4%
Total Percentage Reduction	

Discretionary[4]

Title I education	37.8%
Employment and training assistance	40.9%
Community Services block grant	73.7%
Legal Services	100.0%
Subsidized housing	128.2%
WIC/ supplemental feeding	37.1%
Low income energy assistance	30.8%
Social Services block grant	30.1%
	44.0%[5]

[1] Percentage reduction computed for entitlements based on Office of Management and Budget outlay estimates for current services and OMB estimates of savings from Administration proposals.

[2] Guaranteed student loans do have a means test for families over $30,000, but is listed in the left column because more of its beneficiaries are middle class than poor.

[3] School breakfast and child care food programs are listed in the means-tested column because 88 percent of the children in the breakfast program and over 70 percent in the child care program are low-income children receiving free or reduced-price meals.

[4] Percentage reductions in discretionary programs represent reductions in appropriations (budget authority) and are based on CBO's current policy estimates.

[5] Proposals to rescind over $5 billion in budget authority for housing programs and to seek no new 1983 appropriations play a major role in pushing the reductions in this column to 44 percent. If housing programs are removed from the column the percentage reduction is 18 percent, or 12 times greater than the left column.

Of the approximately 60 million families in the United States, 27 percent of them - and one out of five children - fall below the official poverty line. An additional 25 percent are classified low-income, living between the poverty line and $18,000 annually. About 30 million families fall into these two groups, and about 60 percent of them will have some benefit **slashed** or eliminated.

Another point to note in the discussion of benefits and entitlement is inflation. According to the government's own estimate, as a result of the inflationary effects of the past 10 years, benefits have dropped - in real dollars - about 29 percent. In other words, a $300 check in 1969 has $213 worth of purchasing power today.

Last year's vast social spending cuts were proposed and adopted on the fiscal assumption that the economy would shortly boom. Instead, we now have a brutal recession. Yet, drastic new spending cuts are again proposed.

*   *   *

. . . People who buy $2,000 dresses are viewed as productive members of society, and those who use food stamps are considered a problem. . . So, we should just persuade poor people to save their $2 a day for food and after 3½ years, they could each buy a $2,000 dress and solve our economic problems.

Nancy Amidei
Director,
Food Research and Action Center
(FRAC)

Effects on Specific Programs

Food Stamps

More than 22 million low-income people are served by this program; most cannot work, and half are children. The number of persons receiving food stamps may seem large, until it is compared to the number of Americans who now fall below the poverty line - 29.2 million. The elderly, the disabled, children, and single parents together make up 80 percent of the beneficiaries.

In Fiscal Year 1982, $2.35 billion in cuts were made in the food stamp program. At a time when the announced targets of those cuts were "waste, fraud, and abuse," more than 80 percent of those savings came from reducing benefits to families who fall below the poverty line. All told, one million people, including striking union members, have been dropped under the cuts, and nearly 21 million others have had their benefits reduced. Working families have born a disproportionate share of the cuts, a genuine disincentive to seek or maintain employment. The further reduction of $2.8 billion proposed for FY 1983, is even more harsh and regressive than last year's. Food stamp assistance for 92 percent of all households with elderly or disabled members would be reduced or terminated, while once again, the working poor would be hardest hit. The President, who said he would end exploitation of federal programs by those who could be working, has structured a policy that, in its details, militates against employment as an alternative to welfare. These cuts present just one more reason, amidst a growing number, for going on public assistance and giving up the struggle for independence, self-sufficiency, and dignity.

As an example of the work disincentive, if two families live next to each other, and one gets $5,000 a year from welfare or unemployment compensation, while the other family works and takes home $5,000 annually, in FY 1983 the family that works will get about $300 to $400 a year less in stamps than the welfare family.

Because other public assistance programs such as AFDC and SSI will also suffer large reductions, there will be an *increased* need for food stamps of about $500 million.

Because energy assistance payments will, for the first time, reduce food stamp benefits, many more poor families will be forced to choose between food and fuel.

Housing assistance will also be tied to food stamp benefits; rent subsidies will now include food stamps as income. Dramatic rent increases of 25 to 50 percent would be widespread. Many of the poorest families would find their rent doubling or tripling over the next several years. Of those who would have their rent raised, 85 percent are female-headed households with children, or elderly households. Most of those families have gross annual incomes below $4,000; many are under $3,000.

AFDC mothers and children in the South will be devastated because of the new procedures and cuts, and because welfare payments are so low in that part of the country: $96 a month for a family of three in Mississippi, $141 a month in Texas ($1,152 and $1,692 annually for the respective states).

Despite the Administration's carefully cultivated impression that food stamp recipients are, for the most part, doing quite well, that simply is not the case. The average gross income of households receiving food stamps is $325 per month, $3,900 annually. The average per person per meal benefit is 43 cents. For a person who has no income, the benefit is 65 cents. With all the current talk and complaints about the poor feeding at the public trough, it must be remembered that while the average food stamp recipient receives $622 in annual benefits, the average dairy farmer receives $10,000 a year in government subsidies.

Aid to Families With Dependent Children (AFDC)

AFDC is the only program explicitly aimed at protecting poor children by giving their families income support. Sixty-eight percent of all AFDC recipients, or over 7 million persons, are children. Half are white. Half are eight years old or younger. The remaining 3.5 million recipients are primarily parents living with children in single parent families.

One out of every eight children in America is currently dependent on AFDC for his or her survival. One out of four will, at some point in life, become dependent on AFDC. Contrary to popular opinion, the average AFDC family has two children, and very few "grow up" on welfare: each year nearly one-third of all AFDC families leave the program and are replaced by others. Four out of five AFDC families are headed by women, two-thirds of whom are not high school graduates. Even when combined with food stamps, no state gives AFDC benefits that come up to the poverty line.

In FY 1982, this $7 billion program was cut by over $1 billion, terminating benefits for at least 400,000 families, and reducing them for another 250,000. These families included over one million children. The proposed cuts for FY 1983 are even greater: $1.2 billion. This figure is, in actuality, doubled by the accompanying cut in state matching funds.

These are just a few of the changes resulting from the cuts:

* *Formerly, in determining eligibility and benefit levels, the income of a stepparent could be counted only if he or she had a legal obligation under state law to support the child, or if that income was actually available to the child. Now the income must be counted regardless of whether the stepparent is contributing to the support of the child or can legally be made to do so.*

* *Previously, states could claim federal reimbursement for AFDC from the time a pregnancy was medically confirmed. Almost half the states did so. There will now be no federal assistance for AFDC for first-time pregnancies until the sixth month.*

Moreover, no federal assistance will be provided for benefits to the unborn. This is occuring at the same time that unplanned teenage pregnancies are likely to increase as a result of reductions in family planning services, and the Administration is vigorously attempting to abolish abortions.

* *As a result of Reagan's "New Federalism," by FY 1984 states would be asked to take full responsibility for AFDC. By FY 1988, assuming a federally-imposed minimum benefit until that time, states could opt to get out of the welfare business altogether and more than 7 million children could be left without even the minimal basics of food, clothing, and shelter. If that sounds like an unimaginable possibility, consider the condition of ex-mental patients and the services provided to most of them.*

Low-Income Energy Assistance Program

Since 1973, fuel oil prices have increased more than sixfold; natural gas prices have more than quadrupled; and the cost of electricity has tripled.

Between 1977 and 1980, it is estimated that the energy bills of low-income households rose by $5 billion a year. Yet, in FY 1981, the program received only $1.85 billion, and in FY 1982, it was decreased to $1.75 billion.

The average American family pays about 5 percent of its income for home energy. Low-income households, however, pay about five times as much, while the average low-income elderly household spends more than 30 percent of its total income on home energy costs.

A large percentage of households receiving energy assistance have annual incomes below $4,000, and many are even under $2,000. Yet average energy costs exceed $1,000 a year for low-income households in 21 states; in no state is the yearly average less than $500.

A study done by the Grier Partnership found that if low-income households were to pay no more than 10 percent of their income for home energy (twice the amount paid by the average household, and 40 percent of the amount actually paid by the poor), the subsidy required in FY 1982 would be $4.4 billion. Estimates from the Congressional Budget Office show the actual value of assistance provided, after adjustment for inflation, falling by more than 20 percent this year, 26 percent in FY 1983, and 35 percent in FY 1984.

The Administration has proposed only $1.3 billion in 1983, while, at the same time, utilities have indicated that accelerated deregulation of natural gas, enthusiastically supported by the President, would at least double the average bill. Administration proposals would have the effect of cutting a family's AFDC benefits dollar for dollar for all energy assistance received; food stamp benefits would be cut by $3.50 to $5 for every $10 of energy assistance received.

* * *

Medicaid

For 11 million children, Medicaid, created 17 years ago by Congress, is the only means of financing medical and dental care, and necessary medication or hospitalization. It also pays for prenatal care and delivery services for hundreds of thousands of poor pregnant women.

Children rely on Medicaid more than any other age group. In 1979, 55 percent of public expenditures on children's health care came through this program.

Although anyone who is eligible for Medicaid is poor, eligible children are the poorest of the poor. Income standards for mothers and children applying for Medicaid have lagged far behind those for the elderly and the disabled. For example, between 1975 and 1980, the amount of income a mother and child could have and still qualify for Medicaid rose by 5 percent, while the allowable income level for an aged or disabled adult rose by 26 percent.

FY 1983 proposals for Medicaid include a $2.1 billion cut, bringing the two-year reduction to $4 billion. Consequently, many poor families will have to pay for more of their health services, at the same time that other benefits, such as food stamps and AFDC, are being cut. In addition, changes in AFDC will mean hundreds of thousands of children and mothers will have no way to pay their medical bills. In 20 states, loss of AFDC automatically means a loss of Medicaid.

By the end of FY 1982, it is estimated that 661,000 children will have lost their coverage. The number will easily pass one million before the end of the next fiscal year.

Just as in FY 1982, the President again proposes to cut Medicaid by shifting a major portion of its cost onto the backs of revenue-starved states and millions of low-income families, hardly able to withstand the additional burden. There are other cuts as well: under Administration proposals, nursing homes would not have to accomodate the handicapped and the disabled.

The Reagan Administration is proposing to make two types of reductions in federal funding for Medicaid. First, it proposes to reduce federal funding by 3 percent for "optional" services (i.e., braces, crutches, wheelchairs, prescribed drugs - such as insulin - and physical, speech, and hearing therapy), and it proposes to cut by 3 percent federal funding for Medicaid services provided to "medically needy" families. Medically needy families, although they do not qualify for welfare because they are employed, are, nonetheless, desperately poor. A family of four in Tennessee, for example, is medically needy if its income is $200 per month ($2,400 annually).

Neither the wholesale cuts in services nor the sharing of expenses, is cost effective. Such practices reduce the use of medical services, but not the need for them; patients usually wait until an emergency arises and then use far more expensive care. For instance, a California Medicaid study conducted in 1972 found that as it became harder to get prescription drugs, inpatient hospital costs rose. The ultimate effect of states ending their support for the medically needy may be to force the employed family members off their jobs and back onto the welfare rolls, which automatically entitles them to Medicaid.

* * *

Housing Assistance

A lack of affordable housing and the denigration of a right to shelter have already forced many people onto the street. Thus, it is all the worse that the Reagan Administration is further attempting to eviscerate these programs.

Section 8 and public housing are the two programs that provide assistance to families in need. As of FY 1980, 3.3 million housing units were receiving HUD assistance. Nearly 69 percent of them were occupied by the elderly or one-parent families, divided almost equally.

Far more are in need of help than currently receive it: families eligible for subsidized housing - and badly in need of it - outnumber available units by an estimated 5 to 1. The vast majority of these families are either living in substandard housing or they are paying a very large percentage of their income for rent. In 1976, for example, one-fifth of all households could not afford decent housing; in 1977, nearly 6 million families paid over half their incomes for shelter.

Rents will be increased over a five-year period, until they reach 30 percent. The average annual income for families receiving housing assistance is $4,000. However, the proportion of income considered in computing the family's rent will rise as a result of changes in the kind and amount of "income disregards" (such as child care costs, heating assistance, etc.) used. The average family will now face a 20 percent increase. More "adjustments" are also planned: food stamps will be tied to the income formula in determining rents, resulting in additional burdens for all low-income people, but a far greater weight in states where AFDC payments are low. In Mississippi, for example, a welfare mother with two children would, at the end of the month, be left with $8, after spending 30 percent of her combined AFDC and food stamps for rent.

New subsidized units were also cut sharply; the number of units was reduced from 220,000 to 122,000, a decrease of 48 percent. Section 8 was cut by 31 percent and public housing by 40 percent. About 100,000 families are affected.

Funds for the maintenance of public housing units were cut in FY 1982 to levels that cover only 80 percent of costs. In FY 1983, that will be cut by an additional 13 percent. Not only will some public housing shut down, but other units will quickly and seriously deteriorate.

The Administration is also proposing housing vouchers that will allow families to "shop around" for shelter, a near impossibility in today's tight market. The families now receive an average $3,600 a year, which would be reduced by $1,600 under the voucher system.

*   *   *

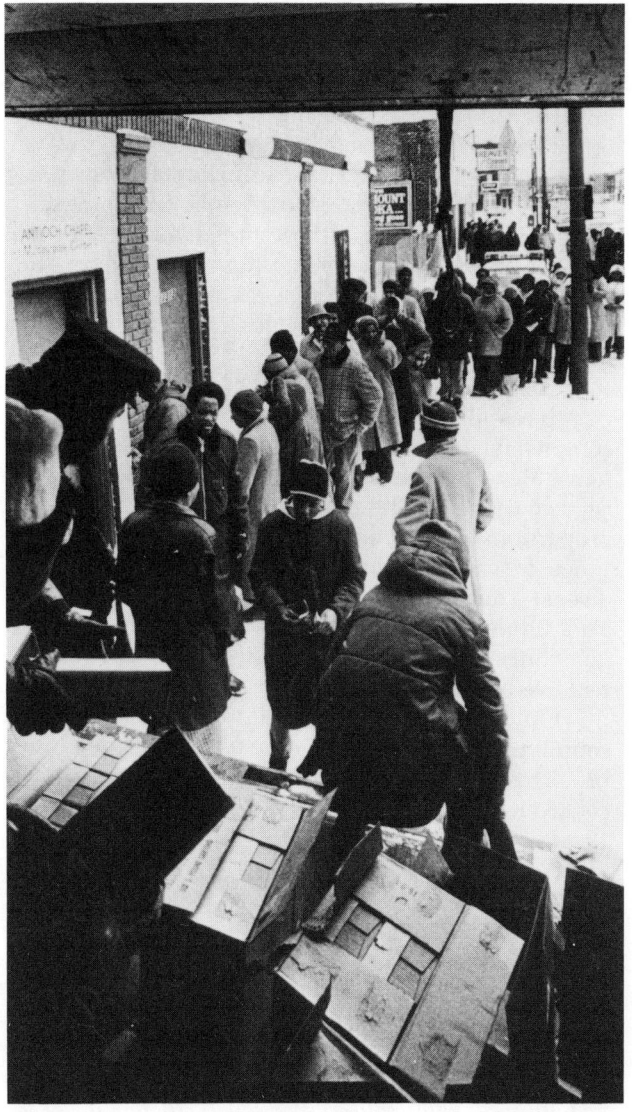

Cheese line in Ohio.

Special Health and Nutrition Programs for Women and Children

Health Care

The health of low-income mothers and children first became a concern of the federal government during the New Deal. There are four major programs that serve 26 million people, 23 million of whom are women and children. The programs are a primary source of funding for community health centers and family planning services. Nearly twice as many people as are served lack adequate medical care, including many families who have no access to health services.

Not only do the programs reach many people in need in both urban and rural areas, but they do so effectively. The health center program offers a wide range of services to those areas of the nation facing a critical shortage of medical care.

For many of those thus served, health problems are compounded by the dictates and conditions of poverty: substandard housing, a lack of clean water or other sanitary facilities, inadequate transportation, and the absence of prenatal care. The community and migrant health centers and family planning programs have alleviated some of these problems. In addition, because they have also reduced hospitalization, they are cost efficient: the family planning program, for instance, has been shown to provide $1.80 in savings for every $1 spent.

The Reagan budget for FY 1982 attempted, unsuccessfully, to eliminate these vital programs completely. Instead, funding was cut drastically. A new Maternal and Child Health Block Grant, representing a 30 percent reduction in funds, proportionately diminished services such as: assistance to crippled children, hemophilia and genetic disease control, rehabilitation for disabled children, and adolescent pregnancy care. Under the new guidelines, states no longer must maintain comprehensive health services.

Funds for the family planning program and community health centers were also integrated into a block grant and reduced by 29 percent. The consequences were grim:

* *40 health centers closed and 80 more faced the same end;*

* *1.26 million people would lose their health services, 199,328 of them immediately;*

* *Children, who represent 45 percent of all users, were deprived of much needed services: 89,697 immediately, and a total of 562,000 in the long run;*

* *441,000 women of childbearing age would lose health services, 69,765 of them immediately.*

The effects in some geographic areas were devastating. Clinic closures, service cutbacks, a reduction in the numbers served, and fewer staff to run the programs mean that not as many people have continuous and effective medical care available to them, and more people will seek assistance only in emergencies. High-risk pregnant women, infants, children who are in need of immunizations, checkups, and treatment, and the handicapped - all are made to suffer.

Lest there be any doubt, the commitment to lay waste or abolish these programs was made clear by the Administration's FY 1983 budget. The WIC program, for instance, was proposed for consolidation into a block grant, with a 35 percent cut in funds. By moves such as these, the Administration achieves a number of things: it freezes funds at past or lower levels, with no provision for inflation, and it wipes out a record of accomplishment. Federal programs, it must be noted, were only developed because the states were not meeting the need. Now, within a few short years, the states are expected to assume the burden for these same services under "turn-back" programs and the Reagan Administration will reach its ultimate goal: an end to all federal health services for poor women and children.

* * *

Food and Nutrition Programs

Supplemental Food Program for Women, Infants, and Children (WIC)

This program is run through health clinics and provides prescription food supplements (such as infant formula, milk, eggs, and fruit juice). It is effective in reaching low-income women, infants, and children who would otherwise receive inadequate nutrition. Although about 2 million people are so served, this group is estimated to represent one-quarter to one-third of those in need. Many eligible persons are either placed on waiting lists or turned away because of program inadequacies; in several hundred counties, the program does not even exist.

For FY 1982, a cut of more than 30 percent in program funds was initially but unsuccessfully sought by the Reagan Administration. Had those cuts gone through, nearly one million women and children - half the current recipients - would have lost WIC services.

The WIC program significantly reduces infant mortality and anemia, and is extremely cost-efficient: each $1 spent in WIC's prenatal component, for instance, saves $3 in hospital costs. Nevertheless, the Administration has proposed for FY 1983 that the program be eliminated and that WIC funds, reduced by 35 percent, be consolidated into the Maternal and Child Health (MCH) Block Grant. If that were to occur, there is no guarantee that block grant funds would, in fact, be used to replace WIC. The cumulative two-year result of 1982 and 1983 cuts, taking inflation into account, would mean more than a 50 percent reduction in maternal and child health care and women, infant, and children (WIC) feeding programs.

* * *

Child Nutrition Programs

Several million children each day depend on federally-funded food programs. Considered the most nutritionally- and cost-effective, the School Breakfast Program serves 3.6 million children in 33,000 schools; "poor or near-poor" describes 88 percent of the children. The School Lunch Program helps 27 million more.

Daycare children from low-income and working-poor homes are served by the Child Care Food Program. The Summer Feeding Program carries about 2 million children through the non-school months with a nutritious lunch.

These programs were mauled by the FY 1982 budget:

> *The School Breakfast Program was cut by 20 percent, ending the participation of 800 schools and 400,000 children, 70 percent of whom were poor or near-poor.*
>
> *The School Lunch Program was cut by 30 percent or $1 billion by altering eligibility standards for free or lower-cost meals and decreasing subsidies. More than 2,000 schools and nearly 900,000 poor and near-poor children were dropped from the program. In addition, children who were paying only 20 cents per meal faced new prices of as much as $1.*
>
> *The Child Care Food Program also lost 30 percent of its budget; fewer meals are served and eligibility standards have been changed. Some centers closed entirely when overwhelmed by the cumulative effects of the loss of staff as a result of CETA cuts and other social service reductions.*
>
> *The Summer Feeding Program was slashed by 50 percent, and many private-sector charitable groups no longer will be able to operate free lunch programs.*
>
> *The Special Milk Program was reduced to 20 percent of its former level, with programs totally eliminated in schools with an existing lunch program.*

For FY 1983, Administration proposals leave the lunch program intact, but exact a heavy price from all of the others. The Summer Feeding Program and the Special Milk Program would be abolished. The Breakfast Program and the Child Care Food Program would be consolidated into a Child Nutrition Block Grant, at a reduced level of funding that would bring the two-year cuts to 50 percent. This would be a permanent level of funding.

These would be the consequences of such a plan: as food prices rise, the number of available meals declines. As schools are then forced to eliminate the program, more children have less to eat. The breakfast program and the child care program would vie for the same dollars at the state level; not only would the less-organized child care constituency lose the contest, but additional programs would be ended in states where educational dollars cannot go to "private institutions," such as many child care centers are.

* * *

Child Care and Education Programs

Head Start

Project Head Start is a model of how well a federal program can effectively serve a multiplicity of needs. Medical, dental, nutritional, educational, social, and mental health services have been provided to 7.8 million children and their families since the program began in 1965. The average annual cost per child for the program is $2,343.

Only 20 percent of those who are eligible are served. More than 9 out of 10 of the 372,100 children in the program are from low-income families. Slightly more than 10 percent are physically, emotionally, or mentally handicapped. A majority of the children are from minority groups and urban areas.

The successes of the program are many. As its name suggests, Head Start offers children opportunities that promise better social achievement, and, as a result, enhanced possibilities in later life. Not only does Head Start decrease the likelihood that children will require costly special or remedial education, but it yields benefits 235 percent greater than its costs.

Additionally, through medical and dental screening and treatment, and a broad immunization program, Head Start children are healthier, and meals provided by the program guarantee improved nutrition.

Another important factor in Head Start is the increased parental involvement and education. Two parents volunteer for every three children in the program, and the results benefit both, especially in family and household life. Parental participation has helped 12,000 earn college credit.

The Reagan Administration originally designated Head Start as one of its untouchable "safety net" programs. A 16 percent budget increase, proposed by the Carter Administration to help the program keep pace with inflation, was turned into a proposed 12 percent cut by the new President. The final result came through Congressional action and consisted of a small net increase. The precariousness of Head Start funding created near-hysteria at the local level; this inevitably affects the quality of the program in areas such as salaries, morale, classroom size, hours and weeks of service.

Head Start has also suffered a "fallout effect" caused by cuts in related programs where Reaganomics was more successful. Termination of many CETA jobs resulted in the loss of 6,000 workers serving over 50,000 children.

*   *   *

Child Care

The traditional two-parent, male-breadwinner household describes only 1 out of 21 families today. In the majority of American homes, all parents are now employed. Nearly 50 percent of all children under the age of 5 have working mothers. The need for adequate child care, that, in many cases, even allows a single parent to hold a job, is critical. About 30 percent of those in need are poor, female-headed households.

Many of these people would have to make a choice if child care were not available. Either they could not work and would, therefore, be forced onto welfare, or they could try to finance child care out of already hard-pressed dollars. For many, the latter is simply not a realistic possibility. "Child care" does not apply only to school hours, either, for working parents need to know that their children, especially the youngest ones, are supervised or cared for until the end of the working day.

The Daycare and Child Development Council estimates that 2.5 to 3.5 million families already need day care and can't afford it. At least 450,000 children, or 50 percent of those presently in subsidized day care, are estimated by the council to be in imminent danger of losing this service because of the cuts. According to the council, 40 percent of those so affected are minority children, for whom such services are important individually and as a way for parents to seek or hold jobs.

Federal funds for child care have been drastically reduced. Working parents or parents in training face a whole new - and, for many, impossible - struggle in trying to establish themselves. Among the programs that receive federal funds are:

* ***Title XX of the Social Security Act*** *subsidizes 750,000 low- and moderate-income children receiving day care.*

* ***Project Head Start.***

* ***Child Care Food Program*** *aids centers, family day care homes, after-school programs and Head Start for meals and snacks. More than 725,000 children were served in 1981.*

* ***AFDC Child Care Disregard*** *provides funds for AFDC families who are paying for child care.*

* ***Child Care Tax Credit*** *gives tax relief to parents who, if they did not have child care, could not work or seek employment. This is the single largest federal expense for programs of this sort, and it serves middle- and upper-income families - 3.8 million in all.*

Under the FY 1982 budget, Title XX services were cut to 150,000 families, many of whom are desperately struggling to break out of a poverty/welfare cycle. As a result of these cuts, many states have reduced income eligibility, making it difficult to obtain subsidized child care. The children of parents who have to be withdrawn from these programs face an increased risk: alternative situations are frequently less stable, not adequately supervised, or simply makeshift. The centers themselves face little choice but to attract more people who can pay higher fees.

Specific alterations in program funding include:

* ***Child Care Food Program*** *- a 30 percent reduction, resulting in higher fees and fewer children served.*

* ***CETA*** *- elimination of the program has caused the loss of thousands of badly-needed child care workers.*

* ***AFDC*** *- limitations on child care cost deductions for working welfare mothers have resulted in cases such as this:*

  In Massachusetts, the replacement of one-third of the pre-school child care slots with school-age slots was reinforced with a new priority for mothers on workfare and mothers receiving welfare. The mothers who are trying to find or hold a job or go to school are given every disincentive not to do so.

* *Predictably, the **Child Care Tax Credit** was increased, a bonus for its middle- and upper-income recipients.*

Fiscal Year 1983 cuts are even more serious. As the result of a proposed 18 percent cut in the Social Services Block Grant, nearly 100,000 families would lose child care. With the Child Care Food Program merged with the Breakfast Program in a block grant, and funds cut by more than 30 percent, the ensuing competition between child care and school lunch users and providers bodes ill for the former, who are much less organized and, therefore, less capable of bringing pressure and influence to bear.

* * *

Employment and Unemployment Programs

There are two sides to the double-digit unemployment spreading like a cancer across America today. One is the human side: the pain and suffering, the fear, the sense of inadequacy, the shattering of illusions, and the long-term diminution of a sense of security and well-being, caused by the loss of a job or the inability to find one. The other is the cost to the American economy in lost productivity, social service programs and supports, and buying power. While the level of unemployment varies widely from industry to industry, and from region to region, higher than average rates are affecting construction, manufacturing, and agricultural workers, and three important industrial states - Ohio, Michigan, and Indiana - have much higher unemployment rates than the rest of the country.

Unemployment line in Connecticut.

Key to the Reagan solution is supply-side economics: the idea that unemployment and stagnation can be reversed and overcome by 1) concentrating capital in the upper reaches of the economy, 2) simultaneously reducing controls on that sector, and 3) letting the wealth "trickle down" to create jobs by a general invigoration and stimulation of the economy. Not only does this overlook the misery that lies between the here-and-now and these jobs-just-around-the-bend, but it overlooks real facts. According to the Full Employment Action Council:

> It takes a lot of capital to insure the creation of one job through the trickle down approach - $200,000 according to the Administration's own figures. In contrast, one CETA public service job costs less than $10,000. Yet all of these jobs have been eliminated by Reagan's program.
>
> Over one million jobs will be destroyed by the Reagan cuts in federal urban mass transit, and jobs programs. At the same time, vital programs to help the jobless are being weakened or gutted - unemployment insurance, job training, trade adjustment assistance.
>
> The key to the Republican "supply-side" job creation strategy is to return windfall funds to wealthy individuals and large corporations through tax cuts.
>
> Has this freeing up of investment funds led to greater U.S. productive capacity? No. Instead, corporations have used these funds to increase dividend payments, acquire other companies, and invest overseas.[3]

Causes of unemployment fall into two basic categories - current economic fluctuations, and a lack of either jobs or marketable skills. The Reagan budget offers relief to neither of the latter two groups. Unemployed and untrained minority youths have as little reason to hope as out-of-work industrial laborers. The President's policies and priorities completely overlook the toll exacted by unemployment, costs both human and social. There are also many more demands on the federal budget - in the form of increased welfare, food stamps, unemployment insurance and diminished tax revenues. When the President takes action such as he did in eliminating the CETA program, it is generous to attribute that action to misunderstanding and ignorance of the human consequences. For FY 1982, CETA funding was slashed more than 50 percent, at the same time that other benefits for the unemployed were cut, and approximately 50 percent of America's black youth were out of work.

Specific employment programs cut in FY 1982 included:

* **Youth Employment Demonstration Projects Act** - cut 80 percent;

* **Young Adult Conservation Corps Project** of CETA - eliminated;

* **Summer Youth Employment Program** - cut 20 percent;

* **Public Service Employment Program** - 310,000 jobs, offering experience and skills to long-term unemployed people, and badly-needed help in public and social service programs - eliminated;

* **CETA Title III** jobs - special job aid for many women, the elderly, migrants, and welfare recipients - cut 64 percent.

Many people on AFDC face new disincentives to finding or keeping a job. The same is true for recipients of virtually every other assistance program as well.

The Reagan budget has failed miserably to come to terms with the reality of the nation's economy. Most people in the United States now agree that we are in a depression. Soup lines, cheese lines, and unemployment lines all testify to the seriousness of the times and the pain felt by many. Yet the President has slashed services for the unemployed, and has heavily wounded the extended benefits programs. The latter worked through a so-called "national trigger" unemployment figure, which in turn activated state mechanisms to extend payments. Several changes were made:

* *the national trigger was eliminated;*

* *the state trigger was raised one percentage point;*

* *the base period of work needed to qualify for the extended benefits was increased;*

* *benefits for those voluntarily leaving the military and not reenlisting were eliminated.*

About 2 million unemployed people were expected to lose extended assistance as a result of these measures. At the same time, as FY 1982 drew to a close, a record 700,000 new claims for benefits were being filed weekly, and for the first time since 1940, unemployment hit double-digit figures: 10.1 percent for the month of September.

In light of the continuing rise in unemployment, cuts proposed for fiscal 1983 are even more threatening:

* *employment and training funds are to be cut further, including total elimination of the Summer Youth Employment Program;*

* *unemployment benefits are to be altered, resulting in heavier taxes, compelling recipients to accept any job that is available; and*

* *mandatory workfare programs in the states will affect virtually all AFDC recipients.*

Besides the programs that assist the relatively recent additions to the unemployment rolls, the Administration's moves against the CETA program most heavily impact on minorities, women, and the long-term unemployed. The wipe-out of CETA is a reversal of the accomplishments of the last 15 years, based not on a realistic appraisal of the situation, but on a political perspective. Once again, the President plans to shift responsibility to the states, at a funding level that cannot even begin to do the job.

To keep to this budget, the quality of the effort would have to be compromised to such an extent that any hope for the future would all but disappear for most young minority people. One of the worst aspects of this plan is that participants would receive no allowance or stipend; they would be paid a below-minimum wage. Given that the minimum wage now yields a below-poverty-level income (under $3000 annually), the Administration's proposals are scarcely cause for celebration among the long-term minority unemployed.

The total elimination of CETA placed a new burden on low-income and minority workers and social service agencies. About half of CETA's 535,000 workers were women. For all of these people, the program represented a route out of poverty and unemployment. Before the cuts, 5,000 CETA workers were employed by Project Head Start; many others also worked for service and charitable organizations. Their jobs were a blessing, for the people they served and the organizations they assisted, and, of course, for themselves. Although the Administration talked of volunteers filling gaps in services formerly staffed by CETA workers, today's economy is such that the traditional volunteers - mothers, grandmothers, and the retired - increasingly must work to make ends meet.

Programs for Older People

When the Leadership Council of Aging Organizations analyzed the FY 1983 budget and the impact on older Americans, it was shocked, even beyond its own expectations:

> *...The LCAO looked at sixteen (16) programs providing services or benefits to the elderly. Of these, more than half are slated for budget cuts below FY '82 levels, and in many cases, below FY '81 levels.*[4]

For almost fifty years, there has been a steady accumulation of meaningful legislation, providing the base for a slowly developing national policy on aging. These programs - Social Security, Medicare, housing aids - stood for a growing sense and acceptance of obligation for the elderly held by most Americans. For many, it is clearly a question of conscience which dictates that our older citizens have earned the right to be assured of food, shelter, clothing, and medical care.

The effects of the cuts in basic social programs have been well covered already. It must be emphasized, however, that *all* of these cuts have a profound impact on older Americans, and particularly on low-income elderly people.

Medicare

Medicare was created in 1965 as part of the Social Security Act. Its primary role is as a federal health insurance program for people 65 and over and certain disabled persons. The program currently covers about 26 million older people and 3 million disabled.

There are two components to the coverage - hospital insurance (Part A) and supplemental medical insurance (Part B), a voluntary program. Together these plans do not cover even 40 percent of the individual health care costs of the elderly. One of the major drawbacks of Medicare is its failure to cover the cost of dental care, eye glasses, hearing aids, long-term custodial care, and certain kinds of prescription drugs.

For older people on fixed incomes, there is a constant consciousness of cost and need. Many elderly Americans recall "hard times" with a sense of personal experience; many are frugal in ways not even imagined by later generations. Most already tend their limited funds with great concern, constantly counting pennies, and conserving wherever possible. Additional financial burdens - particularly those for their own health - commonly exacerbate their anxiety about what lies ahead.

For FY 1982, Medicare was cut by $1.5 billion by increasing the number of costs to be shared by the recipient. The initiation of $1 and $2 fees for certain services may seem paltry, but for the poor, many will be effectively discouraged from seeking health care until an emergency arises. Certain other changes in Parts A and B of the program are designed to spread the costs even further. While federal expenditures are certainly reduced in this way, Administration policies fail to address the rapidly increasing costs of health care, which is primarily responsible for the rapidly rising cost of Medicare.

For FY 1983, an 11 percent increase in the Medicare budget is planned, down from an annual average rise of 16 percent. Given inflation and rising care costs, this is a far more damaging reduction than is immediately evident. It is, of course, a far smaller cut than those reserved for programs that serve the poor, and it is primarily the lower-income recipients of Medicare who will be hard hit by this reduction in funding.

*   *   *

Medicaid

About 3.6 million aged people are covered by Medicaid, which, like Medicare, is also a part of the 1965 Social Security Act. As a federal-state matching program, Medicaid is under special pressure, since many states already were suffering funding problems before the federal approach became one of reducing its own share.

Medicaid's relevance to low-income older people is as the primary public health provider of long-term (usually institutional) care. This type of expense accounts for 42 percent of Medicaid costs. Increasing the share paid by the recipient, also part of the Reagan approach, is to ask more of those who already lack financial resources sufficient to meet the most minimal needs. Another substantial change allows states to seek competitive bids for some services and to restrict Medicaid recipients to specified providers.

For FY 1982, Medicaid cuts totalled about $900 million. The FY 1983 budget requests represent a further 5 percent reduction. These are very severe cutbacks for a program *rising* by three times that amount in recent years.

One aspect of the 1983 plan is a reduction in federal matching funds for necessities such as prescription drugs, dental care, glasses, and hearing aids. Many older people need these services to remain independent; forcing them to pay more for such items and services and calling them "optional" is cruel and deceptive.

A U.S. Department of Health and Human Services report shows that, as a result of 1981 budget cuts, 16 states initiated shared payments for these items, and 20 states reduced or totally eliminated some of these "optional" services.

Another proposal allows the states to require the contribution of some part of the cost of care from adult children of Medicaid recipients who are institutionalized. While the specifics remain unclear, what is predictable is that a new burden is in the making: many of these "children" are of retirement age themselves, increasingly facing the same hard choices as their parents.

*   *   *

Social Security: The Old Age, Survivors and Disability Insurance Program (OASDI)

The Social Security Act of 1935 provided for insuring earned income lost due to any of the causes described in its name. The program's funding and benefits have always been tied to earnings. The program is funded by payroll taxes representing a fixed proportion of a worker's salary and matched by an employer contribution. Benefits are then determined by the worker's average lifetime earning.

Of people age 65 or older, more than 95 percent are currently eligible to receive benefits. About 36 million people are now recipients, while 115 million workers are making payments into the program as employees.

Prior to the present controversy over possible cuts to Social Security, there was, in most quarters, agreement that both immediate and long-term funding problems needed to be addressed. As the nation becomes progressively older, there are certain serious economic difficulties developing simultaneously. While sentiment to maintain the program is overwhelming, there are also critics who believe that Social Security's problems cannot be ameliorated by trimming and slicing in the budget process; more fundamental answers must be found.

In 1981, the OASDI federal cost was $139.6 billion, with $158.1 billion estimated for 1982. According to the Congressional Budget Office, expenditures for 1983 would be $173.6 billion.

The Reagan Administration was unsuccessful in 1981 in its efforts to cut Social Security. The program did not escape altogether, though. The $122 minimum benefit for 3 million new recipients was eliminated. College students' benefits will be phased out, as will parental benefits when a child reaches age 16. The

$250 lump sum death benefit for funeral expenses of Social Security recipients with no immediate dependents was abolished, affecting over 200,000 people. Thus, if any friend or relative who is not legally defined as the immediate dependent of the deceased wishes to claim a body for burial, they are effectively discouraged from doing so, in the absence of other financial resources. The emotional choice for low-income survivors becomes one of incurring debt in order to provide burial, or allowing the government to dispose of the body.

The issues remain volatile and unresolved. Alternatives and criticisms fly in all directions, and their terms consistently overlook the impact on the elderly. To understand the feelings of aged Americans, it is necessary to look at a few facts:

* *In 1980, 56 percent of those over 65 had annual incomes of less than $10,000; 26 percent received under $5,000.*

* *Poverty among the elderly is rising: from 13.9 percent of older people in 1978 to 15.1 percent in 1979 to 15.7 percent in 1980.*

* *A decrease of $20 to $24 per week would immediately raise the poverty rate among the elderly to more than 25 percent.*

* *The average retired worker's benefit is $4,620 a year or $385 monthly. This is only $260 annually above the 1981 poverty level for single people ($4360).*

* *The average couple's benefit is $570 monthly or $6,840 annually.*

When these facts are put next to the cuts made in health, nutrition, and other social service programs impacting directly on the elderly (cuts totalling more than $3 billion), it is easy to see how much the aged have already suffered and why they are so vehemently opposed to further reductions. When inflation's effects on fixed incomes are considered, these proposals can only be seen as a direct and brutal assault against some of our most vulnerable and needy citizens.

*   *   *

The Reagan Tax Policy

On July 1, 1982, the first of the Reagan personal tax cuts took effect. Many people were standing in cheese lines, unemployment lines, and soup lines. The Senate Republican Conference and the American Conservative Union ordered "the world's largest apple pie" in celebration of each American receiving "a piece of the pie," through the new measure. The event was an affront to those who were suffering - and to truth itself.

The tax cuts enacted in 1981 were predicted to yield a federal revenue loss of $749 billion over five years, with the increments rising sharply each year. When placed next to the fact that the entire federal budget is about $720 billion and the FY 1982 cuts are about $40 billion, it is a bit easier to gain perspective on the effects of the tax cuts.

Never before have tax cuts of such magnitude been passed, and never before have they been based on such inequity. The net loss from cuts in benefit programs, despite small tax savings, will average $240 for households with incomes under $10,000 in 1983. Taxpayers earning $10,000 to $20,000 will either lose money - because of program cuts - or break even. Households with annual incomes of $80,000 or more will achieve an average net gain of $15,130.

These conclusions, of course, address the conditions of those Americans who file tax returns; most poor, elderly, and disabled people do not. Nor do these findings reveal the further inequities and privileges conferred by the non-individual tax modifications: oil producers' tax breaks, corporate tax benefits, evisceration of the real estate tax - alterations that aid only those with high incomes.

Igloo, built by homeless people, adjacent to Reaganville.

Reaganville

In compiling material for this chapter, we have read hundreds of reports and news articles. We came away better educated and enraged. Even for those of us who work closely both with the poor and with the issues, policies, and programs that affect them, the magnitude and the seriousness of "Reaganomics" came home with a new intensity.

While statistics can be useful, they can also be dangerous. Our first reaction to what we read was not anger or outrage, but shock. Day after day, as we pored over more material, a numbness settled in; we were overwhelmed by the misery and pain. After all, who among us can embrace and comprehend the agony of millions of people? For a brief moment, we wanted to believe that President Reagan was right about the impact of his policies, and if not right, then at least innocent and unaware of the ramifications of his actions.

But our collective memory is too long, and our experiences are too rooted in the lives of the poor to be distracted more than momentarily by diversions and defense mechanisms designed to protect us from the truth. Initially we were numbed by the statistics; we allowed them to separate us from the people whose pain they reveal. We feel safe in assuming that this material may well have the same affect on others.

For that reason, we have put together the collage that follows.[5] We hope that it returns both depth and pathos to impersonal statistical information. Reaganomics is not an abstraction; it is the rape and defilement of America. Millions of human beings are being driven across the line between marginality and utter destitution. Tens of millions of others are being impoverished. It is the enemy within, the circle of the arrogant and powerful, which threatens the well-being and future of our country.

* Howard Stokes is from Detroit. Like many others from that hard-pressed city, he is unemployed. He lost his job at Chrysler's Mack Avenue stamping plant early in 1981. No longer able to afford an automobile, Howard daily rides the bus to Henry Ford Community College, where he studies electronics. But he will not ride the bus much longer, for the federal tuition support he was receiving has been eliminated in the budget cuts.

* The Joint Economic Committee of Congress recently surveyed the nation's 50 largest cities and found that the majority were cutting back virtually every service that they offer.

* Scores of area agencies in Washington, D.C., report they are being strained far beyond their ability to cope. For example:

* *At Sacred Heart Parish, the number of families receiving church emergency food packages jumped from 70 in July 1981, to 230 in May 1982.*

* *SOME (So Others May Eat), a soup kitchen half a mile north of the Capitol, has seen its daily line grow from 200 persons a few years ago to 600 in September 1982.*

* *In affluent Montgomery County, $30 emergency aid grants given by the interdenominational Community Ministry jumped from 16 a month in 1979 to over 100 in June of 1982.*

* *Catholic Charities reports that "last summer [1981] we were seeing 40 people a month. Now it's close to 100."*

* During the last week of September 1982, Gerald De Toia stood in line in Hempstead, Long Island, waiting to be interviewed for a job. "Real jobs," he said. "They say that they have real jobs in there."

Unfortunately, he stood in line with hundreds, then thousands, of others as word quickly spread that the Marriott Hotel was hiring a complete staff: 296 jobs in all, ranging from dishwashers to desk clerks. Within two days, 4,508 people had applied. More than 1,000 of them stood in line for up to 7½ hours.

* Increasingly, operators of soup kitchens and community centers that serve the poor and the homeless across the country report that unemployment and cuts in social programs have radically altered the profile of the average person served. According to Brother Steve Gilko, for example, who directs Milwaukee's St. Benedict's Meal Program, "Five years ago, it was safe to say that 95 percent of the street people we saw were chemically addicted, to drugs or alcohol or whatever. Today, 70 percent of our guests are just homeless and jobless people, not addicts. They're not out on the streets by choice but because of economic and political forces. Among our guests today, being out of work is the reality, not the exception."

"You can always tell the family or the couple that's new," he added. "Their heads are always down, and they're very grateful for absolutely everything. They eat very quickly, and then they quickly disappear. They're just so ashamed."

* Hunger in New York City is hard to measure, but Donna Lawrence of the Hotline, a service that refers people in need to 35 privately-financed emergency programs, said there has been a marked increase in emergency calls. In 1979, when the hotline started, 20 percent of the 300 calls a month were requests for emergency food. That percentage remained relatively constant, until the fall of 1981. In October of that year, the emergency calls rose to 70 percent. The situation has become so serious, that the food programs no longer allow the hotline to give out their phone numbers or their addresses. They have taken a don't-call-us-we'll-call-you position because they have been thoroughly inundated with requests for emergency assistance.

* City hospitals and clinics will be affected by cuts in both Medicaid and the block grant program. Mercy Children's Hospital in Baltimore, Maryland, for instance, says it will have to absorb $400,000 in Medicaid cuts or face the prospect of "certain death" for infants who receive inadequate treatment.

* Mrs. Gatewood lives in Washington, D.C., on a $388-a-month budget from Social Security. She scrubs all of her clothes by hand and foregoes the use of her oven, because she can't afford to repair it. When she learned that her Medicaid card would no longer be honored and that she would not be eligible for the "medically needy" program, Mrs. Gatewood began to sob. "What's people like us going to do?" she agonized.

* According to a federal study conducted by the National Center for Health Research, the distribution of Medicaid expenditures favoring the poor is offset by the distribution of tax expenditures which favor the high income sector. When the total expenditures were counted, in 1981 the government spent 29 percent of its health care disbursements on the poor, and 28 percent on the rich.

* According to the president of the U.S. Conference of Mayors, "The damage that the FY 1983 budget proposal would inflict on our cities and the suffering it would inflict on so many of our citizens cannot be overstated."

* Dzintra Dowling, 37, lives in a three-bedroom house in the Chicago suburb of Brookfield with her two children, ages 15 and 10. She has been out of work since October 1981, when she was laid off by International Harvester. Dowling is separated and gets no financial support from her husband. Her weekly unemployment check of $199 has run out. "This morning I sat down after my son had gone to school and just bawled. It isn't because I'm worried about myself. It's, my God, what am I going to do with the kids? If it was just me, I could find a room somewhere and live on Campbell's soup and bologna sandwiches. But when you have children, it's different.

* Rick and Penny Thielmann and their two children live in a tent in O'Neill Park in Trabuco Canyon in Southern California. They cook in a cinderblock pit and wash up in camp restrooms. They have been living in parks for over a year, since they were evicted from their apartment. Rick, a roofer, fell behind in his rent because of the construction slump. Families living in both public and private campgrounds are a new, but widespread phenomenon.

* Special Approaches to Juvenile Assistance (SAJA House), is a non-profit organization in Washington, D.C. They provide temporary shelter for runaway and homeless youths whose ages range from 11 to 18. In 1981 they served about 240 young people, who would otherwise have been on the street. The staff tries to reunite them with their families or find alternative placements for them. Last year, the program was supported by a $68,000 federal grant from the Department of Health and Human Services. This year it received $10,000.

* It has been estimated that non-profit organizations could lose $45 billion nationally between 1981 and 1984. Of that, $27 billion will be the result of direct budget cuts and another $18 billion will result from tax law changes that discourage charitable contributions. Currently, annual contributions to non-profit organizations run $2.5 billion in corporate donations and an equal amount in foundation grants.

* In 1980, the St. Benedict's Meal Program in Milwaukee averaged 300 meals a day. In early 1982 it was averaging over 500. So, too, is St. Luke's Episcopal Church in Atlanta.

* In Detroit, social service agencies report a 100 percent increase in requests for assistance from 1981 to 1982, while in Boston, community groups are serving 14,000 more meals per month now than they were in 1980 - a 64 percent increase.

* Alex Chatman, the first black to be elected a county administrator in South Carolina, claims that "the population of the jail has tripled, even though there has been no increase in serious crime. People get themselves arrested on some minor violation so they can get a meal or two."

* At a blood plasma donation center in St. Louis, Director Ron Wilson says business is up 10 percent partly because more housewives and part-time

workers are coming to collect the $8 paid for a pint of plasma.

* Marita Dean is in charge of the Washington, D.C., office of Catholic Charities. She says, "We're seeing people now that no agency ever saw before, people who never had to beg before. They're frightened, so you help them this month, but they're not going to be any better off next month."

* In August 1980, 941 families requested emergency food assistance at an agency in Detroit; 446 were found to be desperate enough to qualify. In August 1981, 1,673 families came seeking the food bags, and 1,078 were found to have no other way of feeding themselves.

* Bill Wilkins, director of health licensing certification for South Carolina, describes the federal health care cuts as "abandonment of the aged." He adds that "we're [soon] going to be right back where we were in the late '60's and early '70's."

* In Chicago, a study of 2,000 patients at an urban community hospital found that 44 percent were admitted with nutritional deficiencies.

* Last year, an official at Einstein Hospital in Philadelphia was quoted as saying: "Now I hate to hear the phone ring. If Reagan gets the cuts he's asking for, we may as well put a tape on the phone and say 'no service available.' I'm starting to feel as though there are no answers."

* The Mayor of Seattle, Charles Royer, says that federal programs turned over to the states will cost $75 billion by 1984, with only $13 billion in revenues to pay for them, "leaving a little matter of $62 billion annually for the local governments to puzzle over."

* In March 1982, a supermarket opened in Dubuque, Iowa, with 55 jobs to fill. Almost 1,400 people applied. Says manager Edward Berberich, "We were deluged with phone calls and resumes - even at home. I couldn't eat dinner. I had to take the phone off the hook."

* At 3:30 A.M., Lorenzo Collins, an unemployed food service manager, was the first to arrive and take a place in the doorway of the Petworth Employment Services Center in northwest Washington, D.C. By 5 A.M., nearly a dozen other people had joined him. When the office opened for business at 7:30, more than 100 people stood in line. Well before nine o'clock, employment service workers were telling those who had arrived after eight that the day's schedule of appointments was already full.

* Friends and relatives said that Kay and Antonio Garza had left their bankrupt company in Ohio to find work in Texas. The couple were found by police in their car, fatally shot. They left a suicide note:

> *We came to San Antonio to work, not to die. But Reagan economics has nothing trickling down to us.*
> *I have gone as far as I can go with our lives. My wife, Kay, and I are hard-working people that have been reduced to beggars almost.*

* A computer analysis by the highly respected, bipartisan Center for the Study of Social Policy of the University of Chicago found that in 24 states, the average family that now lives partly off work and partly off welfare would have a higher income if its members stopped working. Even in states where income would be higher for those who work, the advantage of working would generally be less than under previous regulations.

"The systematic reduction in work incentives hits hardest at families at or near the minimum wage whose work efforts should be supported rather than discouraged," the study said. For many of the 600,000 welfare families who have some outside earnings, "work may no longer be justified by its rewards," the study concluded.

* The Presidential Commission on Housing called for an end to local rent control laws and said that Congress should cut off federal housing funds to cities that persisted in enforcing controls. The commission's proposal would, if adopted, be "catastrophic for low- and middle-income families and senior citizens," according to Republican Representative Bill Green of Manhattan.

* New York City Social Services Commissioner Barbara Blum has ordered her agency - which does the reviews for the federal government - not to drop mentally and physically disabled recipients from Social Security Disability (SSD) or Supplemental Security Income (SSI) benefit rolls simply for failure to mail back a recertification form, a practice demanded by the Reagan Administration. Thousands of mentally incompetent, physically incapacitated, and homeless New Yorkers - those most desperately in need of help - have already lost, or could in the future lose, their benefits in this way, even though they are legitimately eligible.

* Prezell R. Robinson, president of the National Association for Equal Opportunity in Higher Education, in response to the proposed cuts in federal aid to higher education, has said, "Without financial aid, black students are going to be caught in an economic squeeze so serious that if the cuts are effected we could be talking about a loss ranging from 25 percent to 50 percent in enrollment of black students in institutions of higher learning in this country by the fall of 1983." Nearly 90 percent of all blacks pursuing post-secondary education receive some form of government-sponsored aid.

* In a 1980 study, Maine ranked as the 50th state when personal income is measured against the local cost of living. Under FY 1982 cutbacks, almost half of the 20,000 Maine families receiving AFDC lost all their benefits or had them substantially reduced. In addition, about 10,000 people in the state lost their eligibility for food stamps.

* Agnes Dayen, 41, one of those Maine residents so affected, lives in a trailer with her six children. Reporting for duty at 5:30 in the morning, she has been working as a cook at a local roadside restaurant since her husband left her 11 years ago. Her take-home pay is only about $500 a month, or $6,000 a year.

In January 1982, Mrs. Dayen lost the $130-a-month AFDC check she had been getting. She also lost her Medicaid benefits, which had covered all her children's medical and dental expenses. She herself has been too poor to go to the dentist for 25 years.

* James Wilson is a 63-year-old totally disabled man on Medicaid who lives alone in a back-woods South Carolina shack without plumbing, telephone, radio, or television. According to his physician, Mr. Wilson needs seven different medicines to stay alive and out of pain. But the new regulations limit Medicaid patients to three prescriptions a month at government expense.

According to his doctor, Mr. Wilson "is facing the decision of whether to take his medicine for his heart and high blood pressure this month or wait until next month and take his medicine for gout and arthritis instead."

* In February 1982, 1,500 of the 2,500 adult patients served by the Comprehensive Family Care Center in the Bronx were told that they would be turned away at the end of the month if they could not afford the higher fees necessitated by the center's loss of a $350,000 federal grant. An administrator at the clinic said that the reordered operations would affect the working and elderly poor most seriously.

Herbert Harrison, a 65-year-old diabetic who also suffers from hypertension and a nervous disorder, said that he would not be able to afford the new fees. On a previous visit, Mr. Harrison paid $15 for an examination and the filling of three prescriptions. Two weeks ago, he was told he would have to pay $25 for the visit and additional fees for tests and medication. "You're talking $50, $60, $70," he said. "I don't have that kind of money."

* An unemployed Savannah, Georgia man, hoping to get help after two years without a job, robbed a local convenience store and then told the clerk to call the police.

Paul Savage, arrested October 16, 1982, on a charge of robbery, told police he wanted to go to jail and get help. After the robbery, he told the stunned clerk to call the police and drove to a nearby intersection to wait for them.

* An elderly couple living on $425 a month ($5,100 a year) in Social Security benefits now is eligible for $312 annually in food stamps. Under the new proposals, their food stamps would be cut to $108 a year. If the couple also was receiving $30 a month in fuel aid, their food stamp benefits would be wiped out altogether.

* For the most part, the current cuts in health care programs have not meant ending them, but squeezing people out of them. In Washington, D.C., for example, one part-time worker is trying to rush corrective surgery for her 12-year-old son's legs before the Administration's welfare reductions toss the family off Medicaid.

An elderly woman faces another year's wait for new dentures to replace those cutting into her jaw. There are already 384 people in the District of Columbia on a waiting list for teeth.

* In January 1982, about 50 children in a Brooklyn, New York, elementary school returned from winter vacation to find they were no longer eligible for free hot lunches. They were instead fed leftovers from other children's trays. New regulations lowered the amount of money families can earn and still be eligible for free or reduced-price lunches.

Charles Buchanan, an assistant principal at the school, P.S. 219, said he decided to give the children leftovers when he saw them sitting in the luchroom without food. "They were begging for a cheese sandwich from their neighbors," he said, "so we gave them leftovers."

* If Secretary of Defense Caspar Weinberger were to give up his private dining room, according to Marian Wright Edelman, president of the Children's Defense Fund, one million low-income school children could get back their mid-morning snack.

* Robert London was a car salesman in Southern California. His income, at better times, reached $2,000 a month. In 1981, his job disappeared.

Car sales were slow everywhere. He was 54 and unable to find work. Not even his accounting training helped him, since it was dated back more than 30 years, and he was obsolete in a computerized era. With no significant savings, his finances rapidly slid downhill. Because technically he had quit his job, he did not qualify for unemployment benefits. (London explained, "Salesmen don't get fired; they give up.") For the past year he has been at the Union Rescue Mission, receiving meals, a bed in an eight-man dormitory and an $8 weekly allowance.

* Walter Barnes served his country for three years as a machinist's mate in the United States Navy. He returned to St. Louis and began looking for work, but soon discovered that jobs for which his Navy training had equipped him were "not to be found in this city."

Like many jobless veterans before him, Mr. Barnes sought unemployment payments to tide him over. He was shocked to learn, however, that the federal program of unemployment payments for those who chose not to reenlist was abolished a few days before he applied.

* A survey of 48 cities, released in January 1982, noted the following Catch 22: the higher the rate of unemployment, the greater the decline in federal aid and the likelihood that a city has cut services in recent months.

* Cutbacks in the federal government's childhood immunization program could result in new epidemics of polio, measles, rubella, and other serious childhood diseases that have been all but wiped out, according to Dr. Samuel Katz, chairman of pediatrics at the Duke University Medical Center. The programs to be cut saved $10 in future medical costs for every $1 spent.

* Since losing his job as a forklift operator at a mill in Molalla, Oregon, in August 1981, James Wittig, 35, has been scrambling for a job. "I'll try anything, but there's nothing," he says. "If there's a job open in Oregon, there's at least 100 people trying to get it." His wife works as a cook for $360 a month to support him and their two children, but it's not nearly enough. Says Wittig: "I'd like to talk to the President for half an hour. I'd say, 'You're living high off the hog. You're telling us how good everything's going to be in two years. But we're starving today!' "

* Newberry Mills, in Newberry, South Carolina shut down in early 1982. Says mill superintendent Melvin Blackwell, 59, who will also be fired: "You meet people in the store crying. These people put their whole lives in that mill, their whole heart, and they get nothing out of it. Just a closing." Says mill worker Everett Mays bitterly, "I've got two kids in college and the mill didn't give us any pension. What kind of a job can a man get who's 48? Damn right I'm scared."

* Within the general population, this nation's incarceration rate is 250 people per 100,000. On any given day, more than 600,000 people are locked up. Our incarceration rate trails only those of South Africa and the Soviet Union.

More than half of the 5 million people imprisoned each year are not convicted of a crime, but are awaiting trial, and they usually are too poor to make bail. Blacks are imprisoned at 8.5 times the rate of whites.

On any average day, one-quarter of the jail population consists of people arrested for public intoxication. while 600,000 mentally ill people end up in jail for some period of time each year.

* In late September 1982, an unidentified homeless and irrational man, thought to be in his 30's, was found dead inside the polar bear cage at the Central Park Zoo. He apparently scaled a series of fences to get inside the cage and was killed by the animal.

The man had been noticed by guards at the park during the day and had been seen several times going up to the cages, trying to get close to the animals. Each time, he was chased away. At 11:30 P.M., he was spotted inside by the night watchman and was led out of the zoo. At 3 o'clock in the morning, he was again spotted, near the lion cages. As he was led out for the last time, his final words were "Help me."

[*A subsequent* New York Times *column by Sydney Schanberg revealed that the man, Conrado Mones, had immigrated from Cuba in the Freedom Flotilla of May 1980. He was a biology teacher who determinedly studied English so that he could one day teach in a university. Meanwhile, he supported himself in New York with a job at a gas station, eventually becoming assistant manager.*

In mid-1982, Conrado Mones quit his job so he could study English full-time; he went on welfare. Whatever was deteriorating in his life at that point - be it an important relationship, his hope, it is hard to know - took hold. In the end, he was scaling the fence at the zoo.

A final note. The woman with whom he lived was thwarted in her efforts to claim his body and save it from burial in New York's potter's field. Funds which once would have been available from Social Security for that purpose have since been eliminated.]

* Sister Leonard, a Missionary of Charity (Mother Theresa's order), came to Washington, D.C. from Calcutta more than a year ago. She and the other nuns operate a soup kitchen six days a week.

"Some have recently lost jobs, some have not worked in many years. Many are in despair. They see no use in living," says Sister Leonard of those who come to eat.

She adds, "The poor of Calcutta are really poor, but here they are spiritually and materially poor. Washington people are more poor than in Calcutta in the spiritual way, because this country is rich."

* Officials in all 50 states, interviewed by the *New York Times* in February, 1982, expressed surprise at how little response there had been to federal spending cuts by or on behalf of poor people.

Welfare lobbyists in several states said they believed that the current "tranquility" of the inner cities was somewhat ominous because it masked a discontent that might later flare up in violence.

"Contrary to some of the wild charges you may have heard, this Administration has not and will not turn its back on America's elderly or America's poor."

President Ronald Reagan
The State of the Union Message
1982

Footnotes

[1] Significant parts of this examination of the specifics of the FY 1982 and FY 1983 budgets and their impact on the poor are taken directly from Robert Greenstein's analysis in *The Significance of the Administration's New Budget Proposals* (Washington, D.C.: Interreligious Emergency Campaign for Economic Justice, February 1982), and *A Children's Defense Budget: An Analysis of the President's Budget and Children* (Washington, D.C.: Children's Defense Fund, 1982). These two studies have made the budget real in human terms, and we have passed their findings on verbatim in many instances.

[2] Robert Greenstein, *The Significance of the Administration's New Budget Proposals* (Washington, D.C.: Interreligious Emergency Campaign for Economic Justice, February 1982), p.6.

[3] "Reaganomics," (Full Employment Action Council, 1982), p.3.

[4] "The Administration's 1983 Budget: A Critical View From An Aging Perspective," (Leadership Council of Aging Organizations, March 18, 1982), p.1.

[5] Material for this section has been gleaned from a variety of sources. Among them: The *New York Times*, *Washington Post*, *Boston Globe*, *Time*, *U.S. News and World Report*, and various news and wire services.

> *Mental hospitals are the POW camps of our undeclared and inarticulated civil wars.*
>
> Dr. Thomas S. Szasz
> *The Second Sin*

> *If mental hospitals are the POW camps, then ghettos and slums are the battlegrounds. Every emotional breakdown is an inarticulated protest against a complexity of social, communal, and familial conditions and relationships that stifle and threaten the individual's psychic viability. A psychotic episode is a socio-political event and not a medical event.*
>
> Anthony E. Colletti
> "Psychiatric Oppression and Class"

Mental Health, Mental Hospitals, and the Homeless

Since 1965, the population of mental hospitals has declined by 75 percent, as the result of new philosophies and practices in the mental health field. One of the major vehicles forecast to support this exodus has been the community rehabilitation residence (CRR), in theory a facility to provide support in easing the transition from the state hospital back into the community. Unfortunately, no city in the United States has enough CRR slots to accommodate the number of ex-patients in need. In fact, most cities have only a token number of such facilities.

By the hundreds of thousands, patients have been discharged and sent to unfit, unsafe, or unlawfully operated boarding homes and flop houses, without the necessary supportive medical or social aftercare services. Others are given bus fare and the address of a mental health center, and then discharged with neither planning nor preparation.

Since depopulation of America's mental asylums began, the majority of the state mental hospital patients have been released into a world unprepared or unwilling to care for them. They are the victims of a social reform movement aimed at liberating them. Many are now living, and dying, in alleys, parks, vacant lots, and abandoned buildings, with little more than garbage for food, rags for clothes, and no shelter or medical care whatsoever.

In this chapter, and in the chapter that follows, we shall look closely at this process, and at some of the assumptions and philosophies that undergird our nation's mental health system.

Next to a widely circulated belief that our streets are populated by alcoholics, the other well-established image of the homeless is one of "crazies," muttering, puttering souls, laden with baggage, orating at street lights, or shouting at invisible beings. Their appearance tells us that they do not even care for themselves. Their persistent presence in public places tells us, among other things, that they reject our efforts to help and *choose* to remain in miserable circumstances.

It is, in fact, true that many of the homeless are discharged mental patients. The Pine Street Inn is Boston's oldest and largest emergency shelter for men and women. Executive Director Paul Sullivan estimates that more than 50 percent of Boston's street population are ex-mental patients. According to an internal memo written by the New York State Office of Mental Health, in New York City, where there are an estimated 36,000 homeless men and women, 50 percent display signs of mental illness, and one-third have had psychiatric hospitalization. The now-defunct Washington, D.C. Mayor's Advisory Commission on Homelessness conducted an investigation of mental health problems among shelter users. They discovered that more than 50 percent of the men and 70 percent of the women have had contact with the mental health system. Information provided by hundreds of organizations over the past few years leads us to the conclusion that between one-third and one-half of the homeless people in America are ex-mental patients. A bare knowledge of recent history and a look at some of the studies of urban homelessness confirm this.[1] (It now appears that Reaganomics will alter the makeup of America's street population in the next 10 years, in much the same way as deinstitutionalization did over the last 10.) But if there are now many discharged patients, they were once confined, and not all for the same reason.

Emptying the Hospitals

Publicly supported mental institutions were first constructed in the United States in the early 19th century. By 1955, the population in almost 300 state hospitals reached a peak of about 559,000 patients. Nearly half of America's hospital beds were occupied by mental patients. The state hospitals suffered from a lack of funds and staff, and conditions were shameful.

By 1980, slightly more than 137,000 patients were hospitalized for mental illness. Several explanations can be found for the decrease, which resulted in more than 75 percent of the patients leaving the hospitals at the same time that the general population was growing.

First, the prevailing philosophy - that those needing mental health care should be treated in hospitals - shifted to a new ideal that community-based care was the answer. The development of new psychotropic drugs meant that more patients could be maintained outside a hospital setting. The rights of mental patients were increasingly expanded and upheld by legal, legislative, and judicial measures. The federal government assumed more and more financial responsibility for chronic patients being discharged to nursing and board-and-care homes, with Supplemental Security Income (SSI), Medicaid, and Medicare providing necessary funds.

How many chronic patients are there? According to one estimate, "There are 1,100,000 schizophrenics [in America], 180,000 of whom are in hospitals and almost a million in the community." Combined with estimates of elderly and severely mentally disabled patients, the total is between 2 and 4 million.[2]

The alternative of care and support from community facilitites was enunciated in 1961 by the Joint Commission on Mental Health, created by the Mental Health Study Act of 1955. While the commission acknowledged that "the objective of modern treatment of persons with major mental illness is to enable the patient to maintain himself in the community in a normal manner," it also pointed out that "aftercare and rehabilitation are essential parts of all services to mental patients. . . ."

Community treatment was a concept welcomed in many sectors, but it was debilitating to have supporters with both fiscal and humane motivations. While many assumed that community-based facilities and support services would develop commensurate with need, they did not. The establishment of a comprehensive community care system would have undermined the principal incentive of financial savings, since the low cost of community care is tied to the meager services offered. If appropriate support services, shelter, and medical care were extended to former patients, community costs would rise substantially.

Nationally, 1,000 mental patients per day are discharged from institutions. Only 7 percent of those are referred to operating community mental health centers. Not all of those make it to their appointments, and those that do may not find the help they need.

The community mental health centers are presently providing services to the neurotic, borderline patients with a good prognosis: the so-called YAVIS (young, attractive, verbal, intelligent, and successful) syndrome. Treatment of the ex-

hospital patient is of little interest to the psycho-therapeutically-oriented staff at the mental health centers. Any treatment afforded the chronically mentally ill is the most expedient one, namely, psychoactive drugs.[3]

There are differing views of the costs involved with community and institutional care; different studies report different conclusions. In some cases, community costs may appear to be lower because some necessary non-psychiatric costs (food, shelter, clothing) are not provided by publicly-supported community care facilities, but instead are covered by Medicaid and SSI, as well as by family members and private groups. (Further, these costs disappear for the homeless ex-patient.) Direct treatment costs may, however, appear to some to be higher in the community, and other burdens may be added, such as an increased reliance on law enforcement agencies or support for families.

But the fiscal savings theoretically available from deinstitutionalization are far less than had been originally calculated. Many of the costs of a mental hospital are fixed, regardless of the number of patients occupying the institution. As the population goes down, the per person per diem cost goes up. Much of the savings potentially available will not be realized unless and until the institutions are closed altogether and the fixed costs eliminated.

In actuality, a goal of humane and cost cutting deinstitutionalization of patients became instead the dubious achievement of careless and widespread emptying of wards full of patients. The community facilities and support provided to them covered a wide range. Some were "papered out" to spurious living situations with relatives who had no intention of keeping them. Some got a bus token and directions to a mental health center. Some moved to private profit making homes in the community. Some went directly to the street and remained there.

It is not unusual to find a conflict of bureaucratic processes which sequentially 1) dictate a patient's release, 2) begin the qualifying process for benefits just prior to release with the expectation that weeks or months will elapse before the first check is issued, and 3) eventually, see the individual fail to receive benefits because of having no fixed address.

According to a National Institute of Mental Health report, "National statistics show that 38 percent of the discharged mentally ill were not referred to any aftercare services and another 11 percent were transferred to nursing homes and other state hospitals." Other findings of follow-up care report conclusions consistent with the reality of street life; patients (more than one-third in one study) preferred hospital life to the emotional isolation and loneliness they found in the community. Further, one study of dischargees showed that, in the early years of depopulation, about two-thirds of the former patients went back to their families and not more than one-fourth went to nursing or boarding homes. With the passage of time, however, the more "difficult" and more severely/chronically ill patients remained and the distribution of dischargees changed radically: in 1980, only 23 percent of the patients were returning to their own homes.[4]

It must be remembered that these figures reflect "official" outcomes of discharges, as opposed to the obvious reality that many patients simply end up on the streets with no alternatives and no assistance. Follow-up reports on patients outside the hospitals are usually narrow in two respects: they interview patients who have managed to avoid return to the hospital, and they do not locate patients living on the streets, whether those patients went directly from hospital to street or walked away from another situation, such as a board-and-care home.

All of this begins to reveal some of the dimensions of deinstitutionalization and public hospitals. Certainly more has been said eloquently and authentically by those who emerged from institutionalization and "treatment" with enough literacy to pass on their observations and experiences. But the overall invisibility of the homeless places them out of this category for all but the few who strive to form ties with them. The call here is always to examine the burden (rarely the favor) conferred on those most physically weak, psychologically incapacitated, or politically powerless. In this light, the wholesale depopulation of mental institutions during the last decades emerges with a record of neglect and criminal unconcern, resulting in a massive increase in the number of homeless people on our cities' streets.

Why Were They Hospitalized? - The Hospital as Tool

There is a common cause for why, before the age of "enlightenment," these people were separated and segregated, locked up in hospitals for days or years, shocked, drugged, and otherwise "treated." Each of them - in a large or small way - violated the ritual ceremonies that make up society's "norms," as agreed upon by those who prevail (economically, politically, socially, and otherwise). Observed by others, they marched to a different tune. Hospitalization and various forms of treatment followed. (We respond to observable, unacceptable differences as if "normalcy" is a static, immutable reality, not at all fluid or subject to modification, change, or varying interpretations.)

Several obvious questions are thus raised. One concerns how anyone - rich or poor, black or white, female or male - comes to be hospitalized for a state not acceptable to the rest of us, but does not necessarily threaten the health or well-being of anyone. In answering that question, we must consider the justice of the admission process, for if the wards were filled through oppressive measures, what light does this shed on a release process that has been careless and wholesale by many accounts? The second question bears on the "deinstitutionalization" movement of the last two decades and its impact on the number of homeless people in this country.

Any detailed discussion of these topics must do more than repeat the plethora of analysis that has gone on before. It must also take into account more deeply-rooted truths about poverty and justice in our society. Such an examination can be done only briefly here. First, what are the origins of the dividing lines of acceptability and unacceptability?

*... From childhood onward, stories make the invisible forces of life visible by creating images of people representing ideas and social types and assigning some fate to each.... [**Advertisements**] present styles of life telling us what values we should choose and at what price....*

*If deviants didn't exist, they would have to be invented in order to generate a sense of what the norms are and what the price for violations might be.... [**Deviant images**] have developed to deal with the large majority who need to be socialized into roles of conformity and acquiesence and dependence upon stronger and more authoritative types.*

In order to perform these functions, images of deviants have certain characteristics. These images tended to develop in predictable ways to depict menacing forces against whom people need to be

Below:
This grate is known on the streets as "Number 1," located in front of D.C. police headquarters.

> *protected by strong and frequent resort to violence. . . . The first of these is unpredictability. . . . As rationality of a relationship, the aspect of unpredictability justifies irrationality of behavior toward the mentally ill. . . .*
>
> *The second critical aspect of the image is danger . . . constantly reinforced by the label "ex-mental patient" being attached almost exclusively to violent and bizarre behavior. . . .*
>
> *Next, the image of mental illness has to be tinged with a touch of evil. Sin or moral flaws tend to justify the potential irrationality and brutality of the relationship toward the persons depicted, suggesting that they asked for or deserved it.*[5]

When people then behave outside the prevailing norms, when they violate the ceremonies, they have the possibility of being classified and treated as criminals, prophets, geniuses, or mentally ill, the last being the case at hand.

> *. . . Society is particularly concerned about people who do not properly engage ceremony. One must not violate communication ceremony by focusing somewhere other than the listener's face! One must not violate ceremony by speaking audibly to an unseen listener! One must not violate ceremony regarding tests of truth by averring that one speaks directly to a Truth-giving God! . . .*[6]

The establishment of "sanity" for a given person is a value-laden undertaking. It needs a moral framework as well, and that should be broadly defined as questioning whether life itself is affirmed or not. Considering the extent to which personally and collectively destructive behavior is legalized and accepted - e.g., cigarette smoking, driving cars, drinking alcoholic beverages, abusing the public trust, building and threatening the use of nuclear weapons - the standards for deviance, sanity, and criminality are clearly in the eye - or the conscience - of the beholder. A man conversing with a park bench seems infinitely easier to come to terms with than a megaton-mad warrior in public office.

An exclusive group of the "haves" (of knowledge, property, and weapons) consume creative energy and national resources that could take the patient from hospital to community, rather than to street or shelter. Yet it is the poor, minorities, and women - all casualties of disenfranchisement by the norm-setters - who are locked up. They are labelled, and, in many instances, turned onto the streets without shelter or resources, and without the capacity to manage a bus ride, tie their shoes, or report for medication.

Race, Class, Gender, and Society

The roots of psychiatric oppression by race, economic class, and gender are, not surprisingly, well-disguised, for history and psychiatric theory are authored from the same group that issues norms: the dominant class. But the trend has not gone unobserved, particularly by patients themselves, as in the following:

> *. . . Upper middle class women enjoy the boutiquing of psychiatry and engage in private therapy; they are labelled neurotic, and it is considered in vogue. Lower class women are commonly diagnosed as schizophrenic, incarcerated in state hospitals, administered electroconvulsive treatment (shock therapy) and tranquilized into a stupor. Schizophrenia is not in vogue . . . 80 percent of those in state hospitals are so diagnosed. . . . Most of what has been labelled schizophrenia among the poor is dysfunction resulting from the trauma of environmental stress factors. . . . A welfare mother, overwhelmed by environmental and economic stress, falls into a depressed stupor -involutional melancholia or urban stress fatigue? Is she mentally ill or a social casualty?*
>
> *. . . There is a disproportionate rate of dysfunctionality among the lower classes, and this is a direct consequence of the stress they live under. They are not mentally ill; the cure is neither a state hospital, nor shock therapy, nor tranquilizers, but social change. . . .*[7]

Some say this is confirmed as a truth by the reality that, among young blacks (the group aged 15 to 19 whose unemployment rate is the nation's highest, at over 50 percent), the leading cause of death is suicide. Dr. Jay Chunn, Dean of the Howard University School of Social Work, cites chronic unemployment and loss of personal relationships as primary factors leading to what he calls "an epidemic" of suicides.[8]

Ten years ago, some 19 percent of mental hospital admissions were "nonwhite." By 1975, this figure had risen to 23 percent. Per 100,000 people, the admission rate for whites is half that for blacks.

Blacks make up 19 percent of patients in public general hospital psychiatric wards, but comprise only 10 percent of private general hospital psychiatric ward patients. In private psychiatric hospitals blacks constitute a mere 3 percent of patients. (Citation omitted.)

Even more shocking is the source of state hospital admissions for national minorities, who are increasingly being sentenced to mental hospitals by courts for incompetency to stand trial.

The percentage of nonwhites thus admitted is 6.9 percent, 5.5 times the percentage of whites, and the number of Spanish-Americans is 2.5 times the white percentage. Translated into absolute numbers, 5,369 blacks were admitted in 1972 for incompetency to stand trial. That amounts to nearly 1.5 times the absolute number of whites, even though blacks constitute only one-fifth of the state hospital population. This raises the possibility that the custodial state asylums [are] being maintained for an increasingly third world population, and coordinated with a racist judicial system.[10]

Narrowing Choices for Care: Closings and Cutbacks

One way of measuring the success or failure of discharge programs is to examine the scale of readmissions. This factor quite adequately makes the point that many former patients have failed to survive in the community, if the conditions of release ever truly gave them a chance. Most chronic mental patients do not stay in one place too long: insurance coverage usually affords no more than a few weeks in community hospitals, and the state institutions are quick to discharge them because their illness is unresponsive to treatment. According to a California study of a Veterans Administration Hospital, 79 percent of the applicants in a 3-week period were "revolving door" patients, more likely to be homeless and schizophrenic.[11] An equally succinct and illuminating statistic is this one: 50 percent of all discharged patients in New York State return to the hospital within 4 years.[12] Finally, it has been shown that readmission figures skyrocketed in the years following deinstitutionalization, and that the long-term effects on patients in the community are grim: few keep jobs, the majority live in total or moderate isolation, and few remain in aftercare for more than a year or two.[13]

If readmissions signify a failure to survive in the world at large, we must ask how much more difficult this survival is for the poor patient and for the patient who has no support on leaving the hospital? Is there any way to know what portion of the readmission rate reflects the will to survive (i.e., procure warmth, food, a bed) and which part reflects a failure of previous "treatment"? Or must we not ask if the "treatment" of a person in mental anguish does not include the guarantee of these basics?

A 1979 Maryland State Department of Health and Mental Hygiene study estimated that 28 percent of returning patients thought their most pressing problem was acquiring and maintaining adequate shelter. In Richmond, Virginia, where public shelter resources are grossly inadequate, even the option of returning to the hospital is no longer available, for, in April 1982, the Richmond Metropolitan Hospital closed its public psychiatric unit, leaving poor patients with nowhere to go. Community hospitals are unable to provide for them, and the move drastically cut services to those already deinstitutionalized - about 50 percent of those seen by the city's half dozen mental health clinics.

Another facility sometimes available, the Medical College of Virginia, was seeing a 10 to 15 percent increase in mental care cases in its emergency room *before* the closing. Poor patients generally occupy about one-fourth of MCV's psychiatric beds.

While money was the overriding factor in the closing, it is not a consideration when confining poor people who are under a court detention order for care, because these costs are paid by part of the criminal justice system - the Virginia Supreme Court. But at least one mental health center administrator has said publicly that workers are under pressure to "keep people out of the hospitals," and from April to July 1982, with city funds available to hospitalize only 10 people for less than a week, *no* acutely ill uninsured mental care cases with previous hospital histories were able to use city funds for treatment

Costs are the oft-cited factor for many closings or threatened closings in recent years. The long-term community effect for poor people looks to be disastrous. No-frills public services are the only option for many people, and even when these programs are uninviting or saddled with a 9-to-5 effort, they are all that is available to the poor.

A case in point is the threatened shut-down of federally-funded St. Elizabeths Hospital in Washington, D.C., the city's only public facility for mental care cases. In December 1981, Office of Management and Budget Director David Stockman outlined plans to close the hospital or severely cut its funding. As described by Dr. Barbara Tobelman, Executive Director of the Mental Health Association of the District of Columbia, community reaction ranged "from disbelief to outrage."[14] A local union official cautioned that "the nation's capital must not become a psychiatric ghetto."[15]

Virtually all witnesses at a D.C. Mental Health Association hearing on Stockman's plan addressed the impact of closing the sole public psychiatric facility in a city of black and poor people who do not even have a vote in Congress and, until recently, did not have the chance to elect their own officials

Dr. Ruth E. G. King, of the D.C. arm of the Association of Black Psychologists, cited several major consequences of closing St. Elizabeths, given that there are not a sufficient number of private beds available to absorb remaining patients:

* drain on existing D.C. mental health and social service facilities;

* displacement;

* devastation of family systems;

* higher death rates for former patients;

* increased crime from severe economic pressures; and

* devastation of neighborhoods.

"So, in essence, we are looking . . . at the impact of releasing mentally ill patients back into the predominantly black neighborhoods of Washington, D.C. . . ." said Dr. King.

Pointing out that some patients will inevitably end up in D.C. Jail from the hospital, King added: ". . . Where will the patients go? Where will the patients receive needed services? Is Ronald Reagan going to take them in at the White House? Is Stockman or OMB going to allow use of their office building for housing?"[16]

Another witness echoed these views:

> *When the public was first informed of this proposal by way of the public media, many of us thought it could not be true - this was another trial balloon; another effort to formulate social policy through press release. Upon reflection, we must accept the fact that it is probably very true and likely to happen in the near future. After all this is the Administration which was willing to accept the designation of ketchup as a vegetable; willing to give states additional control over monies and programs while cutting the states' amount of federal revenues for these same programs; willing to cut social security benefits for the population most in need of that income and very recently, the Administration which is willing to use tax dollars to fund segregated education.*[17]

St. Elizabeths offers a unique example of the workings of deinstitutionalization, if only because it exists under the federal government. As such, it could be setting benchmarks as a model, implementing the findings and endorsements of previous federal mental health bodies. But, in fact, following the lawsuit brought by the Mental Health Law Project, the hospital has not moved very fast to carry out its court-ordered schedule.

As did similar lawsuits in other parts of the country, D.C.'s *Dixon* v. *Califano* mandated that specific increments of the hospital population be moved to community care facilities over a stated period of time. Not only have the hospital and the local government failed to do this, but some community agencies have cited cases where they have been paid to provide support services and training for a fixed number of former patients, and then have been sent none. While the D.C. government provided the court with a list of organizations and agencies which supposedly provide services to ex-mental patients, on closer inspection many have been found to be out of existence or not especially targeted for former patients.

It costs $20,000 to $25,000 annually to keep a patient at St. Elizabeths, while community placements (in home and group settings) run $2,600 to $3,200. This latter sum comes almost entirely from SSI checks, delivered directly to group homes. The larger amount is paid out when homes have the capacity for more than 50 beds; thus, operators are discouraged from creating small-scale homes.[18]

In the shift away from institutions, there has also been a series of studies of what are called "forfeited" patients: discharged and in need of services, they are least able to secure them, and eventually those charged with their care concede defeat in the struggle. No solid statistical information on how many of them wind up on our streets and in our back alleys has come out of these studies.

Many of these "forfeited" patients are among the 600,000 Americans in need of psychiatric care who are imprisoned for some period of time each year. For instance, in Los Angeles County alone, there was a 100 percent increase in the number of judicial incompetency dispositions following the passage of California's state legislation for mental patients. San Fransisco police find they log more than 800 calls monthly on mentally ill citizens.[19] A study of 500 arrested persons in need of psychiatric care found that all had hospitalization records, but 94 percent were not involved in any outpatient program.[20]

Conclusions

Where does all this lead? There are clearly obstacles to the effective delivery of services to those in need. Given the number of chronic patients among the homeless, how can their needs be assessed, and what are the obstacles to meeting them?

A basic inventory of services would have to include:

* *available and accessible psychiatric aid;*

* *round-the-clock crisis intervention and support services;*

* *programs that instill skills for daily living;*

* *graded housing services for a range of needs; and*

* *financial support, employment assistance, and vocational rehabilitation.*

The obstacles to humane and effective delivery of such services are deep-seated, but not impossible to overcome. They cover the range of problems centered in the institutions and professions themselves - attitudinal, legal, administrative, ethical, and educational - to those that are the burden of non-patients. All of these problems, which have been well covered in other literature, require time and commitment to resolve.

There is also a need for a coherent public policy, with responsibilities clearly assigned at all levels of government and for all sectors of society. Such a policy would include:

1) *a plan of graded and wide-ranging opportunities and services, relying on increased public sensitivity and financial commitment;*

2) *full civil rights for those in need of mental health care:*

   * *a bar on discrimination that is aimed at chronic patients, in the areas of housing and employment; including a ban on zoning discrimination;*

   * *an affirmation and implementation of the right of both voluntary and involuntary patients to have adequate treatment in the least restrictive setting;*

* *promotion and support of an independent system of advocacy services;*

3) *reform of funding mechanisms to insure prejudice toward the patient; and*

4) *accommodation of cultural differences in services, treatment, and community programs.*

In the end, it is not difficult to see why the former patient living on the corner might remain there when the alternatives are returning to the hospital, or going to a shelter that looks remarkably like a jail. But it is obscene that these are the alternatives that allow our consciences easy sleep at night.

Footnotes

[1] A list of these reports appears in the appendix of the book.

[2] Dr. John A. Talbott, "Toward a Public Policy on the Chronic Mentally Ill Patient," *American Journal of Orthopsychiatry* 50(1) (January 1980): 44.

[3] Ellen Baxter, "Deinstitutionalization: A Critical Analysis" (School of Public Health, Columbia University, 1977), p. 8.

[4] Talbott, pp. 44-45.

[5] Dr. George Gerbner, "Dreams that Hurt: Mental Illness in the Mass Media," Plenary Address in *The Community Imperative: Proceedings of a National Conference on Overcoming Public Opposition to Community Care for the Mentally Ill* (Philadelphia, Pennsylvania: 1980), p. 20.

[6] Dr. Joseph Mancuso, "The Mental Illness Metaphor as an Inducement to Rejection, in *The Community Imperative*, p. 26.

[7] Anthony Colletti, "Psychiatric Oppression and Class," *Win* Magazine, August 2 & 9, 1979.

[8] "Suicide Leading Cause of Death Among Blacks," *The Washington Afro-American*, June 20, 1981.

[9] Phil Brown, "Mental Health Policy Problems, Political Economy and Professionalism," in *The Community Imperative*, p. 417.

[10] Ibid.

[11] "Criteria for admission and readmission to a VA Hospital: Decision to admit," The VA Hospital in Sepulveda, California, 1977.

[12] Baxter, p. 4.

[13] Talbott, p. 45.

[14] Comments of Dr. Barbara I. Tobelman, Preface to the record, "Community Hearing on OMB's Proposal to Close or Curtail Services at Saint Elizabeths Hospital," sponsored by the Mental Health Association of the District of Columbia, January 18, 1982.

[15] Comments of Geraldine Boykin, Executive Director, D.C. Council 20, AFSCME, AFL-CIO, see preceeding source, p. 4.

[16] Comments of Dr. Ruth E. G. King, D.C. Chapter of the Association of Black Psychologists, see source in note [14], pp. 10-12.

[17] Comments of Cynthia Roberson, Executive Director, National Association of Social Workers, see source in note 14, p. 36.

[18] Jerome G. Miller, review of *Conscience and Convenience: The Asylum and Its Alternatives in Progressive America*, by David J. Rothman, in *American Journal of Orthopsychiatry* 50(3) (October 1980): 738.

[19] Gary E. Whitmer, "From Hospitals to Jails: The Fate of California's Deinstitutionalized Mentally Ill, *American Journal of Orthopsychiatry* 50(4) (December 1980): 738.

[20] Ibid.

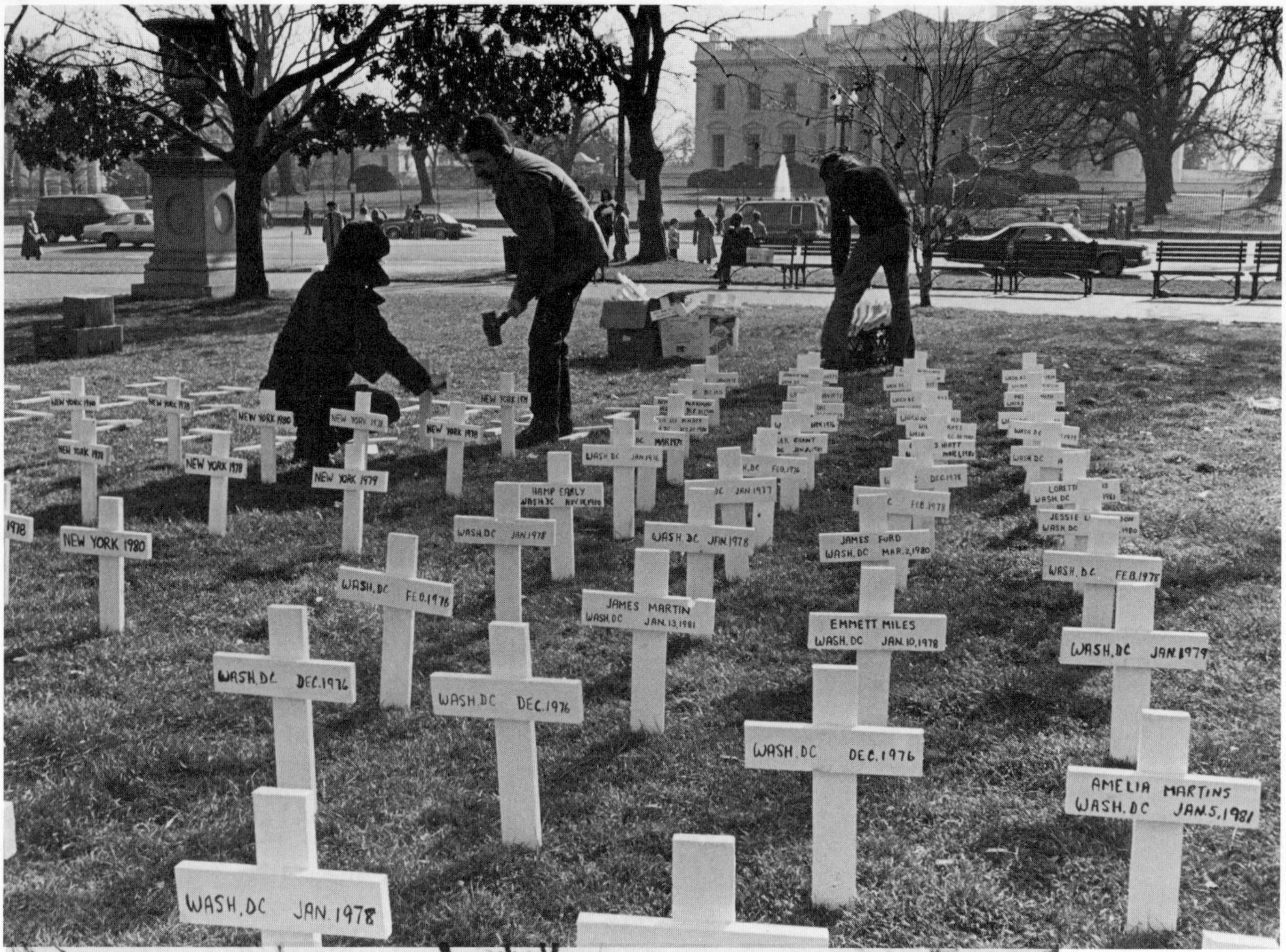
NEW YORK 1980
NEW YORK 1978
NEW YORK 1979
NEW YORK 1980
WASH.DC JAN.1978
WASH.DC FEB.1976
WASH.DC JAN 1978
JAMES MARTIN
WASH.DC JAN.13,1981
JAMES FORD
WASH.DC MAR.2,1980
EMMETT MILES
WASH.DC JAN.10,1978
WASH.DC FEB.1978
WASH.DC JAN 1979
WASH.DC DEC.1976
WASH.DC DEC.1976
WASH.DC DEC.1976
AMELIA MARTINS
WASH.DC JAN.5,1981
WASH.DC JAN.1978

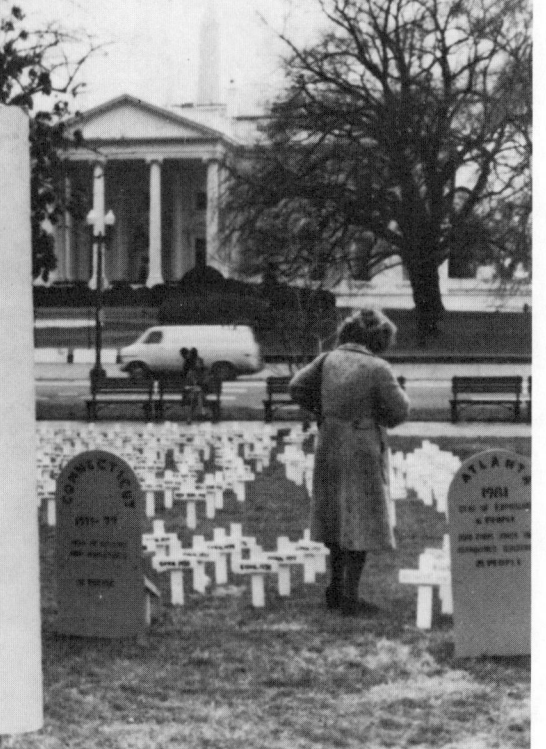

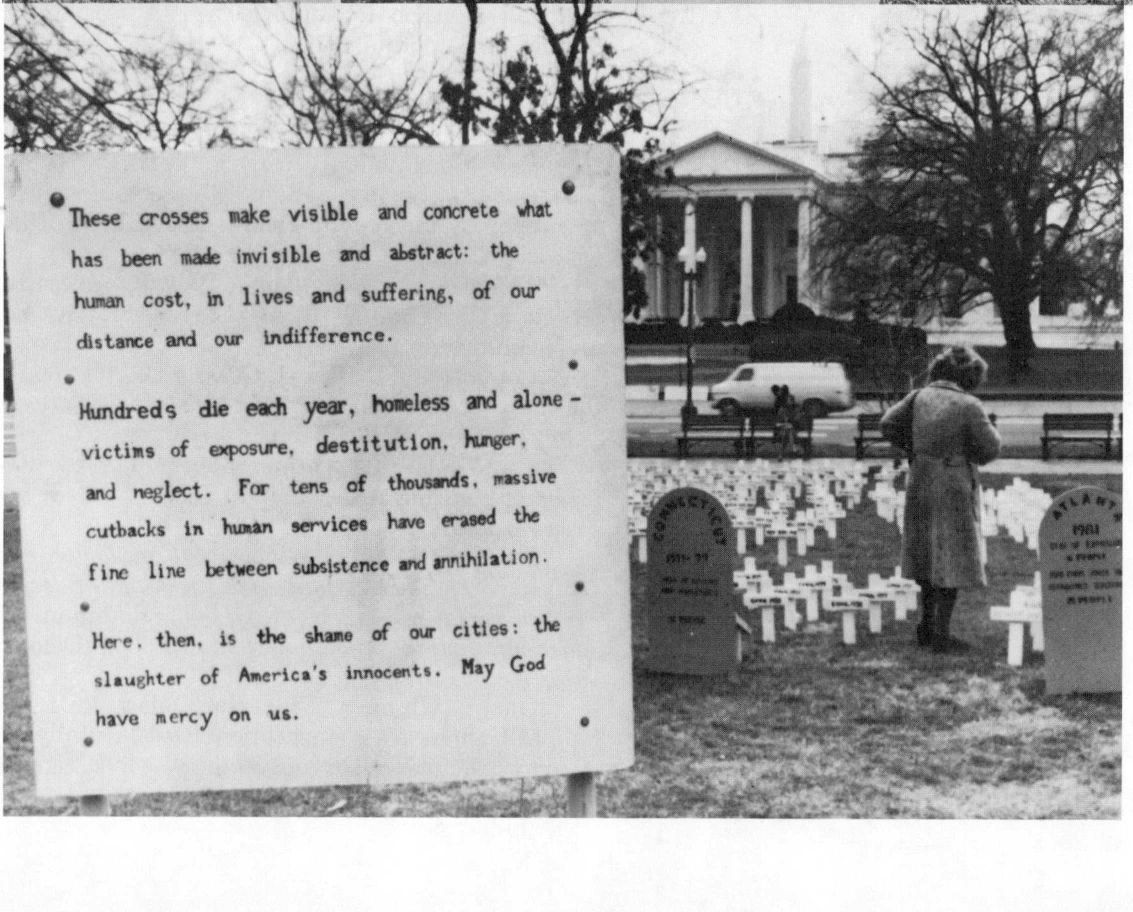
These crosses make visible and concrete what has been made invisible and abstract: the human cost, in lives and suffering, of our distance and our indifference.
Hundreds die each year, homeless and alone - victims of exposure, destitution, hunger, and neglect. For tens of thousands, massive cutbacks in human services have erased the fine line between subsistence and annihilation.
Here, then, is the shame of our cities: the slaughter of America's innocents. May God have mercy on us.

Ceremony marking the addition of a cross for a new homeless victim of exposure, planted in front of Reaganville.

Opposite

Planting of crosses in Lafayette Park, December 28, 1981.

March 19, 1982: crosses from winter-long presence in Lafayette Park are delivered to all members of Congress.

The Woman Who Died in a Box

In the coldest days of January 1982, Rebecca Smith, age 61, died of hypothermia in New York City. She was living in a rug-covered cardboard box on the corner of Tenth Avenue and West 17th Street.

In the days and weeks before her death, she was visited by at least 50 people who offered her food and shelter. Two weeks prior to her death, the Red Cross had informed police of her living arrangements. Following that, she was approached by Human Resources Administration officials, city social workers, a mobile geriatric unit, a Department of Mental Health outreach team, and a psychiatrist. The psychiatrist declared her an "endangered adult" under the first application of New York's Protective Services Law. She died a few hours before the implementation of a 72-hour protective custody order could take effect.

Until late August 1982, Joseph Cruz lived on a 35-foot-long traffic island on East River Drive in New York City. Overhead stretched the elevated southbound lanes of the road. All around him city traffic rushed by, slowing down long enough for sympathetic drivers to contribute food and beer. The 55-year-old Cruz had scavenged a bed and crates for furniture; he had a cooler, and a stove made from an oil drum. He called the city's shelters "pigpens" and refused to stay in them. He, too, was visited by a number of people, including psychiatrists and then the police. The latter forcibly took him to the psychiatric ward of Bellevue Hospital to await legal proceedings to decide whether he should be permanently confined.

Rebecca Smith came to the ranks of New York's homeless from a different sort of life. She was one of thirteen children; she was valedictorian of her class at the prestigious Hampton Institute in her native Virginia. For 10 years, she missed out on the growth and development of her daughter; Rebecca was hospitalized as a schizophrenic and underwent involuntary electroshock therapy. By her daughter's account, it was a different woman who finally emerged from the hospital.

She came to New York in 1959 to live with her sister. Again she was hospitalized. For the next 20 years, she was in and out of hospitals and clinics. During that time, she was heavily drugged. In 1981, she failed to appear for recertification interviews, and thereafter - having lost her public assistance and other benefits - she lived on the streets.

On a public street corner, her human vulnerability to the cold overwhelmed her. She was visible - yet not - to countless people. There were repeated offers of help, official and otherwise. It is telling that, after all of those visits, according to one city official, "Little was known about her other than her name." As is so often the case, we learned the most about her only after her death. We do not know if she understood these offers of assistance or not; custody came too late.

Joseph Cruz was moved to a psychiatric ward when he became *too* visible. He was, in a sense, singled out of the larger crowd of homeless people making do on the streets. In the summer weather and amidst publicity, officials moved rapidly to dislodge him. They did not feel their cause was helped when columnist Jimmy Breslin, outraged over what he considered a blatant violation of the man's rights, took over Cruz's spot, and vowed to remain until his release from Bellevue.

Both Rebecca Smith and Joseph Cruz were victims of exposure - one to the elements and one to the public eye. The circumstances of the two - separately and together - raise profound and vexing questions concerning the nature of options, competency, self-interest, individual civil rights, and the obligations of society and individuals.

The *Washington Post* editorialized on February 16, 1982, that "the story merits attention because there is a real problem here which has not been discussed: the problem of helping people who do not want to be helped." The *Post* is right in one respect: there is a *real* problem here. The problem is in the assumption that undergirds the *Post*'s question: that legions of the homeless poor are on our streets because they choose to be. That is a lie. It always has been and always will be.

During the winter of 1980-81, the mayor of Washington, D.C. decided to offer the press definitive proof that the men and women who live on Washington's streets do so by choice. His implication was that this would absolve his administration of any responsibility for their fate. He gathered two or three van loads of reporters and camera crews and went on a tour of the downtown heat grates. With 20 or 25 press representatives peering over his shoulder and cameras whirring, the mayor stopped at one grate after another and offered to drive the men to a city shelter. They respectfully declined.

No one asked why the men chose to remain where they were, for if they had inquired, they might have learned that there was - and is - good reason for the refusal: brutalization by armed guards; being put back on the streets at 5:30 A.M. in an unfamiliar area, with no place to go for at least two hours; theft of personal property; an abundance of lice and bedbugs. In spite of those problems, many of the men had tried the shelters, only to be turned away for lack of space. There would be no space left on the grates either, by the time they made the two- or three-mile trek back. Given the range of options open to them and previous experiences, the men on the grates had made a reasonable decision.

No one lives on the street by choice; all are there out of necessity. But all too often, people whose only relation to the street is the time it takes them to walk from office to car, decide - out of ignorance, arrogance, distance, and psychic self-defense - that all of those poor souls have freely chosen to live that way.

Being situated in abundance makes it difficult to understand that, even if people are desperately poor and mentally incapacitated, they may still prize self-respect above a forced servile dependency. Without fail, as the range and nature of options open to the homeless has increased, so has their willingness to come in out of the cold.

In calling shelters "pigpens," Cruz perhaps sensed that there were worse places to be than where he was. We do not know if Rebecca Smith understood that offers of help implied concern for her. But, we do know that after more than 50 visits, "little was known about her other than her name."

With due process - which moved too slowly to save Rebecca Smith, and faster than Joseph Cruz' situation warranted - the city acted to make judgments and decisions for each of these people. The belief that society owes us each at least one rescue attempt - whether our "deviancy" is mental illness, homelessness, drug addiction, or alcoholism - is widely held, though inconsistently applied with regard to urgency and effectiveness. What should be done? A temporary loss of freedom may be outweighed by the saving of a life, yet the balance has to be between fathoming the individual's own perception of danger and choices, and the state as Samaritan.

When the state undertakes the role of Samaritan, it does so within its own very great limitations. Rebecca Smith is a case in point: "The social worker who occasionally visited might have wanted to provide styrofoam sheets so that Mrs. Smith could have been more comfortable in her home... But if she was assisted in this way by the government, the government would be admitting a kind of 'approval' of what Mrs. Smith was doing." These are the comments of a man who himself had lived on the streets for a month, offered to the *Washington Post* in response to the flurry of letters and editorials that followed Mrs. Smith's death. The most important insight to be gained is that when government does reach out to help, it does so in a way *it* can understand and accept, in contrast to the kind of desire for understanding that is reflected in the following case.

A few years ago, a man was pictured in the *Washington Post* as he lay sick and cold on a heat grate behind the State Department. He had refused official offers of help, though local residents and shopkeepers had kept him going with coffee and sandwiches. Harold Moss, a CCNV member and a black man of about the same age, took two blankets - one for each of them - and joined the man on his grate. Moss had a considerable amount of experience working with the homeless, but it still took him two days and nights to begin to communicate with the sick man. By then, due process has run its course, and the man was taken away in an ambulance against his will. For the moment, he had been saved.

Our response when confronted - explicitly or implicitly - with the different and the needy is a telling expression of our values and our goals. We cannot know how many people passed by Rebecca Smith. Perhaps they have since begun a journey back toward human caring, for to pass her by and not act is to allow oneself to be changed for the worse. Responding in a helping way, which is to say, offering some alternative that is perceivable, accessible, and acceptable to the Rebecca Smiths and Joseph Cruzes of the world, requires first that we distinguish between the different and the dangerous and expand our values likewise. It is a task that requires time and concern.

The choices facing kind and caring people are presented as polarities - should someone's rights be violated so that his or her life can be saved, or should we demand that those in need accept options which may not be seen by them as viable ones? The questions produce agony and frustration in those who consider them. The violation of rights or the acceptance of intolerable options are not the only alternatives. By looking for generalized truths, we miss the individuality and uniqueness of homeless people, and thus make impossible the construction of workable solutions that serve those in need. In our dilemma, we move only within the parameters and possibilities that we already comprehend. If there are other answers, we will wait for visionaries and theoreticians to give them to us. While we wait - uncertain even about testing ourselves - the Rebecca Smiths and Joseph Cruzes will continue to suffer and die.

The Example of Geel

> ... [*The*] *negative public attitudes toward the disabled and those who are different are defined, structured, and reproduced by the fundamental values on which our society is based; the form community care has taken reflects the fact that "true" acceptance of differences or "deviancy" is antithetical to the dominant ideology of this country...* [1]

But the disabled and the different can be integrated and accepted, with full respect for their humanity and their perception of reality. In Geel, Belgium, a very different concept of "deviance" and the accommodation of it is at work and has been for several centuries.

The system of care in Geel for the mentally ill and retarded is based on a religious tradition stemming from the legend of St. Dimpna. According to legend, supplemented by bits of historical fact, an Irish king made incestuous demands of Dimpna, his daughter, after the death of his wife. Dimpna fled the country accompanied by her confessor and tutor, Gerebernus, in a boat across the North Sea and landed in Belgium. The two travelled overland and hid in the region of Geel. The king pursued and beheaded them both with a sword in approximately 600 A.D. At the moment of Dimpna's beheading it is said the king's sanity was restored. Dimpna became endowed with miraculous powers to drive the devil or evil spirits out of persons possessed by such forces, the supposed cause of insanity at that time. A shrine was built and pilgrims, usually accompanied by relatives, travelled long distances in hope of cure. They performed rituals of penance by crawling barefoot under the reliquary containing the bones of St. Dimpna. Today, the stone floor around the reliquary is worn by the feet and knees of those who sought to be freed of their malady by Dimpna. The pilgrims were cared for in sickrooms adjacent to the church. When these became overcrowded the homes of parishioners surrounding the church were used. By the middle of the 15th century there was a sizable and steady flow of pilgrims. Although records of the church attest to the miracles performed by Dimpna, certain pilgrims did not benefit from her curative powers. In such cases, the natural family returned home and paid a family of Geel to house their "possessed" family member. Initially, the motivation to house a pilgrim was primarily religious, although monetary incentives did strengthen the caretaker's piety. Over time, patients were sent to Geel by welfare administrations of nearby European cities as an inexpensive and convenient way to dispose of the "deviants" in their region. The expenses of wealthy patients were provided by their natural families and came from places as distant as Russia, Brazil, and the United States.

Currently 1,000 families within this town of 30,000 citizens have in their private homes one, or a maximum of two patients, or boarders as they are called. Families care for a total of 1,100 individuals; the back-up central hospital houses 250 in-patients. There has been no recruitment of caretakers by the central administration; in fact, a waiting list has always existed. The families are not given any specific training, psychiatric history or diagnosis before they receive an individual boarder. They are expected to rely on intuitive understanding and skill which they have developed over years of continual exposure to other boarders within their own home or neighborhood. Hundreds of families have housed mentally disabled persons for generations.

Excluding the families who "inherit" a boarder from their parents, other caretakers are initially motivated to take a patient for the supplemental income it offers and the work he/she will do with the family... [The] policy of limiting the number of patients to two per family insures that it cannot be the sole source of income... Children and boarders develop attachments, the boarders become involved in family festivities and crises, and over time, emotional bonds develop which turn the boarder into an integral part of the family group.

The boarders are considered to be a chronic population in need of supportive, long-term care, the majority of whom were referred from other traditional institutions... Many of the boarders in Geelian families are severely mentally ill and retarded individuals who are not considered to be suitable candidates for the majority of community care programs in the United States... Taking into account the type of patient Geel attracts, mainly chronic patients with no viable family or community ties, these individuals would otherwise spend their lives on the back wards of state hospitals.

To the dismay of professionals... Geelians just do not see the boarders as psychiatric patients. Boarders are included in the work and recreational activities of their families and are also free to participate on their own in the community sphere. Boarders are quite visible in the churches, cafes, local fairs, the movie house, and at sports events...

Cafes, of which there are 143 in the town, are places of social interaction for all Geelians. Boarders socialize with others in cafes, some spend their time actively hallucinating at a corner table, others cannot be distinguished from "normal" customers...

Although bizarrely dressed individuals may talk to themselves among a group of schoolchildren and others may endlessly pace up and down store aisles, the community does monitor certain forms of deviant behavior in public places. When a boarder begins to take off his/her clothes or begins to direct traffic, a passerby will intervene and take the individual home.

The police, too, tend to be protective of the boarder... According to the chief of police, Geel has a lower crime rate than the surrounding communities.[2]

The question is not what to do for or about a person who does not "want" to be helped. The real question concerns our love, care, and acceptance for those among us who are different. To what extent are we our brother or sister's keeper? Have we, in fact, so limited the options for the needy that the only choices before them are life in hell or danger and death on the streets?

Footnotes

[1] Ellen Baxter, "Geel, Belgium: A Radical Model for the Integration of Deviancy," in *The Community Imperative*, p. 67.

[2] Baxter, pp. 68-71.

Still I can point to one or two things I have definitely learned by being hard up. I shall never again think that all tramps are drunken scoundrels, nor expect a beggar to be grateful when I give him a penny, nor be surprised if men out of work lack energy, nor subscribe to the Salvation Army, nor pawn my clothes, nor refuse a handbill, nor enjoy a meal at a smart restaurant. That is a beginning.

George Orwell
Down and Out in Paris and London
1933

A Quiet Violence: The Homeless Poor in New York City, 1982

by Kim Hopper

A quiet violence. When Joseph Heller said it a few years ago, nobody thought that so vague and disquieting a phrase would ever apply to the state of our cities. To our anxious lives, shattered hopes, and uncertain relationships maybe; but not to the tilt of the urban world as a whole. Riots we'd had, but they at least were visible, and over, for the time being. Heller's warning was about unseen forces, insidious changes, things that are not noticed until nagging apprehension gives way to wholesale alarm. Spend a few days - or, better yet, a few nights - on the streets and you'll see what he meant. Something happened. Though it isn't clear at first glance what did, the signs, at any rate, are everywhere:

Kim Hopper is a research associate at the Community Service Society in New York City. He is co-author of Private Lives/Public Spaces: Homeless Adults on the Streets of New York City *and* One Year Later: The Homeless Poor in New York City, 1982.

New York City, winter 1980-81: By 7:30 each morning, most of the 300 men and women who come to St. Francis for coffee and sandwiches have scattered. Nobody knows exactly where they go. But if one looks closely, a trace of their presence can be detected: the lower five feet of the beige brick wall they stand alongside is several shades darker than the rest of the wall. Over the past 50 years, thousands of men, and increasingly, women, have made their way to the breadline. This stain is their signature, a mute reminder that, in this most affluent of societies, there exist large numbers of people who lack the minimal possession of social life - a home.

Washington, D.C., March 19, 1982: A curious scene is enacted just across from the White House. Forty crosses are driven into the ground of Lafayette Park. The crosses are meant to commemorate this winter's toll of reported street deaths in six cities. They join over 500 others already in place, unmourned casualties of the last five years in 11 cities.

Denver, winter 1981-82: Over 400 people slept in church pews each night, a scene repeated in Baltimore, Atlanta, Minneapolis, Seattle, New York, and Washington, D.C.

The Salvation Army announces plans to reopen soup kitchens closed for 50 years. Record numbers turn out for free food programs in Cleveland, Detroit, Milwaukee - but with a noticeable difference, according to kitchen workers: they don't look like Skid Row types anymore.

In a one-week period in March 1982, major news stories on the homeless poor in America appeared in Newsweek, U.S. News and World Report, *and the* Wall Street Journal *- not notably among our more alarmist broadsheets.*

The Manchester Guardian *of England put it this way, not without a certain measure of astonishment:* "You could be dead and they would just step over you." *(October 21, 1981)*

Sydney Schanberg of the New York Times *calls them the "expendable people." (December 15, 1981)*

Who are they? This is the tricky part, because, as quickly as they've been noticed, they've been tagged - whether as the "lumpenproletariat" in the nineteenth century, or as the "underclass" today - and the anxiety that accompanies their notice is quelled. In a sort of grotesque substitution of the part for the whole, we discovered "bag ladies." We've resurrected words

Saint Francis breadline in New York City.

which had fallen into disuse: words like vagrant, transient, derelict. A little reflection reveals that such words serve as anodynes to still the growing suspicion that something is desperately wrong in a society where people are scrounging to survive on the streets.

In a profound sense, as Denise Hinzpeter has observed, such a livelihood mimics the social identity of "street people."[1] Surplus, redundant people themselves, they exploit the surplus use-value, the "waste" potential, of public facilities: using waiting rooms for sleeping, restrooms for laundry, trash bins for food, and subways as resting places. One anticipates the appearance of a new round of outrage against such "parasites" every time a neighborhood is approached about the possibility of opening a shelter in its midst.

Drawing on the work Ellen Baxter and I have been doing for the past 2½ years, I'd like to sketch something of an overview of the situation of the homeless poor in New York City. By virtue of our approach, this will be something of an underview as well. But first, a brief historical prelude.

A Tradition of Neglect

The current Administration's obsession with whittling down the ranks of the "truly needy" has an honorable pedigree, one which harks back to the philosophy of "less eligibility" written into the reformed English Poor Laws by chief architects Jeremy Bentham and Edwin Chadwick. The idea is alluring in its simplicity: in dealing with unproductive, dependent populations - the elderly, incorrigible, unemployable, disabled or merely mad - the state's policy will be to make relief an option of last resort. Conditions in the workhouse are intentionally to be deplorable. Thus, needy individuals will avail themselves of any alternatives before turning to the state for aid. Families, charitable associations, churches, mean and degrading work: these were to be the next-to-last line of defense before relief. When families are overburdened, charitable and religious groups unable, and work unavailable, however, the state would step in. "Reluctant relief" best characterizes the policy.

Of course, conditions could not be so bad as to spark a general uprising of the poor, as has happened on occasion through the state's miscalculations of the limits of endurance possessed by the indigent. Further, some civilizing influences were exerted by philanthropic groups, social reformers, and the like. Their legacy (and that of medieval charity) is most keenly felt, however, in the provision which demands that the state justify such niggardly policies as were in effect.

Relief must not be made merely efficient; it has to be presented as fair. Typically, the state has justified its paltry sustenance in two ways: first, by appealing to dissatisfaction of the populace at large with the cruel necessity of work; and second, by portraying needy groups as "undeserving." In the post-Depression era in this country, both methods have been in force. Antipathy toward "Skid Row" denizens trades on the deep-rooted resentment of the tramp's refusal to work, and the equation of "homeless" with "derelict" insures that only minimal relief need be extended toward so unworthy, so degenerate a form of life.

Howard Bahr detected a third factor, more elusive and difficult to discern but one which *Time* magazine saw fit to acknowledge.[2] By their very existence, Skid Row men are an affront to the verities of a well-ordered society, refusing not only to work, but to take family responsibilities seriously, to take care in their appearance, to give shame its due and duty its claim. They are a standing challenge to the self-evident truths most of us accept as centrally ingredient to our settled sense of the world. Their world is manifestly unsettled, and their contentment with it, equivalent to social apostasy.

Such appeals work so long as the population of Skid Row could be seen as alien, its life-ways forbidding and its practitioners defective. But something happened. And it happened quite recently.

The New Face of Homelessness

Radical changes have occured in the size and make-up of the homeless population in the last 15 years - changes that challenge the legitimacy of traditional relief measures. In the first place, "Skid Row" is no longer a geographically confined way of life. The subways, bus and train depots, doorways and abandoned buildings, public parks and loading docks, alleyways and sidewalks - these are home for thousands of New Yorkers each night. With startling suddenness, women have appeared on the streets and their numbers are growing. (Only 15 years ago, sociologists were assuring us that they were a "relatively rare" phenomenon, indicative of widespread social disruption.) No longer are homeless families found on the streets only as a result of being burned out of their apartments. Young, minority men now make up the majority of the Bowery's population. Chronic alcoholism - long the mythic affliction of *all* Skid Row men - is no longer even the dominant scourge it once was. The presence of large numbers of disturbed "street people" is so prevalent as to be an almost clichéd feature of contemporary city life. At no time since the Great Depression have the homeless poor represented so broad a cross-section of American society as they do today.

The face of homelessness has changed because the forces responsible for it have done so as well. In times past, homelessness was typically confined to migratory laboring men and women. It took the dislocations of war, famine, plague, or civil strife to deprive people of their homes on a massive scale. Today we have the scale of deprivation without the antecedent catastrophes. The former sources of displacement have been succeeded by less obtrusive ones: unemployment, the depopulation of mental hospitals, the dramatic shrinkage of the low-income housing market. Let us look at each in turn.

Unemployment: The national unemployment rate stands at over 10 percent, closer to 12 percent if "discouraged workers" are included. Regional rates go as high as 20 percent, with rates upward of 60 percent not uncommon among minority youth. In its effect, unemployment has always been a great equalizer, demoralizing with ease the high and mighty and the low and menial. But it is a flail with a decided preference for the already vulnerable. It strikes, as Elliot Liebow recently put it, "first, hardest and repeatedly at those who can least withstand it, especially the poor, the young and minorities."[3] A quick glance at new male applicants for shelter in New York City provides indirect support for Liebow's claim. Their average age is 36, they are overwhelmingly black or Hispanic, most never finished high school, and fully a quarter of them find themselves applying for shelter owing to loss of a job.

Depopulation of state psychiatric facilities: New York State records show 126,000 releases over the past decade or so. Excluding expected deaths and readmissions, an estimated 47,000 ex-patients live in the metropolitan area. For many of them, this has meant a different kind of confinement, rather than an alternative to it. During much of the state's 14-year history of intensive deinstitutionalization, inadequate discharge planning, weak follow-up efforts, and scarce supportive housing were the rule. When combined with rampant inflation, rising rents and fixed subsistence-level incomes, these factors virtually insured a swelling of the ranks of the homeless. By the mid-'70's, psychiatric problems rivalled alcoholism as the predominant clinical disorder of homeless men. Depending on the count, anywhere from one-third to two-thirds of the homeless population as a whole are thought to suffer from significant psychiatric problems. When outreach workers first entered the city shelters in 1981, they found that 25 percent of the 219 men they examined in their first 16 days of operation were disturbed enough to warrant immediate hospitalization.

To these causes must be added an even more recent one: severe cutbacks in the social service sector. If reports from other regions, for example, in Minnesota,[4] are any indication, we may expect new casualties on the streets. In New York, the impact of more aggressive review procedures on the part of the Social Security Administration has been felt already: manifestly unemployable people are being dropped from the ranks of the "deserving" disabled because they fail on paper to meet more stringent eligibility requirements, and they lack the wherewithal to contest the decision.

In a word, it is disenfranchisement - from work, from decent housing, and from appropriate care and support - and not defectiveness, which is the hallmark of today's homeless poor. Under such circumstances, circumstances which challenge the root assumptions of fault and failure - or "dereliction" in short - on which traditional relief policy was based, prospects for a new approach improve. Simply put, the legitimacy of minimal efforts on society's behalf is no longer self-evident.

Private Lives/Public Spaces

For 15 months, beginning in December 1979, Ellen Baxter and I investigated the conditions of the homeless poor in New York City as part of a research project for the Community Services Society. By most standards of survey research, our methods were primitive: we spent time on the streets, usually at night, and in the public shelters and flophouses, getting to know the terrain and the people who made it their home. The regularity with which we ourselves were taken to be homeless, despite our favorable appearances (we made no effort to dress in tatters, carried no shopping bags) and good health, was both telling and a bit unnerving. We tried not to exploit the fiction - explaining to those we interviewed that we were researchers (or writers) doing a project (or story) on homelessness - except on those occasions when we deliberately posed as homeless ourselves. (Ellen passed herself off as homeless in applying for a bed at the women's shelter; I did the same in the flophouses and pulled a stint as a housekeeping worker in a Catskill hotel which formerly employed a number of Bowery men.)

Our findings will, I think, be of interest both for what they suggest about present sheltering arrangements and for what they imply about possibilities for a different approach. Very briefly, we found:

(1) Contrary to both popular and official opinion, the notion that the homeless "choose" to live on the streets, victims of deranged minds or infirm judgements, is - in the cheap sense of the term - a myth. Whenever decent, humane shelter has been made available, willing recipients have made ready use of it. Actual demand for public shelter

cannot be taken as a valid index of the true extent of need. The reason, I suggest, is two-fold: first, once the supply of public shelter reaches a certain level of oversaturation (usually signalled by a nearly full lobby in the Men's Shelter), demand falls off - a sort of spontaneous recognition that the market has been exhausted; and second, given the nature of the personal costs exacted when one submits to the regimens and conditions of the public shelters, many homeless people decide to fend for themselves on the streets.

(2) At the time of the study, public shelter was more of a voluntary prison than a refuge. The deplorable conditions in the flophouse and Men's Shelter, routine contempt meted out to applicants, and historical association of the Bowery as the abode of "bums," all conspired to make public shelter an option of desperation for many homeless men. For different reasons - namely, exclusionary policies, limited beds, and exacting regimen - the Women's Shelter could effectively serve only a small proportion of the women in need, The deterrent power of public facilities was especially strong, we found, for those homeless people afflicted with disorders which render them acutely sensitive to the slightest trace of menace in their surroundings. In light of such observations, we felt, the city's claim that no one who applied for shelter was turned away, took on something of the character of a cruel joke.

Since we began our study, things have changed significantly. Prompted by the twin spurs of a protracted class action suit and a slowly dawning sense of the crisis they face, city and state officials have improved both the supply and the conditions in public shelters.

(3) Finally, we rediscovered something on which George Orwell had remarked some 50 years ago: "the terrible complexity" of dire poverty. Mere survival on the streets is a wearing and demeaning pursuit, highly vulnerable to a host of natural hazards and social rules. It was a little short of daunting to witness the courage and resourcefulness of those who - homeless, and sometimes crazy, too - were "making it," if only temporarily.

*   *   *

Six months after *Private Lives/Public Spaces* was released in March 1981, the class action filed on behalf of homeless men (*Callahan* v. *Carey*) was settled in court. The impact of the suit was immediate and far-reaching: after an initial ruling in December 1979, the city opened an emergency shelter on Ward's Island. The following winter, upwards of 625 men were quartered there nightly. While by no means a model shelter, it did offer some men an alternative to the streets and flophouses.

The significance of the consent decree signed in August 1981 was even greater. It strengthened the initial recognition of a right to shelter which the court had supported in December 1979, and then went on to establish certain qualitative standards that all public shelters must meet. By October 1981, attorney Robert Hayes was back in court, charging the city with contempt of the consent decree they had signed a scant six weeks earlier. By that time, 220 men were sleeping in an intake center which met none of the standards by which the city had agreed to abide. The judge ordered the city to open an additional 400 bed facility within 24 hours; the next day a former public school in Brooklyn was converted into an emergency shelter, and men were bused to and from the facility. Within two weeks of its opening, it was filled to capacity. In the ensuing two months, two more emergency shelters - both state armories - were opened. Facilities for women were expanded as well, and a new shelter for women was opened on the Lower East Side.

In the past year, the city has also funded two 24-hour drop-in centers. Over 150 homeless individuals made use of them each night this past winter. During the latter part of the winter, dozens more have found respite courtesy of a number of churches and synagogues which have opened their doors to the homeless. Both of these latter efforts are standing testimony to the fact noted earlier: that many homeless men and women find the public shelters too forbidding to avail themselves of them, but they will gladly accept refuge when it is offered in a non-demeaning, non-invasive fashion.

Beyond Shelter

Shelter is not the answer to the problem of homelessness; homes are. Having said that, I hasten to add that emergency shelter is an indispensable part of a more general solution - a necessary holding action. Significant progress has been made by the city in this regard in the past two years. The new shelters are not sufficient. Most were, after all, set up on a crisis basis and do not meet the qualitative standards of the *Callahan* consent decree. But they are promising.

Yet shelter, no matter how decently it is offered, by its very nature confirms an uncertain status: one is still on the margin of polite society, neither belonging nor quite in exile (although being quartered on an island separated from the city by a moat may lead one to wonder about that last claim). What is needed is a comprehensive approach, one which recognizes that while the diversity of today's homeless population means that a variety of supportive services will eventually be needed, still their shared and prior need is for decent housing.

The New York Coalition for the Homeless has found it useful to discuss such a comprehensive solution in terms of a three-tiered approach. The basic features look like this:

Tier
I: basic emergency shelter, made as undemanding and accessible as security and hygiene considerations allow, which provides the minimal amenities stipulated by the *Callahan* consent decree: decent, clean bedding, wholesome food, adequate security and supervision. Armories, church basements, school buildings may all serve such a purpose.

Tier
II: transitional accommodations, a step up from emergency shelter in demands on residents and services provided, which will achieve some differentiation by need of the homeless populations. Intensive efforts to secure appropriate entitlements as well as necessary clinical linkages could be made here. A step in this direction was approved by the State Office of Mental Health some time ago and has been the subject of considerable and intensive discussion at the City Department of Mental Health. To date, however, no substantive commitment of funds or personnel has been made. The Parker Street Shelter in Boston - at least in the form it took in the winter of 1980-81 - was a pioneering effort in this regard.

Tier
III: long-term, not-for-profit operated supportive residences - homes, in short, with the appropriate service and aid modalities built-in as part of the structure of everyday life. The city- and state-supported St. Francis Residence is an excellent example of such a facility.

The St. Francis Residence warrants detailed attention here. Owned and operated by the St. Francis Friends of the Poor, it is paradigmatic of a humane and cost-effective long-term approach to urban homelessness. Nor can the charge sometimes made - that St. Francis has "skimmed" the homeless population for its more intact and well-functioning members - be sustained: many of the residents at St. Francis were formerly tenants of a since-converted SRO hotel - and before that, had spent much of their lives in and out of mental hospitals. A significant number have also logged time on the streets and in the shelters.

What St. Francis demonstrates (for the primary population it serves) is that when genuine "community psychiatry" is tried, it has a real chance of success. Here as elsewhere, even severely disabled people can live decently and well when appropriate support is provided. The trick is not to treat social and clinical needs as though they designated separate domains of concern and action. They are intimately linked for this group of people, and with this recognition, residences can be designated with the supports built in, rather than tacked on. At St. Francis, assistance with meals, medication, and money is provided in the same matter-of-fact, non-stigmatizing fashion. Clinical attention and emergency intervention are both available as needed: the requisite back-up services have been secured. But the key to its success lies less in an armamentarium of therapeutics than it does in the simple - and sometimes not-so-simple - effort to build community for a group of people who have repeatedly been told they don't belong.

Ironically, all this is accomplished in a way that not only saves lives but money as well - a not inconsiderable fact in these parlous times. The daily cost per resident of the temporary accommodations at the Keener public shelter on Ward's Island is calculated to be $18.90. This includes staff and operating expenses, but, of course, makes no allowance for personal stipends of any sort to the men. Staff and operating expenses for the St. Francis Residence come to a total of $6.78. If one adds as well the daily living allowance secured under public entitlement programs and the dollar-value of the donated services of the Fransiscans, one arrives at a total figure of $13.18. Note, too, that the total capital cost of the 400-bed Keener expansion currently under way amounts to nearly $7 million, or $17,500 per bed. By contrast, acquisition and renovation costs of the St. Francis Residence together amounted to $850,000, or $8,500 per room. This latter amount is roughly what the city and state spend per man in emergency shelters over a 15 month period.

By Way of Conclusion

The New York situation as I've recounted it here offers, I think, grounds for hope on a number of levels. First, it demonstrates both the power and limitations of litigation as a tool for advocacy. Nothing moves city administrators quite like the threat of a suit, and whatever effectiveness the Coalition can claim in negotiating with public officials draws heavily on the continued presence of that threat, whether stated or not. At the same time, quality is a matter of details, and judges are exceedingly reluctant to involve themselves in the day-to-day specifics of running a public shelter, or to set any but the most general guidelines for such conduct. (The consent decree, signed voluntarily by both plaintiffs and defendants, circumvented that difficulty because the specific qualitative assurances were arrived at through the negotiations of the interested parties, not through judicial decree.) Then , too, policy-making by judicial fiat has meant, in effect, lurching from one court order to another; it has yet to eventuate in a comprehensive plan on the city's part.

Second, it is fair to say, I think, that the public attitude toward the homeless has changed markedly in the past year. The press and electronic media have proven generally to be worthy allies in recent months, dutifully depicting the shame of the streets for the public scandal it is, and increasingly voicing suspicion of official dithering in place of real policy-making. Slowly, images are changing. "Derelict" no longer appears quite so often as a blanket description of the homeless; mere eccentricity is no longer the sole concern of "human interest" stories. Blame is no longer extended so handily to men who are homeless - as one discovers upon asking them - because they have lost a job. In short, homelessness as a modality of disgrace has been muted somewhat.

In partial testament to this change, as well as to the organizing work of Coalition for the Homeless members, a number of Community Boards and political clubs in the city have passed resolutions welcoming the establishment of residences for the homeless in their neighborhoods. Once communities understand that sheltering the homeless need not mean re-creating the Bowery - and for many this is a novel realization - the way is opened for a variety of initiatives. Here, I think, a deeper factor comes into play. One of the more impressive features of this effort is the eagerness of ordinary citizens to give lie to the dominant myth that the public couldn't care less. It is difficult to escape the notion that, in some small way, this gesture helps combat the pervasive alienation of the secular city, the re-charged fear of nuclear annihilation, the numbing sense of being utterly at the mercy of forces beyond one's control or ken.

Finally, although I anticipate the times somewhat, there is the forced conviviality of shared misfortune. Massive conversions and elevated pricing have placed many former housing resources (like SRO hotels) beyond the reach of welfare or SSI recipients. In this regard the homeless find themselves increasingly in economic kinship with other vulnerable (if, for the time being, housed) groups: the elderly, the unemployed and marginally employed, the working poor with children. The precariousness of the position of these "deserving" groups can only increase as the recession deepens.

The underlying causes of homelessness - structural unemployment, inadequate community-based psychiatric care, housing scarcity, and social service cutbacks - show every sign of continuing unabated, if not, indeed, intensifying. Newly-initiated review procedures are returning disabled recipients of federal entitlements to the ranks of the merely poor. For the homeless poor effectively to plead their case for relief, it will be increasingly critical for them to make common cause with other neglected or victimized populations, to force the issue away from idiosyncratic pathology and into the realm of common suffering. Only in this way will an effective constituency of demand - the initial first step in the redress of grievances - be mobilized.

These are not grounds for celebration, but they are grounds for believing, I submit, that hope is something other than a fool's errand.

Footnotes

[1] Denise Hinzpeter, review of *Shopping Bag Ladies: Homeless Women Speak About Their Lives,* by Anne-Marie Rousseau, in *Working Papers*, March/April 1982.

[2] 28 February 1969.

[3] *San Diego Union*, 6 December 1981.

[4] *Minneapolis Tribune*, 29 November 1981, and *Minnesota Daily*, 7 January 1982.

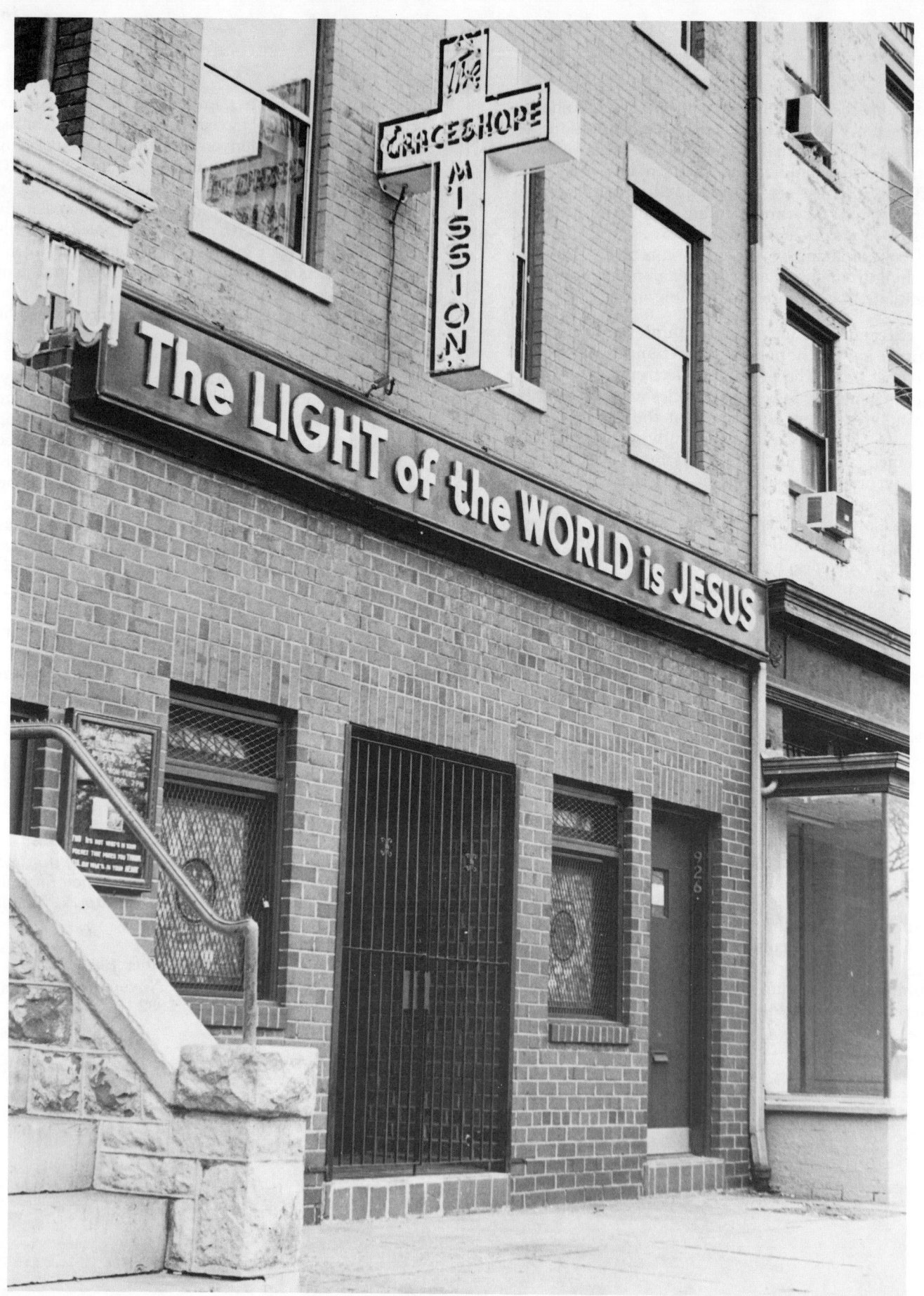

HOME FOR THE HOLIDAYS?

Richmond: Southern Hospitality for All?

On the day after Christmas, 1981, the Richmond *Times-Dispatch* ran a photo entitled "Home for the Holidays." It showed the silhouette of a man living in an abandoned bus. "The homeless man spent Christmas Day in the shelter of the old vehicle," read the caption.

In Richmond, Virginia, awareness of homelessness and the level of concern is such that this photo and what it symbolized did not cause many people to move out of the camp of the disinterested. There was no outcry or public debate - as there would be over the death of Rebecca Smith in a cardboard box in Manhattan. Those who experienced revelation at this printed sight did so quietly and privately.

The Salvation Army has been working in Richmond for 94 years. It is, as in many other cities, the prevailing force in non-government welfare services, and the acknowledged expert in analyzing needs and goals. While it does not have its own physical plant out of which to provide food or shelter, the homeless are served a meal in a facility five blocks from the Salvation Army headquarters, and they are housed in rented rooms 1½ blocks away. There is space for 10 people per night, and an average of 25 requests for emergency shelter per day. The Salvation Army's policy here is to provide a free bed and meal one night per month to any single transient man. Lodging, meals, and job referral services are offered on a seven-day-a-week basis, with a daily sign-up program from 4:30 to 9:30 P.M. The city government has chosen not to take any steps of its own to provide for the increasing numbers of homeless people on the streets of Richmond.

The Salvation Army announced plans in 1976 to build a new facility to feed and house men, women, and children. Zoning problems forced it to look for an alternate location, but, with the agreement of the city, the group eventually returned to the original site. Early in 1982, both the Planning Commission and the City Council cleared the way for the Salvation Army to begin construction. In the meantime, $630,000 in contributions for the building program had been gathered, as well as $112,000 in pledges.

The Salvation Army has a golden reputation as resident experts and providers of emergency services. Along with various private missions, it has been the traditional local source of assistance where the municipal government, individual churches, and independent groups have not been directly involved. When faced with a housing crisis, the conventional and comforting response is to make certain that the Salvation Army is involved.

* * *

Emergency Shelter, Inc. (ESI) first came into existence in February 1981. Volunteers and staff members of more than 30 churches and social service agencies had become concerned about what they perceived as a growing problem: homelessness. Each of these groups had been limited in providing emergency services to people in need of temporary housing, and they coalesced their concerns into ESI as a way of filling gaps in existing services and documenting the city's need for additional shelter space, according to Valerie Marsh, a professional social worker who was ESI's major promoter, first executive director, and subsequent program director.

With an organizational structure in place, ESI turned to the city for support. They didn't come away with much. The city's reaction was political and predictable: to appear concerned, and produce a response without becoming involved. Being somewhat naive, it took ESI a number of months to see how empty the city's efforts really were.

One step the city took was to form a Mayor's Emergency Shelter Task Force. On the task force, along with a city council representative and the assistant city manager for human resources, sat several attorneys, a U.S. Attorney, a utility executive, a newspaper executive, a United Way official, a minister, and a Salvation Army officer.

As a public body, the task force had several advantages. It had respectability and legitimacy, and the efforts of the task force appeared to be a serious attempt to examine the problem of homelessness and the availability and adequacy of existing resources. By

June 1981, it had, in fact, produced a study on the subject: *Report and Recommendation of the Mayor's Emergency Shelter Task Force*. However, the end product was not only a very cursory examination of Richmond's problem, but one written from a traditional point of view about the homeless, and heavily biased toward solutions being offered by the Salvation Army. By patting ESI on the back both in its report and its public presentation, the task force diffused ESI's potential to force concrete demands on it. The report and the task force created the illusion of city action and involvement in the shelter issue without having to develop a program or spend any money.

If there had been equality between ESI and the city, or, if ESI was equipped with a better understanding of political machinations, they might have raised their demands or lowered their expectations. The net result was obfuscation; the city could fall back on a wide-spread desire to avoid new and expensive programs, while pointing to what it *had* done to help: i.e., the task force and its study. Not surprisingly, the outcome of the study was this:

> "... The Salvation Army's proposed emergency shelter program provides the best permanent solution to the unmet emergency shelter needs of [*local residents, newcomers, and deinstitutionalized adults.*]
> Report and Recommendations of the Mayor's Emergency Shelter Task Force (page 4)

The Salvation Army, however, has been unable to commence construction because of ongoing litigation arising out of neighborhood opposition to its plans.

The task force was also to support ESI in its search for a permanent location, but its official efforts were not the determining factor in ESI finding a home. When ESI finally located a building, the city did not move to help ease the logistical and legal problems that accompanied it.

ESI's record has been a laudable one for a new group moving on an unpopular problem. Its first temporary operations (from February 4 to April 5, 1981) were in a city firehouse. In that time, ESI served 490 different people, providing 1372 bed spaces, and turning away only 71. Staff members were inclined to shelter as many people as space permitted in the firehouse; the number of people turned away later rose. In its first 11 months of operation, ESI served 1,100 different guests and turned away 1,727 others for lack of space.

From May to October 12, 1981, ESI provided shelter through a contractual arrangement with several hotels. In this way, 52 to 75 people per month were given emergency housing assistance.

The actual difficulties ESI encountered in attempting to establish a permanent shelter are the traditional ones, set in the usual net of archaic laws, outdated attitudes and stereotypes, and ignorance: zoning problems, building code violations, and neighborhood opposition.

With the formation of the task force in February 1981, and the verbal support of Richmond's mayor and city council, ESI began to search for a permanent location. With the task force lacking the will or the means to solve ESI's problems, ESI had to labor on its own behalf. After a lengthy search, a building at 2 East Main Street was selected and rented, and repairs begun. After a substantial investment of time and money by ESI, the owner ceased cooperating with the attempt to obtain an occupancy permit. A complex legal battle ensued, and the owner eventually agreed - in mid-August 1981 - to allow ESI use of the building for 21 months.

Thus, ESI was able to open at the East Main Street site on October 13, 1981, with both salaried staff and volunteers. Its 1982 budget, about $76,000, represented $41,000 from United Way and the remainder in contributions from churches, civic groups, and individuals.

The shelter offers services seven nights a week from 7:00 P.M. to 7:00 A.M. In keeping with ESI's policy of filling gaps in existing services, guests, are, for the most part, referred by other agencies. Out of a total of 20 beds, a limited number of walk-in spaces are available. There is a maximum stay of 10 nights a month, though this rule is somewhat flexible. The staff provides information and referrals for daytime services. For instance, shopping privileges at a local thrift store are arranged through the issuance of a chit, so that guests can procure needed clothing and household items. In addition, returning guests must provide three daily verifications of efforts to resolve the "cause" of their homelessness: e.g., SSI interview, housing search, a job application.

The primary standard for acceptance of guests is that they are homeless and ineligible for services from other sources. Most guests therefore are victims of:

* vandalism;
* lost, stolen or delayed checks;
* accidental utility loss;
* illegal eviction;
* domestic violence ineligible for YWCA
* assistance;
* relocation to Richmond and ineligibility
* for Traveller's Aid; or
* unemployment.

Dinner is served on weekends when other programs do not operate, and breakfast is served daily. Both meals are prepared at the shelter. In addition, laundry facilities are available, and showers are provided for those who wish to use them.

Because many of the guests stay at the shelter through referrals, those with the most deep-seated causes of homelessness are served the least. They either do not initiate the assistance process or they are viewed as chronic cases who cannot be graduated to other parts of the welfare system, and they are discouraged from returning. Further, there is a greater availability of information on referrals since more extensive records of interaction are kept on them. Finally, because "successful case follow-up" is important to an atmosphere of productivity, there is an effort to link shelter users to other parts of the system that can offer them long-term aid. Thus, guests are passed on to other agencies for solutions to their immediate problems, i.e., loss of a check, housing, job placement.

Despite these factors, a look at some of the records is enlightening:

Reasons given for homelessness

relocation	708
unemployment	384
family dispute	158
travel problem	133
waiting for check	107
eviction	105
medical problem	61
mental problem	45
other	15

NOTE: These figures cover guests from October 13, 1981 to March 31, 1982. Guests may offer more than one reason for their homelessness. For the months of March to May 1982, the ranking of these has shifted somewhat, with unemployment being most frequently listed. Second is relocation, with travel third.

Several comments on these trends are appropriate. Recently, unemployment is the most commonly given reason for need of shelter, no doubt because people are attracted by Richmond's relatively low level of joblessness (4.5 percent), which, in turn, is swelling the ranks of the unemployed. Of course, the unemployment disguises the problems disproportionately faced by minorities, those with few marketable skills, and those with little education. The three leading causes of homelessness here point up the Depression-like search for jobs that is underway.

As a result of this situation, a trend on the increase in Richmond is the sight of single men and women and whole families attempting to relocate to the city. They have fled dismal conditions elsewhere, coming from as far away as Washington and Oregon. Many tell tales of being bounced from one town to another, given a meal and a night's hospitality, and then told to move on. It is alarmingly reminiscent of the 1930's.

While the racial make-up of those who have used the shelter was originally estimated to be about 60 percent black and 40 percent white, it has shifted to about 50-50. Tracing a pattern of deinstitutionalization among adults has been more difficult. Though Marsh says her intuition tells her the number of patients released without previous planning is high, only about 15 percent of ESI guests acknowledge prior mental health contacts. (Most ex-mental patients are incapable of dealing with the bureaucratic maze that confronts them when they seek assistance from traditional sources, and hence, never make it to the shelter.)

From the October 13, 1981 opening to March 31, 1982, 861 guests were sheltered at 2 East Main Street. Of these, 483 were single men, 123 were women, and 94 were children. Sixty were on some form of welfare, and 46 were SSI recipients. Guests stayed an average of 4.5 nights, though 23 guests stayed longer. The staff computes that between $10 and $12 was spent to shelter each guest each night.

The types of assistance provided fit the description offered earlier:

employment counseling	*314*
welfare referrals	*121*
housing counseling	*108*
hospitalization	*35*
vocational rehabilitation referral	*19*
other	*160*

"Successful case follow-ups" were reported at 303.

Time and experience have helped Marsh and her staff hone their awareness of the magnitude and nature of the problem. An example: a long-awaited shelter fire drill, weeks in the planning, resulted in a gain of guests that night as some of the homeless people simply joined the crowd re-entering the building and by-passed the admissions procedure.

Volunteers have been hampered in their efforts to undertake a street census (nearly impossible under the best conditions), primarily because they lack entrée to unfamiliar areas where the homeless can and do remain invisible during critical periods of the day and night. Necessary personal relationships and a keen awareness of survival techniques are in their infancy here, existing at a sufficient level that staff can point out nearby cars as available sleeping quarters when the shelter is full, but inadequate when it comes to checking out vacant buildings or highway overpasses where the homeless take refuge.

A new factor has now inserted itself in the summary of shelter in Richmond: the Capitol Hotel. With 113 rooms that have rented at $26-$28 per week, the downtown hotel is scheduled to be sold. Neither shelter nor low-cost housing is among its potential uses. In a city where few services exist in duplicate, the loss of one such facility spells greater need and increased demand.

The Capitol is one of the hotels that ESI used before acquiring a permanent facility. The city currently places families with children there, as well as people awaiting their first allocation of benefits.

ESI itself faces problems in expanding to meet the need it already sees. Currently one floor of its East Main Street shelter is unused, with the other two floors serving as segregated quarters for men, women, and children. Ten additional beds could be located on the unused floor, were it not for permit requirements that would also demand 30 parking spaces. The ESI staff is willing to hire the additional workers needed to facilitate the expansion, but they have not been successful in overcoming the permit problem. Though staff members have pointed out to city officials the absurdity of such a parking requirement, there has been no breakthrough.

Who will meet the additional need? While the Mayor's Task Force quickly came up with recommendations that paved the way for the city to sit back and do nothing, members also put a finger on the central difficulty for city residents who have not yet come to terms with the reality of growing homelessness. From their report:

> *The Task Force is convinced that there will be some neighborhood opposition to a permanent shelter wherever it is located. We believe that this opposition is largely the result of a misunderstanding of the program and the people it serves.*

Report and Recommendations of the Mayor's Emergency Shelter Task Force (page 8)

While litigation and permit disputes drag on, real human beings suffer and die. The Richmond Office of the Chief Medical Examiner verified that 23 people died during the winter of 1979-80 with hypothermia the major cause. Thirty others perished with exposure as a contributing factor, in a city not known for its harsh winters. While it is not clear how many of these deaths occurred among homeless people, they are, of course, most susceptible to exposure. The homeless are hit hardest when food, shelter, and care are the missing resources. When compared to deaths reported in other major northern cities, these figures appear to be very high: exposure-related deaths in Richmond are greater than those reported by New York and Chicago combined. It is, in fact, difficult to settle on an explanation. Politicization of death reports and conscious under-reporting elsewhere, as well as an easily manipulated standard for hypothermia may play a part in the figures that are finally released.

Conditions have worsened through early 1982, yet figures pre-dating the Reagan Administration's budget cuts show that needs and resources did not even come close to each other then. Statistics for a two-month period during the winter of 1980 illustrate this clearly, though shelter workers say the figures are understated:

	Seeking aid	Not receiving aid
Richmond Crisis Intervention	23	14
Grace House	45	42
Oasis House	N.A.	25 (12 less than 20 years of age)
Daily Planet	85	74
Salvation Army	2760	1080
Traveller's Aid	187	69 (54 adults, 15 children)
YWCA	61	39
United Way	42	19 (11 children)

Source: Report and Recommendations of the Mayor's Emergency Shelter Task Force, Appendix B.

ESI has estimated that the city needs at least 200 additional beds, with services directed at single men and families. But support, both political and financial, is hard-won. The report of the Mayor's Task Force is seen by many as a significant attempt to diffuse attention. As Valerie Marsh points out, "Though they have been requested to provide funding, buildings, Community Development Block Grants, supplies, and even assistance with linen, these requests have not led to concrete results. The city's action has taken the form of endorsement of the cause and the declaration of a 'Shelter Week,' which went unpublicized."

Atlanta:
I was Homeless and You Offered Me Shelter

If there is a good example of a city where the religious community has played a major role in creating shelter for the homeless, Atlanta would be the nominee, and the story would be dramatic and moving.

Atlanta is no exception to the rule that things urban are built on contrasts; here is a Southern setting, a black city, a new spot on the map of international finance and business, a rare bird now governed by a black former United Nations ambassador who also succeeded a black mayor.

As Atlanta has put on the traditionally Eastern glitter of commerce, wealth, and nightlife, the contrasts have become more stark, and they do not exclude the homeless. The major downtown business organization, Central Atlanta Progress, maintains a special Derelict Committee, yet nothing akin to a public bathroom exists in the city. Downtown Atlanta is filled with new offices, shops, and hotels; a modern airport is close by. People do not freeze to death here; they die in fires in vacant buildings. The city suffered during two recent years under the weight of unexplained killings of young black men, creating divisive racial tensions and heightened perceptions and distrust of those who are "different." Where is there room for the homeless?

* * *

The Reverend Ed Loring was pastor of Atlanta's Clifton Presbyterian Church in 1978, when some of the congregation's 30 members decided to initiate a closer relationship to the poor. The next year was spent altering and renovating the church building in preparation for a "night hospitality" program. The congregation was so thoroughly exhausted by the physical preparations that they no longer felt capable of creating an emergency shelter. They contacted CCNV's Mitch Snyder, already scheduled to travel from Washington for an intensive weekend exchange about hospitality, and told him: We don't think we can do this.

"We rationalized," says Loring. "We were too far from downtown. We didn't have much money. We were just too damn tired. But Mitch 'promised' to come anyway, and, when he did, he offered a clear direction: 'Not only *can* you do this, you *must*. You must open the doors, because people's lives are hanging in the balance.' " The weekend was compelling, fearful, transforming. On the surface, it was a tough job and inconvenient timing. Amidst the tears and doubts, a small group of people took their first step into the unknown and said "yes."

* * *

On November 1, 1979, the Clifton Presbyterian Church opened space for 30 homeless men. On the church's floor was plastic sheeting to protect the carpet, and foam mats on which the guests could sleep. This simple yet serious effort would yield abundant fruit.

The opening of even this small space at Clifton appreciably increased opportunities for Atlanta's homeless to get off the streets. "The Salvation Army has only 14 beds for transients, and the men get only one free night every six months. At the Union Mission, there are three free nights *per lifetime*. Even if luck goes your way, you have, at most, four free nights of shelter in this city," stated Loring.

The hosts and guests still had to find and get to know one another. Clifton's program was modest in its approach: to find those in need, volunteers simply drove around Atlanta's darkened streets, offering baked potatoes and a ride to the church.

In a short time, the church was filled, and a pick-up point for guests was established. Seven nights a week, volunteers set up the mats, prepared hot drinks and a simple meal, and drove the van. They offered showers, laundry, extra winter clothes, and, most important, friendship. No questions were asked, no rules administered save two; no violence, and please check liquor bottles overnight. In the morning, a hot breakfast and bus fare eased the journey back.

Meanwhile, the core group was rethinking its position: the original estimate of those in need was raised to "hundreds," and "we discovered new needs every day," said Loring. Church members adjusted to the few stains that appeared on the sanctuary carpet; they were part of the price of what they had undertaken. Parishioners found themselves re-examining old values, images, and expectations.

"I became very angry when people were called 'bums,'" recalled Loring. "They are broken. If they could even steal successfully, they wouldn't be on the streets. We have been taught to distrust the poor as people who freeload. In opening our church to the down and out, we are in a constant struggle of faith, and so we grow."

Three months into the winter, a change took place among the men at the church. Without being asked, they began to relieve the few volunteers of the housekeeping duties that were draining them night after night. The dishes were washed, the tables wiped, floors mopped, needs met.

*

Clifton's efforts were a story of loaves and fishes when the next winter arrived. Realizing the inadequacy of their own facilities, they began knocking on other church doors. Their request was simple and direct: sanctuary for the poor. The Central Presbyterian Church, across from Georgia's Capitol in downtown Atlanta, opened its doors to more people - and with more services.

On January 14, 1981, Central began sheltering 180 men and 6 to 12 women each night. The men stayed in a fourth floor gymnasium that provided only floor space, while the women used a separate area. From 7:30 P.M. to 6:30 A.M., a small group of volunteers provided sandwiches and tea. Here there were the same basic rules: no alcohol, no violence. More than 200 volunteers were involved. For each of those volunteers, life would never be quite the same.

The Reverend Archbishop Pope Saint Charles Tyler Cavanaugh.

By the summer of 1981, Loring and his friends were not only seasoned at the business of offering shelter, but were also developing their own ideas of the shape and magnitude of homelessness in Atlanta. A repertoire of evidence makes the problem understandable and provides grounds for movement; the Atlanta workers were becoming well-versed in facts to which others had no access:

* About 50 percent of those staying at Clifton each night used their bus fare to travel to one of the 10 or so area labor pools. "The labor pools fill a vacuum where the churches and government have failed," according to Loring. "Many of these people are unemployable, but the 'pools' let them come in, sit down, and use the bathrooms."

* St. Luke's Episcopal Church has served a meal to 200 to 500 people per day, five days a week, for five years. Other than this and the labor pools, there are no daytime services for the homeless.

* In a city of 2 million people, shelter volunteers had personally known six homeless people who died during the previous winter. In addition, the workers had become all too familiar with the city and state offices and hospitals that were repeatedly admitting, refusing, and releasing the guests in a seemingly endless cycle.

* Under Mayor Maynard Jackson, there was a consistent and official denial of homelessness as a problem, though city streets were sometimes "swept" of the destitute. But there was hope for responsiveness when challenger Andrew Young won the mayoral election. Press coverage, on the other hand, has always been sympathetic, timely, and helpful.

* Shelter workers, probably the only people besides the homeless themselves who could approach an estimate of numbers, raised their rough projection to two hundred women and thousands of men.

Other facilities in Atlanta are the traditional ones: the Salvation Army and a mission. At the Salvation Army there are 14 beds each for men and women, the low numbers being part of its national organizational trend to accept federal halfway-house contracts in lieu of performing traditional hospitality. (However, this should not be seen as a contradiction of the group's recent encouragement of soup kitchens and shelters for the new Depression.)

While not aimed at the truly destitute, the women's Union Mission provides fifty beds at $7 per night. This includes all day access to the facility and three meals.

The men's Union Mission offers three free nights per lifetime and otherwise charges $2.50 per night. One hundred beds for transients and 100 beds for semi-permanent guests are available. It is primarily older men who use the latter. There, two separate and unequal meal lines correspond to the sleeping arrangements, with the semi-permanent guests paying $1.50 for the better meals. Guests are searched. The mission opens its chapel on nights when it is especially cold in Atlanta.

In addition, 90 beds are available at a recovery center for alcoholics in the form of bunks and dorms. The center, located across from one of the labor pools, is described by Loring as "filthy." At $3.50 per night, guests must also report to the labor pool as a condition of their stay.

The Reverend Robert Bevis of Central Presbyterian Church credits Ed Loring's work as an inspiration for his church's opening. He was also moved to act when he was awakened late one night to aid a street woman who had been badly beaten and raped repeatedly.

"Anyone who pastors or works in a church on Peachtree Street deals with these people daily," said Bevis in a news story afterward. "But bringing in church volunteers to help was a challenge.... I must admit that it's been like pulling teeth. Some of Atlanta's clergy are long on words, but short on action. ... It is time for the churches to get back into the business of meeting the needs of Atlanta's poor."

And help they did. After six years as pastor, Ed Loring and his wife, the Reverend Murphy Davis, left Clifton Presbyterian Church. With their family and another, they began the Open Door Community in downtown Atlanta, now a welcoming spot for the homeless as well as for prisoners and their families. In December 1981, the Open Door began its work of sheltering 25 men and 7 women. The guests are served breakfast, and in addition, lunch is served to about 30 people and dinner to 50. In May 1982, the community also opened a daily kitchen to even out its services.

Clifton backed up its members' venture by voting to continue its hospitality program. Central Presbyterian re-opened in mid-December 1981 with gratifying results. Over 500 volunteers representing all major faiths participated, and the St. Vincent de Paul Society provided a coordinator. Sandwich-making for the shelter besame a popular act of voluntarism, resulting in the donation of 30,000 sandwiches over the course of the winter.

First Presbyterian Church provided the now-basic offerings of mats, showers, food, and tea for 12 women, with the willingness to continue beyond cold weather. All Saints Episcopal Church in the downtown area opened for the winter for 60 men, and Oakhurst Baptist did the same for 12 men. Trinity United Methodist Church offered shelter for 30 non-smoking men for February and March, and they had no difficulty finding men who were willing to comply. At least seven churches will be open for the winter of 1982-83.

A long distance to come in just three years? Some might say so, but such an answer would deny certain fundamentals of history and faith. When the elements have worn the crucial rock to a point where it moves and starts an avalanche, the old terrain cannot hold it back. Those who must contribute to this movement can choose no other way; when it is their time, they must act. If only a small number are available to be thus used, so be it.

The city of Atlanta has yet to offer any acknowledgements or solutions in regard to the many people on its streets, although Mayor Young made himself available for a meeting with religious leaders who have been involved in the rapidly multiplying efforts. The churches have shown that they can and will act, but, in Atlanta, government and business are yet to be heard from.

Rainstorm on a wet steam grate on the Ellipse.

There are no epitaphs carved in marble here. The tombstones are men and women. The epitaphs are chiseled in sunken shadows on their cheeks. These are dead men and women. They are ghosts that walk the streets by day. They are ghosts sleeping with yesterday's newspapers thrown around them for covers at night. I can see that these are ghosts that groan and toss through the night. I watch. From time to time a white splotch gets up off the ground. He cannot rest for the rats and the cold. This is a restless ghost. Or maybe it is the gnawing pain in his belly that makes him restless and sleepless. The ground is hard. Damp and hard.

. . .We do not ask questions about each other. There is nothing to ask. We are here. We are here because we have no other place to go.

Tom Kromer
Waiting for Nothing
1935

The site was unpromising. The river ran sluggishly across a flat plain to the lake. A low ridge eight miles inland cut the connection between Lake Michigan and the water route that ran westward to the Mississippi. No promontory, no hill caught the eye. The lake alone was arresting.[1]

Chicago: Does It Work for the Homeless?

Probably none could have predicted that Chicago - the nation's second most populous city - would rise on such inconsequential topography. The black pioneer Jean Baptiste Pointe du Sable surely did not have an inkling when he built the first settlement there in the 1770's, nor could he know that the city would, in time, mirror his own ethnic diversity as the son of a Quebec trader and a freed slave.

But Chicago became all this and more. The city was strongly influenced by geography from the time the first settlers approached. Natives, traders, and trappers all appreciated the strategic location at the convergence of lake, prairie, and river. The area quickly became a major link to all corners of the continent.

The city got a slow start in the marsh land that was so well situated. Only 50 people lived in Chicago in 1830, but by 1837, there were 4170, and so much demand for housing that contracts often called for one-week construction time.

When Cyrus McCormick came to the city in 1847 to produce his reaper, manufacturing in Chicago took the first of many steps that would see it become a major center for metal and machinery work, and iron and steel. For all industry, it would become "The City That Works."

All at once came the establishment of the largest rail center in the country, the outpouring of manufactured goods from city factories, and the influx of huge numbers of immigrants: German, Irish, Italian, Mexican, Puerto Rican, Scandinavian, East European, Southern blacks. Virtually every group found a corner of the city to call home, and thus the tradition of strongly identified neighborhoods that remains "Chicago."

The Civil War made Chicago more prosperous, and the period to World War II was one of tremendous growth: trade, finance, iron and steel - all came to the city on the lake. With them came the political, economic, and social problems of all urban centers, but with a difference: a powerful Democratic machine came to life and remains effective today.

The dire predictions that followed the Great Fire of 1871 never materialized - the city came back stronger than ever. New identities came too. As an industrial hub, Chicago quickly became a center of both a labor movement and pioneering social reforms. The Democratic machine and the Roman Catholic Church (Chicago is the world's largest archdiocese) were instrumental in the institution of health, school, and child labor laws.

World War II had striking effects on Chicago. The production of war materials brought iron and steel to the forefront, and also brought a huge influx of Southern blacks and Appalachian whites in search of jobs and opportunities.

The '40's brought efforts at reducing the inner city decay that accompanied rapid change. Acres of dilapidated buildings were cleared but not redeveloped. Low-cost housing became a scarce commodity, and racial segregation did not break down. The racial and economic divisions were so sharp that Martin Luther King, Jr. began a major civil rights campaign in the city in 1966, calling it "a prototype" for racial problems in the North. Inevitably, some of the most hard pressed, the most unsuccessful seekers, became homeless, added to the ranks of the destitute as the consequence of economic fluctuation and disparity.

In 1923, Nels Anderson wrote:

A survey of the lodging-house and hotel population, supplemented by the census reports of the areas in which they live, indicates that the number of homeless men in Chicago ranges from 30,000 in good times to 75,000 in hard times.[2]

Anderson may have thought himself on firm ground when he presented those figures almost 50 years ago, but the picture in Chicago today is so fragmented that few would venture estimates. Two years ago, prior to the onslaught of Reaganomics, the situation was termed "extremely serious." Estimates of the number of homeless people on Chicago's streets varied wildly. Not unpredictably, the Interagencies Task Force, made up of Chicago's major social service agencies and voice of the local administration, estimated that there were at least 1,000 people living on the streets. Yet the Pacific Garden Mission, the city's largest, offered different estimates. Having housed 104,255 persons overnight in 1979, Pacific Garden says the homeless comprise at least 6.5 percent of the city's 3.75 million population, or nearly 250,000 people!

As Chicago has changed and grown, borders have become fluid, new waves of immigrants have appeared, and gentrification has announced itself loudly. In the face of these forces, the homeless remain political orphans and geographic nomads. This is not to say that Chicago has never spawned efforts to feed, clothe, and shelter the down-and-out. In fact, five of the missions mentioned by Anderson in his study are still in existence, and at least two others not mentioned by him also date from that period to the present.[3]

But the traditional missions, with their emphasis on single men, prayer, and alcoholic rehabilitation, do not address the radically altered and varied makeup of the homeless or a changed perception of the differences between social or religious charity and justice. A look at their facilities attests to this:

The Chicago Gospel Mission offers daily worship and an evening meal to between 40 and 50 men.

The Helping Hand Mission serves a seated afternoon meal to 45 men, with beds for those who "want to work on their problems."

The Olive Branch Mission provides daily worship and a morning meal to about 75 men. Housing, for a few men with an alcohol problem and for a few families, is available.

The Holy Cross Mission, with an evening soupline, serves 250 to 300 men and women, and it can also lodge several dozen in exchange for their participation in rehabilitation programs.

Chicago Christian Industrial League serves 850 to 1,000 meals per day. It provides an alcoholism program (Alcoholics Victorious) for 155 men, with shelter for others on a space-available basis. In addition, it provides family shelter for about 40 people.

Cathedral Shelter has space and a meal for 12 men, with a daily religious service.

The Salvation Army's Harbor Light residence offers alcoholic rehabilitation and shelter to 200 men.

The Gospel League Home for stranded women and families holds twice-daily worship for the 60 women and children who stay there.

The Brandecker Lodge, also a shelter for women and children, houses and feeds about 100, offering them religious services and counseling.

That many of these long-lived programs are narrowly defined in scope does not negate their use or their value. They are never lacking for guests or program participants; they fill a need. Many staff people are quite frank in admitting that they both turn people away and see the necessity for many more facilities and services. The missions have other strong points. The personal and religious commitment of many of the workers is an asset. Some of them have themselves come from the streets; many of them have devoted their lives to the work through good times and bad - in the absence of interest by the rest of society.

But by no account do these programs and facilities address the magnitude or the diversity of the problem of homelessness today. Nor, in the public arena, do their workers attempt to demand more accountability or action from the religious community or the city government. Their approach is invariably traditional and non-confrontational. That suits local officials since, in the final analysis, even prompting the creation of basic shelter space - with or without rehabilitation programs - would constitute an acknowledgement of the severity and urgency of the problem that revenue-starved local governments are most unwilling to make.

Elaine Lamy has attempted to combine concern for the homeless with a demand for accountability by the public sector. She and her husband, Dan Burke, came to Chicago in 1979 as members of the Jesuit Volunteer Corps. Both had gained experience as shelter and soup kitchen workers in the politically-charged atmosphere of Washington, D.C., and there they saw the commitment and creativity that progress for the homeless requires.

Their Chicago involvement began at the neighborhood level, in their own Uptown area. Emergency shelter facilities did not exist for the hundreds of homeless in Uptown, though food, clothing, and health centers did. A committee was formed to find space, and in the 1979-80 winter, two local daytime drop-in centers were opened to provide emergency overnight housing. One sheltered about 20 women per night, and the other took in 60 to 70 men.

At the same time, the group approached the city Department of Human Resources to gauge its awareness of the problem. A meeting with four deputy commissioners resulted in verbal support for emergency shelters, but little else. A promise to explore available space died from lack of interest and follow-up.

Lamy realized that no group in Chicago had a concrete hold on both knowledge and action. Her subsequent efforts led to the adoption of a "Shelter the Homeless" project at the 8th Day Center for Justice. A first step was to develop the research that could shed some light on the problem and would, in turn, result in specific approaches and programs.

In late 1980, Lamy began interviewing DHR commissioners, who had little interest in talking or doing anything about the situation. It became increasingly clear that the city was not concerned about homelessness and felt no pressure to respond. Their best offering had been a crisis intervention team that responded to cases of fire and eviction. The chronically homeless went unnoticed and unserved.

The city's basic policy was to shelter those in need on a contractual basis at other facilities; they had done so for some time at the YWCA, which could house about 200 people at $9 per night per person. They also opened Hamlin House, a Far West Side facility, capable of housing several hundred people. But, again, the intent was to provide shelter for emergency cases, not for the chronically homeless.

Devastating information came to Lamy from unexpected sources. One DHR employee revealed to her that many people approached the department for shelter, but they were sent away after being pronounced "not homeless." Another DHR source told 8th Day Center that 7,500 families had contacted the agency for shelter in one period. Of those, 1,200 were permanently placed, 1,200 were temporarily placed, 2,000 were placed and "lost," and 1,700 were not placed. (These figures didn't add up for them either.)

Lamy also contacted the city morgue to inquire about winter deaths among the homeless. She was casually told by a worker that "one or two" unidentified exposure victims per week were brought into the facility. Without further documentation and even when this estimate is reduced on several fronts for likely inaccuracies, it still has explosive potential. Similarly, a January 1981 Chicago newscast reported 50 recent burials in the local potter's field. Somewhere in Chicago, people were silently dying for lack of shelter.

The 8th Day Center took as its task the raising of public consciousness and the development of emergency shelter. Its primary route was through the churches, in a city with strong religious-ethnic ties. The group sponsored several community meetings; it sought to translate the interest of social service agencies into concrete action and participation.

Additional shelter space resulted. On the Far North Side, a facility opened in response to the migration of the homeless from other areas, the result of a process publicly known as "urban renewal," but familiar to the poor as "urban removal." Organized by several social service agencies, the North Side shelter is tightly structured in an effort to minimize conflicts with the neighborhood and thus it also falls short of meeting the not-so-predictable or easily regimented needs of the inveterate homeless.

On its own initiative, St. Pius V Catholic Church also opened a shelter for about 30 men. The Dominican-run parish in Chicago's Mexican-American area of Pilsen responded to what it felt was an obvious need. Its shelter for the winter of 1981-82 was housed in an old furniture store that has since burned, but Father Gerard Cleater says they will reopen in the fall of 1982 in a newly-purchased building. The church has steered away from seeking either government or diocesan support for the project, feeling that it is their responsibility. Donations will buy and renovate the shelter, and volunteers will provide hospitality to 30 to 40 men. In addition, St. Pius serves a meal to 80 people per day twice a week.

*   *   *

Lamy's efforts have been most intense in her own Uptown area, and that is where a political identity for the homeless first surfaced. While night shelters were operating during 1979-80, it became apparent that not only was the city not offering support, but it was sending guests to the soon-overflowing effort. There were people willing to contribute time, money, and resources to the shelter, and there were local churches prepared to open overflow space for the remainder of the winter.

As they looked toward the winter of 1980-81, the group added the services of a Jesuit volunteer whose primary task was to locate additional shelter space. A few Sunday sermons in suburban churches by Lamy and Burke sent them home with almost $5,000 in cash offerings, but not even money could find a shelter. Space that was physically acceptable was not "available," and space for rent was often not suitable for shelter. Everywhere they faced severe pressure from gentrifying areas that did not welcome the homeless, or - in areas where the homeless already abounded - the added visibility a shelter created.

On November 15, 1980, a make-do facility was opened in the basement of the American Indian Center, just west of Uptown. It had serious fire code violations, and the layout required women guests to pass through the men's area. Yet, about 80 men and 8 to 15 women found a warm spot to sleep.

Unexpectedly, on January 6, a city inspector appeared at the building and ordered an immediate closing for code violations. The visit was the end product of pressure that the neighborhood had exerted on the alderman. With no notice to guests, the doors were shut.

When the homeless showed up as usual that evening, many were willing to join a procession of volunteers from the shelter to the alderman's house. A crowd of about 150 formed. Press coverage was heavy.

The city attempted to respond. Police were dispatched to ferry the homeless to precincts for DHR processing to shelters - with no questions asked. The question that should have been asked was *where* the shelter was, as guests found themselves traveling 10 miles by bus, arriving at their beds at 3:30 in the morning. Return transportation did not materialize until 1 o'clock the following afternoon.

The events of that night caused DHR to attempt to respond to the obvious need for shelter. DHR would keep its crosstown facility open while volunteers sought a new location. But, as the weeks went by, even the most stalwart homeless dropped out of the process, for it was just too difficult to make the long trip to the shelter each night and back again each day.

The emergency shelter committee itself was split over future directions: should efforts at creating space prevail over a public campaign of education and sensitization for the need of and right to shelter? A series of slip-slide steps followed, and all of them

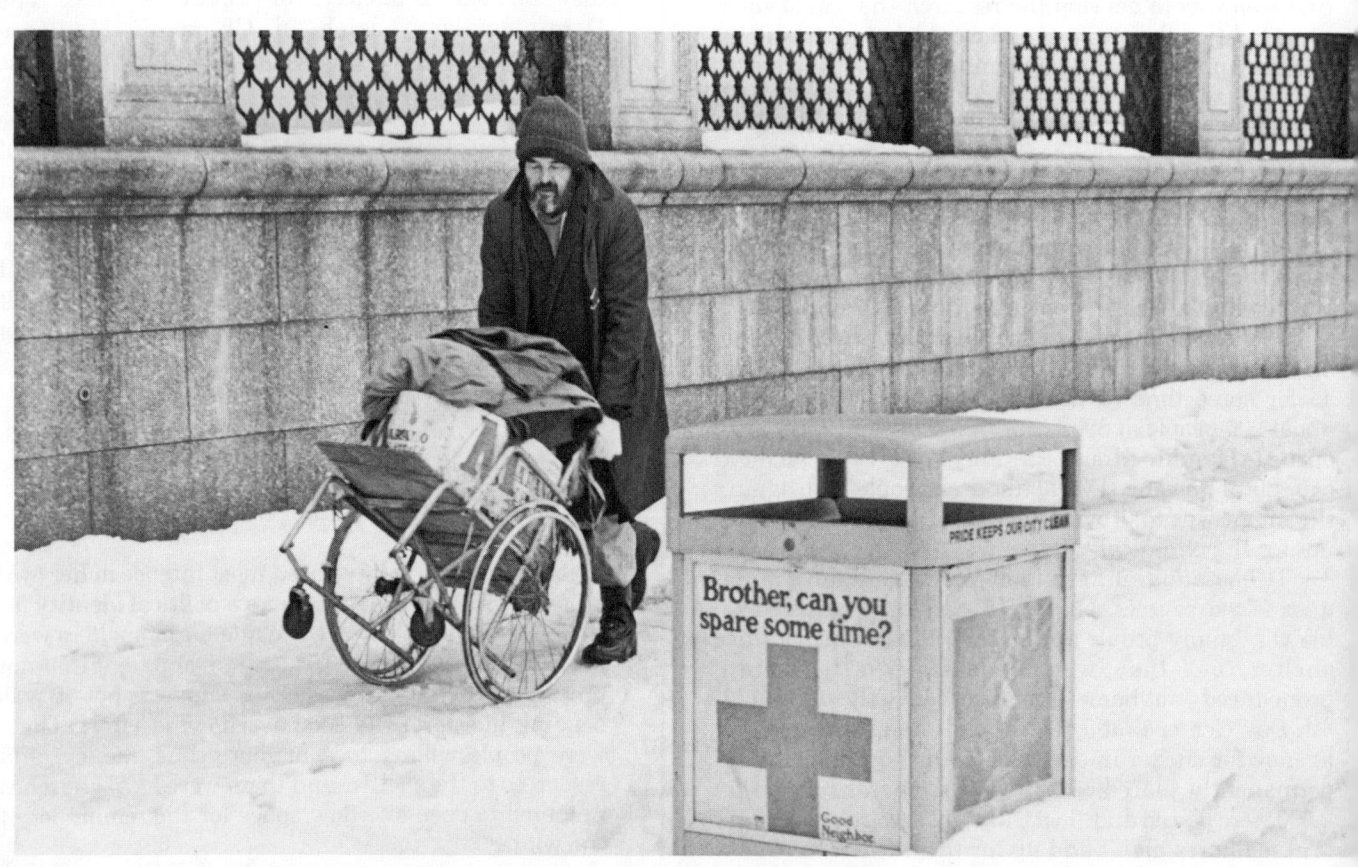

showed one thing: the city would respond only as long as the pressure was maintained. DHR held a community meeting to discuss shelter alternatives. The owner of a transient hotel offered two community rooms for rent, but the move to the Northmore Hotel lasted only five days, with a re-run of the alderman/shut-down scenario. The committee split again, and all operations were suspended until spring.

A new approach was tried. The committee met head-on with the Uptown Chicago Commission. The commission decried the proposals, but the committee had done its homework by soliciting an impressive list of community endorsements and the depth of support became obvious. Ideal space was located in a former day care center. When the shelter was opened, the official harassment and inspections didn't abate, but neither did they result in confrontation or closing. Press coverage continued unsolicited.

The day care center was not promised to the group for the 1982-83 winter, and it is likely that future shelter developments will follow past patterns. A toehold has been established, an introduction to the politics of poverty has been made, and the process of education will continue. The Gospel Family, a Chicago religious community active on the shelter issue, put it this way in their Spring 1982 newsletter: "The battle lines are already drawn for the next winter, when there will be Christians trying to reopen the shelter, and others will try to keep it from happening."

Chicago, like every other urban area, has been hit hard by Reaganomics. These are not times in which most cities are considering the opening or reopening of municipal shelters or soup kitchens, even though the need is evident. The Chicago Municipal Lodging House, opened in 1901, reflected changing ideas about the times and the people it served. It was first an arm of the Chicago police department, then was switched to the health department, and finally to the public welfare division before closing.[4]

Homelessness in Chicago was the subject of Nels Anderson's 1923 study, and several of his recommendations are worth noting today. Not only was it advised that the Municipal Lodging House be reopened, but the study suggested that a clearinghouse for counseling and support services be started and that further support should come from the opening of municipal laundry and bath facilities for the homeless.[5] Such services are still desperately needed.

> *Both on the road and in the city, they are at all times subject to arbitrary handling and arrest by private and public police....*
>
> *The attitude of Chicago, like that of other communities...has been a policy of defense....*
>
> *Social service for the homeless...has for the most part been remedial rather than preventive, unorganized and haphazard rather than organized and coordinated.*[6]

One must ask whether things have changed at all in Chicago in nearly 60 years.

Footnotes

[1] Harold M. Mayer and Richard C. Wade, *Chicago: Growth of a Metropolis* (Chicago: University of Chicago Press, 1969), p.3.

[2] Nels Anderson, *The Hobo: The Sociology of the Homeless Man* (Chicago: University of Chicago Press, 1923), p.3.

[3] In the first group are the Salvation Army, Cathedral Shelter, Helping Hand Mission, Pacific Garden Mission, and Chicago Christian Industrial League. In the second group are the Olive Branch Mission and Holy Cross Mission. The Bible Rescue Mission noted in Anderson's study closed in 1980.

[4] Anderson, pp. 260-61.

[5] Anderson, pp. 269-274.

[6] Ibid., pp. 266-67.

willie

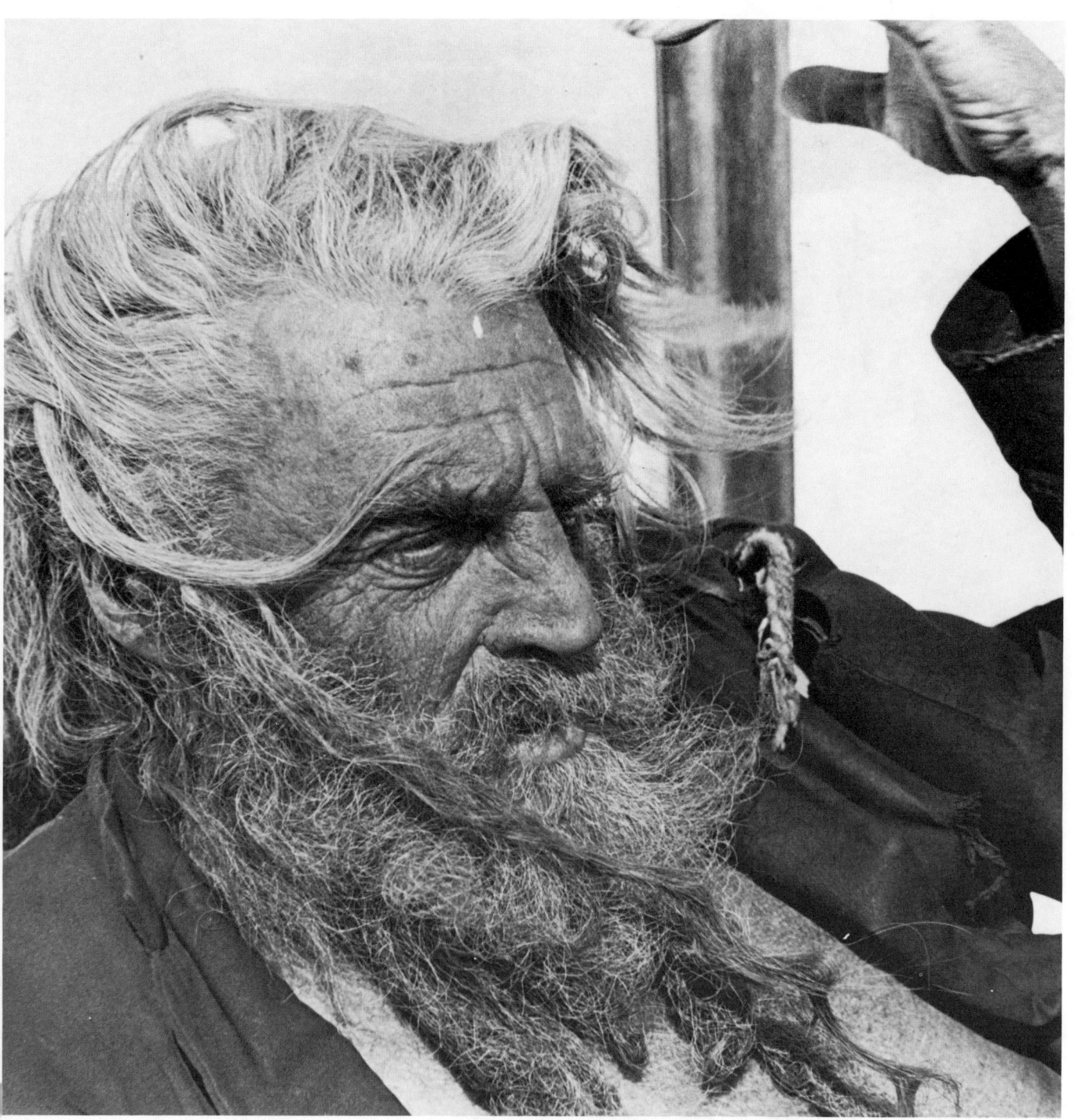

Thanksgiving Dinner 1980 at the Drop-In Center.

Spacious avenues that begin in nothing and lead nowhere, . . . It is sometimes called the City of Magnificent Distances, but it might be termed with greater propriety the City of Magnificent Intentions.

Charles Dickens
American Notes
1885

Washington, D.C. : City of Magnificent Distances

After reading your article on how the Union Station/National Visitor Center is going to be converted into a flophouse for skid-row types, I was appalled. . . .

Now, when passengers arrive at Union Station and walk through the Visitor Center, instead of being greeted by red caps, they will no doubt be harassed by the "street people" (which is the new word for bums and vagrants), bumming money for the night's booze.

Letter to the Editor
Washington Post
December 6, 1978

If you are not careful, the newspapers will have you hating the people who are being oppressed, and loving the people who are doing the oppressing.

Malcolm X

Big Red used to live on a heat grate at the Corcoran Art Gallery, making him, as mentioned elsewhere, one of the President's closest neighbors. Red and other homeless men found a bit of warmth on cold winter nights by taking to the grates surrounding the gallery. By all indications, this arrangement was not very popular with the Corcoran's patrons or decision-makers. A couple of years ago, the grates at the Corcoran were turned off; Red and the others moved on. The message was not very subtle.

Red has been on the grates through several Administrations and a couple of local mayors and commissioners. After his eviction from the Corcoran, Red took up residence near the State Department. His new neighbor was another long-termer, Willie.

Willie would not be difficult to spot in a crowd. His hair and beard cascade down in dirty and knotted profusion. Willie's clothing, much like his diet, is chronically and woefully inadequate. He is like a deer, painfully shy and vulnerable. But Willie is not a deer; he is a human being who, in the past 15 years of his life, has not had a bath or slept in a bed. He has lived on one heat grate on the corner of Virginia Avenue, virtually all of the time. Big Red and Willie's grates are not simply their homes - they are also a window on reality. In all of the years that Red and Willie have spent on the downtown heat grates, millions of people have walked or driven by them, but only a handful have stopped to talk, to see if they could be of any help. Some furtively scan the scene; others stare in amazement. For most, expressions do not change. Red and Willie, their pain and their loneliness, are invisible. If not invisible, then surely untouchable; just as the hundreds of other people whose broken bodies are scattered around the Federal Triangle. But, occasionally, that curtain may be lifted for a moment or two.

No one knows for sure whether Red saw his picture when it accompanied a national news magazine story on homelessness in early 1982. Perhaps some reader recognized him and finally stopped to talk. In any event, Red is still on his grate, passed by thousands of civil servants and tourists daily, and perpetually vulnerable to a variety of attacks. Many homeless men in the District and elsewhere have been beaten, slashed, or set on fire. Another kind of assault occurs when local officials seasonally make well-publicized tours of the grates to point out that "these people choose the streets," no matter what kind of shelter is offered.

It is true; Red is still on his grate. He remains homeless, as do thousands of others who are holed up in abandoned buildings, cars, alleys, and bank lobbies, taking the best refuge they can find. Others are not so lucky. At least 46 have died of exposure and homelessness in six recent winters; many more have lost limbs and minds to the rigors of the street.

Washington is a city where what is most visible is taken as fact and norm, yet what is most prominent is a misleading indication of what exists. In actuality, Washington is a minimally integrated Southern town with a veneer of sophistication. It is a city with a double identity; some have called its contradictory portions "the marble mask" and "the secret city." Simultaneously, there is the monument-studded public self, ruled over by federal officials and existing for the rest of the nation, and another, less familiar side: a community where three-fourths of the population is black. Attendant to that single fact are several bits of history about a city John Dos Passos long ago called a "drowsy sun parlor."

The slave and slave labor tradition of Washington has been strong since its earliest days, from the auction block just across the park from the White House to the slave pens where the Mall now stands. Slaves built much of the city and rebuilt more of it after the British burned it in 1814. Not surprisingly, tour guides at the U.S. Capitol do not volunteer the fact that it was built by slaves. As laborers, they gave way before the only other group to rival them as immigrants: the Irish. Blacks continued to serve those who ran the city, well into the 20th century. "The Four Hundred," black professionals of long lineage in the District, by and large enjoyed their own society separate and apart from the white rulers. They continue as a third force that relishes its distance from the poor blacks and often transient whites who make up the rest of Washington. In a city where power is a credential in itself, race is an equally important factor. The black-white ratio reversed itself in the years between 1942 and 1976, with blacks growing from 30 percent of the city's population to 76 percent. More changed than that, as many more blacks now hold a variety of positions in the federal government. In contrast, in 1938, 90 percent of the blacks in government were janitors.

But, in many respects, while there have been certain significant changes, the city still has slaves - of the economy as much as of race. More than 250,000 people in the metropolitan area live below the official poverty line; the vast majority of them are people of color. The homeless sleep where the slave pens and auction blocks once stood.

As is true of much else, the way homelessness takes shape in Washington, D.C. is both the exception and the example for the rest of the nation. That thousands live on our streets is rarely disputed publically any more, but the "how" and "why" are the result of a complex matrix of factors.

The city is a mecca for young Southern blacks, but with an unemployment rate hovering around 11 percent, there is little to make the promise a reality. Housing is even more scarce, and, as the needs of the long-term poor meet up with the increasing numbers of needy people in the Maryland and Virginia suburbs, there is little hope for relief.

A center city building boom has accompanied the not-yet-completed D.C. Convention Center, but the focus of construction has been offices and hotels. Not only have low-cost housing, soup kitchens, and services for the down-and-out been swept away in the center's path, but its "local jobs" slogan ignores the skilled workers imported from as far away as Baltimore and Richmond. Less than a block away from the site is a day labor center, where hundreds assemble at sunrise each morning to angle for a handful of low-paying jobs.

Yet the convention center is a star in the crown of the local government, a favored project pushed by both D.C. officials and the Board of Trade, a business and real estate organization acknowledged by many as a government unto itself. With a Congress once labelled "a brotherhood of distinguished bigots," they share several goals and views. One is that the D.C. government is a kind of unmentionable embarrassment to be overlooked whenever possible. An enduring goal is the sanitizing of the Federal City, the wholesale removal of all that is poor, unsightly, or old. When performed federally, this is called "urban renewal"; at the local level it is called either "progress" or "building the tax base."

The resulting machinations of the economy and the skyline yield service jobs that feed an empire of government workers, conventioneers, tourists, and downtown businesses. The lucky few get the jobs; the enterprising and able go door-to-door in season with snow shovels, looking for work; the hopeless sit on street corners or walk across town for a bowl of soup. For even a dishwashing job, the old refugees - of racism, poverty, and geography - must compete with the new wave of immigrants - the Central Americans and Asians.

In the end, we have a city of contradictions. A fiftieth birthday party was thrown for Mickey Mouse in the train station; the mouse himself put in an appearance. Outside, a homeless woman rummaged through the garbage can for leftover cake.

The day and night personalities of the District are as dissimilar as the insulated affluence of upper Northwest and the high-pressure ghettoes of Anacostia where even the barest survival is not guaranteed. Washington is a city where the physical constraint presented by its borders causes economic and real estate convulsions that find people living on the streets of Georgetown (a poor neighborhood just 50 years ago), as well as in vacant homes in the worst slum areas (where senators and Supreme Court justices once lived). New construction, conversion, and renovation have cut a wide swath across former low-income areas, turning boarding-house and cheap hotel residents into urban nomads and drastically narrowing the choices for all but the affluent.

Into all of this fall the homeless. Their presence and their needs are as welcome as a movement to relocate the cause of Washington's existence - the federal government - to another city. Despite the local government's apparent acknowledgement of the problem, thousands of people in this city have no homes and shelter space is inadequate. The city's assessment of the availability and adequacy of emergency shelter is inaccurate and misleading; it offers no real or proportionate solutions, since its major initiatives have been aimed at closing space rather than creating it. People are suffering daily and dying - in all seasons - from the lack of shelter.

If Washington provides a model as a city, it is as one where a sensitized and committed core of citizens has prodded an ever-reluctant government to make minimal provisions for the homeless, then dug in both to provide alternatives and to see that city services stay in existence. However, not all of these efforts have been successful. Institutionally, the response of the religious community has been disconcertingly similar to that of the government: characterized by defensiveness and an unwillingness to become directly involved in the lives of the destitute.

Prior to 1975, the city had no relationship with single, homeless people, nor any involvement with the provision of emergency shelter for them. The city did operate two small apartment buildings as family shelters, yet each was capable of housing only 20 families at a time when an estimated 10,000 people were being evicted annually. The Central Union Mission had 50 beds for men (offering 4 free nights per month) and 12 beds for women. The Gospel Mission housed 150 men, with one free night each month. In addition, the Salvation Army had space for 10 women.

There were a total of 22 beds for women and 200 beds for men. No shelter worker could recall a time when all the women's beds were not in use.

*   *   *

The Community for Creative Non-Violence (CCNV) began in late 1970 as a response to the war in Vietnam. In those first months, the community's focus was on education and outreach. Through a series of speakers, workshops, and retreats, we tried to bring people together in an atmosphere of urgency and seriousness, to address questions of war and peace, violence and non-violence.

At the same time, we understood that words without action are like flesh without bones: they simply will not stand up. So, while we continued to talk of peace and justice, we also prepared to make peace and practice justice with our more immediate neighbors. Within a few blocks of the White House, people were going to bed hungry. Many didn't even have beds. Thus, in 1972, we opened the Zacchaeus Community Kitchen. Within a short time, we were feeding about 400 people a day, seven days a week.

In more fully sharing our lives with the poor, we were able to discern quickly some of their other obvious needs and respond to them. The woman or man who comes in for a bowl of soup is also the person who lacks shelter, adequate medical care, or any semblance of protection from those who wield power and authority. We soon opened hospitality and pre-trial houses, as well as a free medical clinic.

We see the sharing of bread with the victims of injustice as a responsibility born of faith and our common humanity. Because we see the equivalent need to resist values, institutions, and policies which victimize all, we have aggressively involved ourselves in the shaping of public policy and consciousness.

In all that we do, we serve as volunteers, living mainly off America's waste and excess. Food, enough for 1,000 to 1,500 a day, clothing, furniture, appliances, even our cars are scavenged or cast off by others. We are non-hierarchical in structure, and decisions are made consensually. Our work is sustained by small donations. The community is not tax exempt, nor a corporation. We believe that people should give at a personal cost and not at the expense of the state. We do not accept contributions that are encumbered in ways that could impair, reduce, or delay our ability to respond to the dictates of conscience or the needs of others. Nor are "gifts" accepted that require the growth of structure or the pushing of paper as the price of their use.

The common thread which brings us together is the recognition of the need to blend within the individual and the community the elements of spirituality, direct service, resistance, constructive action, and the personal integration of justice. That thread binds together the fabric of our community; its pattern and texture are woven out of shared experience.

* * *

For several years, it was our custom on Christmas Eve to keep the soup kitchen open through the night to offer warmth and shelter to those on the street. On Christmas Eve 1976, unbeknownst to us, we were nearing the end of a year-long struggle to free a city-owned abandoned building for rehabilitation and use as an emergency family shelter. A recently-evicted family of 15 had also been taken into our home. All of these events combined to make us acutely aware of homelessness.

Our work in providing emergency shelter traces its roots to discussions we had on that Christmas Eve. Our understanding and our lives wove together with the grace of the moment to bring us to a simple, but previously obscured, thought: all people have the right, on any night of the year, to get inside.

On Christmas morning, the few people who had passed the night at the kitchen began drifting out. As they did, we wondered where they would spend the next night, and the next. We decided to find out.

Within a few days, we had, reluctantly, but with a sense of inevitability, decided to open our own home to the destitute. It is embarrassing to admit, but it took a couple of nights of driving and searching before we found our first guest. On New Year's Eve 1976, we found Big Red and a few others on the Corcoran Gallery heat grates. It was one of the coldest nights of the coldest winter in 50 years.

Each night, we would drive around the city, searching for the homeless. Baked potatoes and hot tea were offered to those who preferred to stay behind. In less than a week, 40 or more people per night were sleeping on our floor.

More space was critically needed, for it was immediately apparent that many people were still on the streets. We wrote and called all 1100 area churches, temples, and mosques and invited them to do what we had done: make shelter space available. Luther Place Memorial Church, in the heart of D.C.'s "red light" district, said yes.

For the rest of that winter, 60 or more people were sheltered at the church each night, in addition to the 35 to 45 at CCNV. The opening of Luther Place set in motion a process with several outcomes. There was a slowly growing recognition that the religious community had an obligation to share in this work, and an awareness that there were, in fact, many more people on the street than anyone had previously assumed. The need for separate facilities for men and women had quickly become clear, and a search was begun for space. A small but growing group of volunteers was becoming involved with the homeless, learning where to find them, and developing relationships with them.

Thus, in November 1977, separate men's and women's shelters were able to open, at St. Stephen and the Incarnation Episcopal Church and again at Luther Place. There was space and a meal for 100 men and 30 to 35 women each night. With a few exceptions, guests arrived on their own. Volunteers continued to make the rounds of heat grates, empty buildings and parking garages, doorways, alleys and barrel fires in vacant lots, delivering warm food and a few words.

No real demands were made on city officials until the winter of 1977-78, when media attention was focused on the freezing deaths of three men on the same night. D.C. Department of Human Resources Director Albert Russo said in a series of interviews that there were sufficient facilities to meet the needs of the homeless. He attributed the three deaths to extreme temperatures, alcohol, and bad luck, but not to a lack of shelter - a conventional and predictable point of view. But reporters also interviewed shelter workers, and what they said directly contradicted Russo's assertions.

Subsequently, Russo and CCNV members met and discussed the situation. Two days later, a vacant city-owned building, 456 C Street, became D.C.'s newest shelter. DHR staff opened the doors to 22, 52, and 68 men during the first three nights. Stated capacity was increased from 50 to 75; within a few days that figure was also surpassed. A replay of events, including the threat of confrontation, resulted in the replacement of 456 C Street with the 150-bed Blair School.

Thus, from December 1976 to February 1978, the number of beds available in the city rose from 22 to 52 for women and from 200 to 450 for men. At the same time, a very different kind of shelter - city-run - developed. City funds were used to pay utilities and building expenses, as well as salaries (the largest budget item). Dinner was prepared - at no small cost - by a private catering service, despite the presence of a usable kitchen in the old school building. Blankets and cots came from former civil service reserves, in contrast to the bales of homemade quilts that were donated by the Mennonites and used in the church shelters.

The biggest difference resulted from the attitude and atmosphere that was created by the use of city workers in the shelters at C Street and Blair School. From admission logs to the filing of "unusual incident" reports, the city workers conveyed a sense that the homeless were not people to be served so much as regulated. The guests, and their hours spent in the shelter, must be boiled down to a sameness that promised no surprises or trouble on an eight-hour shift.

Demonstration in response to city's closing of women's shelter.

456 C Street, D.C.'s first city-run shelter.

95

The National Visitor Center, site of 1978 men's shelter operated by CCNV.

Wagon carries body of unidentified exposure victim "John Doe" in funeral procession down D.C.'s 14th Street to City Hall.

Such an all-night shift was defined by late openings and early closings, and the men would find themselves back on the street by 5:30 or 6:00 A.M. The workers were motivated by overtime pay, since a hiring freeze was in effect for the city. Thus, while staff might come to know guests individually, might even have known them in a "previous" (pre-street) life, uniformity required the erection and projection of barriers: recording of names, checking of identification, screening and rejection of those receiving benefit checks, storing of all possessions (not always to see them returned), one serving of food per person, and an armed and uniformed guard at all times. It was prison voluntarily entered.

The pressure of lives being risked and lost resulted in the opening of the shelters and also caused advocates and guests alike to tolerate them as they were. A foot in the door marked "progress" demands a certain amount of "wait and see." There were 150 more men being sheltered than only a few weeks before, and that was a good thing. The previously vacant city-owned building was now put to good use.

The same idea - that publicly-owned and under-utilized buildings could at least be opened as warm space for the homeless - was put into sharper focus in late 1978. Luther Place Church had once again opened its doors to women, but St. Stephen's had decided not to. Nor could any other church be located that would allow itself to be so used. It was apparent that the more numerous men needed additional shelter space.

For two weeks in late November 1978, CCNV members Mitch Snyder and Ann Splaine, a crippled woman, moved to D.C.'s streets to eat, sleep, and live as homeless people. They moved from place to place, seeking warmth, food, and protection. As they described it, they disappeared into a separate reality, an endless, solitary, forced march to nowhere. But, before making the move, they wrote Secretary of Interior Cecil Andrus, telling him that, at the end of the two weeks, they and their homeless friends would move into the National Visitor Center (NVC).

The NVC, in the old Union Station, was an enormous federal white elephant, once likened to a carpeted moonscape. Originally planned to supplant ordinary train station functions (at a cost of $45 million) the center was to provide a Bicentennial welcome to D.C. tourists. To say that it was unpopular would be an understatement: it was, in fact, a big-budget disaster.

The acres of multi-media experience were boarded up when Congress refused to appropriate funds for completion. As a focal point, it was a perfect example of the facilities that are available in many localities. It was underutilized, enormous, centrally located, and known by the homeless.

Interior officials were not pleased at the proposed use of the Visitor Center. But an arrangement was reached after a series of meetings, including one that took place on a bench in Lafayette Park. The night spent on a heat grate or in an alley beside the Interior Department provided a strong counterpoint to meeting in their executive offices the following day.

On November 30, 1978, amidst a grest deal of local and national media attention, the National Visitor Center was opened as an overnight shelter. There were separate areas for men and women. Hundreds of people came each evening. There was room to spare and more than enough food. In one corner, late arrivals enjoyed hot stew and tea. In another, volunteer drivers compared notes on people awaiting rides to the shelter and areas not yet investigated that evening. On another carpeted hump, a guest quietly strummed a guitar, while others enjoyed a last cigarette and some conversation before claiming a mat and blanket. The ambience was tangible.

In spite of the mild weather and the constant risk of expulsion (the question of a continued stay was raised daily in banner headlines), hundreds of homeless men and women used the facility each evening. It was becoming an embarrassment to the city government, which was repeatedly claiming that existing facilities were adequate. Soon the weather would break, the cold would arrive, and hundreds more would flock to the NVC.

On the tenth day, the temperature was falling rapidly, and the forecast was for a brutally cold night. The Department of the Interior chose that time to declare the "experiment" over. Twenty-four people were arrested after spending the night in the middle of Massachusetts Avenue in front of the Visitor Center. Hundreds were turned away from the former shelter. (As of November 1982, the NVC is still empty, unused, and deteriorating.)

The press had closely followed events at the NVC, and the public response had shown a reluctant but growing awareness of the magnitude and nature of the problem of homelessness. The opening and closing of the Visitor Center drew public attention as well, since there were arrests for three nights, and CCNV member Mitch Snyder was badly beaten by the police. As a result of the focus, the city was successfully pressed to provide additional shelter and to relax some rules in effect at the Blair School shelter. They designated an additional vacant building - Pierce School - as a backup facility to handle Blair's overflow.

DHR consented to eight specific proposals to improve the operation of the city-operated shelter and encourage more men to use it, although it was nearly always full anyway. The changes made identification and showers optional and allowed a later morning closing time. The centrally located and unused 456 C Street building would be put into service again as a decentralized hospitality and pickup point, and the use of volunteers in the shelters would be encouraged.

Further, the department made two specific long-term commitments. One was "to provide sufficient space to meet the overnight shelter needs of homeless men and women." The other was to "accept and support" the establishment of an oversight committee of local residents, the homeless, and others to monitor the operation of the shelters. Members of the group would maintain an unannounced presence in the shelters and report directly to the DHR director.

CCNV also agreed to staff Pierce School with volunteers and shelter users for 30 days and to develop a model shelter program in that time. It was not difficult to do. Within three days of the transition, Pierce was at its capacity of 150 men, and within a week, numbers swelled as high as 216. Men slept on floors and tables while waiting for another building to open. Blair School remained full.

It was obvious that a difference in atmosphere quickly attracted more people. They served one another meals, and helped maintain the building and staff the shelter. They began to assume the duties for which they had a responsibility and to which they had a right. Along with control over their environment came some of the dignity and self-respect they had been denied.

Coinciding with the CCNV staffing of Pierce School was D.C. Mayor Marion Barry's public announcement on February 14, 1979, that he was adopting as city policy the position paper authored by the recently-established oversight committee. At that time, Mayor Barry stated, "We are serious about trying to stop the needless deaths of our homeless people." Further, he created the Mayor's Advisory Commission on Homelessness and announced its first appointments. About one-third of these original members were homeless people and shelter users; others were community volunteers and agency representatives. But the mayor kept the commission at a distance, denying it even the barest support and ignoring its statements and ideas. The chairperson resigned as an act of protest, and the commission was thoroughly debilitated well before the mayor summarily dissolved it in May 1980.

The city reneged on a promise to open a much-needed shelter in the Northwest quadrant, and no additional buildings were forthcoming after Pierce reached capacity. As a result, it was decided that a new shelter would be opened without the cooperation of the city, so guests and staff took over the Lenox School building themselves. It soon filled.

Overcrowding was temporarily offset by this move, but major problems remained. Supplies were erratic at best; dirty towels could be sent to the laundry on one day and replaced with a shipment of shorts the next. Buses, to pick up people at the hospitality center (456 C Street) each evening and return them downtown in the morning, were either late or didn't show up at all. The city refused to provide lunch food for the newly-formed resident staff (in spite of the potential savings of $1 million in DHR staff salaries). Even after we were told that lunch food was "out of the question," ten cans of previously ordered tuna fish arrived, but, instead of ten cans, ten *cases* were delivered. The resident staff of Pierce voted to divide it with the men of Lenox. The meals were also a constant source of aggravation: either they came late or they were inadequate.

It seemed as though the District government could do nothing right, nor did officials seem to have other or higher standards for concerned care for these, the poorest of its poor. Suspicion and dislike for the guests seemed to define a policy made largely by black officials for other black people.

The case was made, however much difficulty the bureaucratic mind had with it. Many men, who had not previously perceived shelter as being available or accessible to them, were now staying at the schools. If the conditions and the atmosphere were optimal or even improving, a larger number would emerge from the invisible world of the street; then the true proportions of the problem could be seen. Undoubtedly the formula is alien and elusive for many officials: we can only know how many people are on the streets, we can only quantify the problem, *after* we have resolved it by bringing the homeless inside.

While local officials continued to complain that our estimate of 5,000 to 10,000 homeless people in the District was absurdly high, we later learned that by the city's own estimates - not for public disclosure, of course - more than 12,000 men had used the city-run or city-funded shelters in 26 months.

By its own hand, city policy was laid out in that season of 1978-79, but there were other benefits to the long-range assault on homelessness as well. The system of participation by guests instilled in many a sense of possibility and the dignity that comes of being in control of one's environment and of service to others. A large pool of experienced shelter volunteers emerged. Since many of them were college students and young working people, they spilled over into other cities to continue their efforts. Attention was also focused on D.C. by other cities, for few were taking serious or innovative steps to address the growing problem.

*   *   *

Attention and efforts have remained focused on city policy, but other fronts have also developed. These contributed to a growth of awareness in the city, to the point where many ordinary people have a basic understanding of the problem and issues. While recent national press coverage has not looked closely at Washington, the city has had its own continuing exposure to the reality of homelessness.

Blood poured on District Building in response to winter's first exposure death of a homeless person.

January, 1982: memorial service for Jesse Moore, held in Western Plaza on Pennsylvania Avenue, opposite D.C. city hall.

CCNV has, on numerous occasions, conducted public events and demonstrations to focus attention on homelessness and force a response from both the religious community and the local government. Activities undertaken during the last four years have included:

* Community members poured blood on the altar at St. Matthew's Cathedral, after cathedral officials refused to keep the building open during a snowstorm, and two people died of exposure within the next three days.
* The mayor's testimony during D.C. City Council budget hearings was disrupted as laughing boxes were set off whenever he spoke of the adequacy of shelter programs.
* CCNV's census forms were publicly burned because census bureau procedures failed to count the homeless.
* On the first anniversary of the mayor's policy statement on homelessness, a similar press conference (on his administration's commitment to reduce infant mortality), was disrupted with a reminder that he had not yet fulfilled his pledge to create adequate shelter.
* CCNV members conducted a public fast to secure additional shelter space for women. After three days, it was successful.
* The community confronted a wealthy Roman Catholic parish on its selfish use of resources. A $400,000 renovation program was planned by a congregation that spent more money on magazine subscriptions than they did on the poor.
* A banner was unfurled on the steps of city hall with a quote from the mayor's February 14, 1979 press conference: "We are serious about trying to stop the needless deaths of our homeless people." Blood was also poured on the building in response to the recent exposure death of a homeless person.
* An alternative Fourth of July celebration was held in a downtown park, under a huge banner that read "Don't tread on us." The event was a reminder that, for the hundreds of homeless people who gathered in the park that day, the revolution still was a distant dream.
* Community members were twice arrested and removed from the Hilton Hotel for distributing copies of the Beatitudes to the U.S. Catholic Bishops at their yearly conference. The church was being asked to be more sensitive and responsive to the needs of the poor.

*   *   *

CCNV has also conducted public services for people who have died. In January 1980, members were able to claim the body of "John Doe," an exposure victim and a homeless, unclaimed man. A horse-drawn cortege led a funeral procession through downtown Washington. The subsequent service in front of city hall was an accomplishment in itself, for the city had taken legal action to prevent the funeral from occurring, and it took a D.C. Court of Appeals ruling to force the release of the body.

On December 28, 1981, the Christian Feast of the Holy Innocents, a field of crosses was planted in Lafayette Park across from the White House. Each cross bore a name or date of death of a homeless person and was a graphic reminder of the suffering and death that occurs every year. The more than 500 crosses were hammered into the ground by several dozen advocates from a handful of cities. The crosses remained all winter, visible day or night to passersby.

On a sunny morning that began the last day of winter, many of the same people gathered again. Each called out the name of a homeless victim of the season just ending, and new crosses were planted. The hundreds of other crosses were then taken up, and each was delivered to a member of Congress.

In January 1982, an unusual service was held, again across from city hall: a 24-hour vigil and public funeral for Jesse Moore, a popular homeless man who died in an abandoned building. The event changed abruptly when press coverage leading up to the day accomplished what the city and its investigators failed to do in the previous weeks since Jesse's death: the man's family was located. They chose to have a private funeral, and the snowy memorial service became a poignant tribute to all the homeless.

Public funerals and memorial services are a reminder to the community that the homeless are suffering and dying. But the drawback of such events is the same for both the public and the people who work more closely with those in need: the homeless remain as anonymous in death as they are in life. Their personalities, their human qualities, the stories of their lives - all are lost to us. When we manage to find out something about a person, it is usually too late, and we have learned it from a death certificate. This, then, is an attempt to add a bit of depth to the statistics which are so easily and impersonally digested.

Willie Brass, 51, was found semi-conscious about 3 A.M. in the 1300 block of H Street NE. He was just one block from the overcrowded Pierce School shelter, where he had often stayed. He died shortly afterward at the Washington Hospital Center. He was found on the coldest Christmas morning in 108 years.

Willie Pender, age 42, also died on Christmas Day, 1980. He was found on the steps of New York Avenue Presbyterian Church, just one block from the White House. Willie was a laborer, and, as he said more than once, "There just ain't no work." Both he and Willie Brass died of exposure to the cold; both men had been drinking to keep warm. The temperature was 12 degrees, and fierce northwest winds knifed across the area.

Dinner line at CCNV's Drop-In Center.

CCNV's I Street Center for older people, located around the corner from the Drop-In Center.

James Martin died in mid-January, three weeks after he was found in an abandoned building on Christmas Day. He died of bronchial pneumonia following a coma, hypothermia, and exposure to cold, according to his death certificate.

Willie Brass' body was claimed by his wife, Barbara, of nearby Takoma Park, Maryland. Willie Pender was claimed by his brother, Johny, of Oxon Hill, Maryland. James Martin, a widower and a retired Hostess Company baker, was claimed by his niece, Joan, of Lynchburg, Virginia.

On March 1 and 2, 1980, a storm moving up the Atlantic Coast dumped inches of snow on the D.C. area. Cold temperatures accompanied the storm, with an almost record low of 13 degrees. The cold claimed three lives in as many days.

James Ford died on March 2. He was found at the rear of an abandoned building in the 1800 block of Biltmore Street in the changing neighborhood of Mount Pleasant. His legs were so badly infected from frostbite and gangrene that, when his body was found, the police were driven back by the stench. James could not possibly have walked the three miles to the nearest city shelter, Blair School. He was just a few blocks from another vacant school building that the city had reneged on opening as a shelter, after repeated promises to do so.

James received his mail at CCNV's Drop-In Center. A letter had arrived the day before he died, but he never claimed it.

James Ford's 90-year-old mother, confined to a nursing home, asked that her son's cremated remains be given to CCNV, so his life and death would not be forgotten.

Charles Hiatt died March 1, 1980. He was found in the stairwell of the D.C. Employment Security Building.

Johnnie Mack Speller was found in a parked car not far from where Charles Hiatt died two nights before. He had apparently broken into the vehicle, which was parked in an Amoco gas station, after being turned away from an overcrowded mission only a few feet away.

The deaths of James Ford and Charles Hiatt on two consecutive nights were the impetus for the blood-pouring at Saint Matthew's Cathedral on March 3. Following that action, the protesters were informed of Johnnie Mack Speller's death.

James Ford and Jesse Moore had been close friends - "walking partners" - as people on the street say. After James died in 1980, Jesse became frightened that the same thing would happen to him. He spoke often of his dread of freezing to death - homeless and alone - in some abandoned building or doorway.

Jesse was a popular man, well-known and well-liked by Mount Pleasant shopkeepers and long-term area residents. He was a good carpenter who, for months at a time, could ply his trade in a professional and responsible way. At times, Jesse worked long enough to save a few dollars and rent a room. Then, he would talk of reuniting with his wife and family. Jesse and his family, even after all the years of separation, loved each other very much. Occassionally, his wife would come to the neighborhood and talk with him.

But Jesse Moore had a problem, one which he did not understand and could not control. He was an alcoholic. Try as he might and dream as he did, Jesse could not stay away from the bottle. It separated him from his wife, who cried when she learned of Jesse's death, although she had known for years that such news would come. It separated him from his son and daughter, both police officers in Virginia. It sometimes separated him from his work. It kept him on the street, and, in the end, it killed him. He died in the cold in an abandoned fish market.

It was because Jesse was so popular, and because his friends requested it, that a public funeral was held for him when he died.

* * *

Reaganville: Population Growing Daily

In the 1930's, little settlements of shacks sprang up across the country. These "Hoovervilles" of poor and homeless people were a direct contradiction of the notion that "prosperity is just around the corner." The existence of growing numbers of suffering people has also been denied by the Reagan Administration, which has authored budgets and policies that have heaped new pain on the poor and added to the rolls of the impoverished.

Thus, on Thanksgiving Day 1981, a statement of the new era was delivered in Lafayette Park, across from the White House. A Thanksgiving dinner was served to about 700 poor and homeless people that afternoon, and they were justly treated to every dish the average American was enjoying at home.

What followed dinner has become history: "Reaganville," an encampment of nine tents where the homeless could gather to communicate in the only real way open to them: with their bodies, and through their very existence. By Thanksgiving Day, CCNV had already lost two rounds in a battle to open the tents as places the homeless could sleep during the course of their demonstration. The Interior Department had denied a permit for that purpose, and their decision had been upheld in federal court. A small band of CCNV members and homeless people persevered, however, and spent Thanksgiving night there. Early the next morning, they were arrested and the tents removed.

While awaiting further court action, CCNV brought the tents back under a permit that prohibited sleeping: for the moment the symbol would have to suffice, minus the controversial element of sleeping homeless people. A large "CENSORED" was stenciled across Reaganville's sign. The tents stood as a reminder of a still-invisible population. The homeless could have been there, as they were on Thanksgiving, talking about themselves and their lives with reporters and passersby. But absent their eloquence and pain, the empty tents would have to do. The dead would also have to speak: 41 crosses were planted in front of the tents to memorialize some of the local victims of five previous winters.

Twenty-four hours a day, CCNV members and volunteers were present at the tents, talking to those who stopped by and carrying out the unpleasant duty of preventing the homeless from sleeping there.

Then, on December 22, Federal Judge Charles Richey surprisingly reversed his previous decision. He was enlightened by two hearings and the testimony of CCNV's Mitch Snyder, who talked of his experience living on the street. Richey ruled that the homeless had been discriminated against and could sleep in the tents, since others - farmers, veterans, and blacks - had been allowed to do so.

The Interior Department lost a subsequent Court of Appeals ruling, and the tents were opened for the remainder of the winter. It was clear that the government began to worry about the winter of 1982-83 even then, as they began to prepare new regulations. They selectively overlooked the growth of a surrounding community of the homeless. Makeshift tents and lean-to's abounded, but with a common goal, perhaps best expressed by a sign erected in the park: "Wanted: Wisdom and Honesty." Interior was building its case: This is what happens if people are allowed to sleep in the tents. They exercised none of the controls available to them, even allowing the squatters to be there without permits.

In June 1982, The Interior Department officially changed its regulations to prohibit any repetition of Reaganville. The tents had come down on the first day of spring, although the independent demonstrations had continued and then moved to the White House sidewalk. What the government could not reverse was the sight seen by millions who passed by during the winter. What they could not change was the awakening of volunteers who regularly spent a shift in the cold tents, talking to the homeless. What they could not take away was the memory of all who gathered on a snowy January day to plant a cross for a new victim of the cold.

Six people were arrested at Reaganville, on the day after Thanksgiving; each was charged with demonstrating without a permit, camping in a prohibited area, and unlawful entry. Four of the six were charged as repeat offenders, previously arrested for unlawful entry. Four people faced 1½ years in jail and two faced 2½ years as a result. The government vigorously carried forward the prosecution of these cases, and filed the punitive "repeat papers" as if there had not been a civil decision on Reaganville that declared the defendants' activity to be protected constitutionally. It was with obvious reluctance that the U.S. Attorney finally dropped charges.

In August 1982, the case of *CCNV* v. *Watt* went back to court in an effort to rebuild Reaganville for the upcoming winter. Also planned was "Congressional Village," an extension of tents at the Capitol as a reminder to Congress that, with their approval of two Reagan budgets, they too are responsible for the increasing suffering and deprivation.

* * *

Another series of events that has educated both press and public while having mixed results for the homeless, has been a succession of court cases aimed at keeping city shelters open. In May 1980, Mayor Marion Barry abruptly dissolved his Advisory Commission on Homelessness and prepared to close the Blair and Pierce School shelters without written notice and within 72 hours.

Breakneck legal work by volunteer lawyers and CCNV members found the case in federal court on a Sunday morning. The effort was successful; a court order kept the schools open from May 1980 through June 1982. During that period, the city contracted the running of the shelters to the Washington Council of Churches, under whose control they remain.

On June 8, 1982, Federal Judge Thomas Flannery ruled in the men's shelter case[1] that it was sufficient protection for the homeless to submit written comments in response to a notice of closing. It is not necessary that they be enabled to express themselves in another fashion. Judge Flannery's ruling has been appealed.

As a result of these activities and the constant application of pressure, 178 beds for women and 700 beds for men were available by the winter of 1981-82.

Offering volunteer time or participating in litigation are clearly ways of helping homeless people. But, for depth, nothing compares to two alternatives - voluntarily living the life of a homeless person and documenting the help that is offered daily. In 1980, both of these areas were exposed to the public as never before.

By a coincidence of timing, *Washington Post* reporter Neil Henry broke a series on the homeless in Washington and Baltimore just as the *Williams* v. *Barry* men's shelter case was heard. The 12-part series was the result of Henry's two months spent living on the streets in the two cities. He stayed in the local shelters and missions, ate at the soup kitchens, and reported the conditions as he saw and experienced them, excluding none of the violence or indifference he found indoors as well as out.

At a shelter in Northeast Washington, the bums warned me of a burly security guard who clubbed several of them every night for sport. I slept on a heating grate in Foggy Bottom with three men who preferred the rats and the cold to contending with the degradation of the public shelters.

Neil Henry
"Exploring the World
of the Urban Derelict"
Washington Post
April 27, 1980

We staggered out of the [mission] every morning at 5:30, a dawn processional of bums trooping down the streets in twos and threes, alone in the city. . . .

The [weather] forecast was important to us because most of our time was spent on the streets. This was a life of interminable trudges - more than 10 miles daily - between soup kitchens uptown and warm daytime shelters. So I quickly learned of certain anchors to the daily schedule. Just as a business executive knows where he will park his car in the morning or where he will meet a colleague for lunch, the homeless know where to go to eat, to use the bathroom, to get a few bucks, or simply to pass the time. . . .

Weekends were the toughest days for the homeless and destitute because so many retreats - the blood banks, labor pools and soup kitchens - were closed. Saturday and Sunday thus became the hottest days for bus station security guards who were kept busy bouncing bums from waiting areas and rest rooms.

Neil Henry
"The Bum's Life in Baltimore"
Washington Post
April 28, 1980

. . . I discovered my appearance was my greatest drawback.

By now I was close to two weeks into this assignment. I had showered at the mission but my clothes smelled foul and stubbles of hair were beginning to spread on my face. My clothes absorbed my own perspiration, as well as the faint sweet-sickly odors of urine and old sweat emitted by sheets and blankets at the mission. I was getting little sleep because of the cold at night, and my eyes were turning red. I had developed a painfully sore nerve in my left foot and was limping badly. I was not a presentable sight.

Whatever dignity I felt at the beginning of this journey had eroded to a point where I felt comfortable only with other bums. . . .

Neil Henry
" 'Work!' Brings Cheers at Local 194's
Hiring Hall"
Washington Post
April 29, 1980

First the wino collapsed like a dead man, smacking head first onto the cold pavement. Then Norton, the nightstick-toting security guard, viciously beat two old geezers across their backs and ribs and sent them howling into I Street NE. . . .

. . . [Norton] knew that nothing panicked Washington bums more than losing their places in lines - be it outside the soup kitchens on O and L Streets NW, St. Vincent de Paul, The Chinatown missions or the Northeast shelters.

Their days and nights, their sustenance and shelter, are ever defined by the line - first come, first served. Whenever a scuffle broke out among the bums of Washington, if it wasn't over that last bit of booze, it was usually over a place in line.

Neil Henry
"In D.C., Raw and Threatening Things"
Washington Post
May 4, 1980

The series and the civil suit played off well against one another. On the one hand, Henry presented a picture of official brutality and abuse of dignity. He said the same things we had been saying, but now they were being said by the *Washington Post*.

At the same time, concerned people who were close to the homeless, and the homeless themselves, were fighting to keep these places open and to improve conditions, giving exposure to several hard truths. The shelters deserved their reputations as snake pits, unimaginably degrading and dehumanizing. They offered beatings and ice-covered shower room floors, where the chattering of teeth was the only sound heard.

No longer under total city control, the shelters have improved, but they still punish the homeless for unknown sins. Nevertheless, they are always full, and people continue to come to them. True, many would rather die than subject themselves to this treatment. But that is precisely the nature of the choice: death by degrees, or life in hell. Many choose to live.

Another source of new information resulted from the defense investigation for a 1980 criminal case stemming from the arrest of several CCNV members and homeless people who sought refuge in the local Episcopal Washington Cathedral and the Roman Catholic St. Matthew's Cathedral during a February snow storm. The intruders reminded church officials of the relevance of the admonition to shelter the homeless on a night when it was a matter of life and death, and they demanded that the cathedrals keep their doors open to the homeless through the night.

Instead, they were arrested, removed, and charged with unlawful entry. They worked with a team of Antioch Law School students to prepare a defense of necessity, i.e. the breaking of a law (in this case the unlawful entry statute) to prevent the greater evil: the possible death or injury of homeless people, on a bitterly cold and snowy night. The trial was seen as an opportunity to expose the nature and magnitude of the problem of homelessness in the District of Columbia. An investigation of the interaction homeless people have with medical facilities and the criminal justice system resulted in the following findings. It must be remembered that the figures so reflected have only increased, and also that these figures represent only those people perceived to be homeless. For instance, not many judges, clerks, or hospital personnel recognize the street addresses of shelters, yet a homeless person might offer this information in the course of being processed.

The homeless resort to hospital emergency rooms as both a place to rest for the day or evening, and also as a longer-term aid for exposure-related problems. Numbers in winter months are high, particularly since none of the city-run shelters are equipped to provide hospitality to the physically handicapped and disabled. Several hospitals frequently used by the homeless report the following:

George Washington University Hospital: a few homeless people each night.

Veterans Administration Hospital: one or two a day, always malnourished.

Washington Hospital Center: at least one per night, with one or two each week sent to intensive care with frostbite or low body temperatures — usually around 82 degrees.

D.C. General Hospital: 10 or 12 such patients per night; many of them slept over. Some stayed for days.

Howard University Hospital: about 10 homeless patients per shift, or about 30 people per day, in the winter. Many are admitted to the wards for weeks at a time simply as a humane effort to keep them off the streets.

Extrapolating the figures provided by physicians, nurses, and case workers at these hospitals shows a total of 50 visits per day and approximately 1500 visits per month for all the hospitals combined. Needless to say, the complaints range from the vague - the motivation to get inside - to frostbite, heat stroke, gangrene, seizures, sleep deprivation, intoxication, bronchitis, pneumonia, malnutrition, and more.

The following is a sampling of patients and their diagnoses at Georgetown University Hospital's Emergency Room during a recent winter. These entries are from the Emergency Room log.

January 1, 2, 3, 4 - L, male, dehydration secondary to ETOH [alcohol]
January 9 - J, female, 19-year-old transient; weakness. Unknown if sent to shelter.
January 10 - J, male, admitted to hospital for hypothermia.
January 13 - W, male, paranoid schizophrenic; sent to the Blair School.
January 20 - C, female, 32 years old, had many somatic complaints, no findings on exam. In past she has stated that she has no place to go.
January 24 - C, female, 22 years old admitted with frostbite and gangrene.
February 5 - H, female, 63 years old, came in at 7:19 P.M., no place to live, was sent to House of Ruth.
February 6 - W, female, 79 years old, multiple myeloma, social disposition.
February 9 - C, male, 60 years old, detoxification, sleep deprivation. He is an ex-con who was recently discharged from serving a life sentence when it was learned that he has terminal lung cancer. He has been an inpatient here. Unknown to me if he has any resources.
(There were three other cases where people claimed to be homeless, yet outwardly appeared clean, decently dressed, and regularly fed. These people were perhaps borderline schizophrenics in need of mental health care. . . . They were offered transportation to DHS, but refused to go.)
February 28 - L, male, 79 years with bronchitis. He is definitely a street person, with some psychological problems, who somehow survives.

*   *   *

The D.C. courts provide a good example of the degree to which the problem is neither recognized nor comprehended within the very institutions that have primary contact with the homeless. Interaction with the court is inevitable, since it is nearly impossible to be destitute and live within the confines of the law. Drinking, urinating, defecating, or changing clothes on the street: all are illegal. Yet, quite often, there simply is not the opportunity to do these things indoors. The D.C. Superior Court does not statistically differentiate people who are homeless and people who have been arrested for common petty offenses - such as disorderly conduct, or urinating in public. There is no official recognition of the thousands of arrests that occur on these charges, the thousands of dollars posted and forfeited $10 at a time as collateral, or the accumulated years of jail time done by those with no funds. Among judges, attorneys, and most other court personnel, there is little real knowledge of the existence and operation of shelters, so much so that defendants are routinely released to shelters where they have no guarantee of a bed.

The only clear picture to emerge from the D.C. Superior Court comes from the Pre-Trial Services office, where director Tim Murray states that services for the homeless "have not changed one iota" in the 10 years he has been there.

There are high costs attached each time a homeless man or woman makes use of a publicly-supported service or institution whose services exceed the person's need; for example, when a homeless person is hospitalized for a problem that arises from being homeless. What the person really needs is shelter. The difference in cost between a bed in a hospital or a shelter is astronomical.

Likewise, there are costs attached when neglect is a policy in itself, when chronic problems *must* become acute before they are recognized or addressed. A jail cell, a stay in a hospital, or an ambulance ride - all these costly and readily available services are substitutes in an ill-conceived policy of care. In 1976, the cost of such "overinstitutionalization" in the District of Columbia was estimated to be $16.1 million in D.C. and federal funds each year. In contrast, for FY 1982, the budget for the Blair and Pierce School shelters for men - each housing an average of 120 men per night - was $701,000. That comes to about $8 per person per night.

For some other institutions where homeless people may go as a last resort, the costs are these:

According to the Budget Office of the D.C. Department of Corrections, the FY 1981 cost of incarceration, per day, at D.C. Jail is $38.65, and $37.49 per day average for longer term prisoners at Lorton.

Although many persons on the street have been released from St. Elizabeths Hospitals, they return there either voluntarily or through contact with other institutions. According to the Finance Office, the FY 1981 patient cost per day is $144.16.

While many people are allowed to stay in D.C. General Hospital's waiting rooms and hallways, others are admitted out of sympathy for their condition. Many others require hospitalization as a result of exposure. Without advanced care, the per day cost was $558 as of FY 1981.

What are the alternatives? Will there ever be enough space for people to sleep? The city has shown, again and again, that it is not prepared to lead the way. The efforts of the religious community have been, at best, only piecemeal and reluctant. As suffering has increased, local churches have responded slowly and with temporary measures. In the coldest weeks of the winter of 1981-82, three Catholic parishes opened their doors, but two closed within a few nights, and the word passed on the streets that the third was a poor alternative. Decentralized shelters are a necessity for keeping people alive, yet the churches - generously located in every neighborhood - are locked tight. The Catholic archdiocese, which had not previously run any men's shelters, now seems ready to postpone delivery on a promised facility in a poor neighborhood. Almost without exception, a sense of urgency - born of understanding and proximity - is missing from these deliberations. The church is not behaving boldly in the face of great pain.

Both men and women now have centers available where they can rest, clean up, and get a change of their clothes. They can have a cup of tea, make a call, wash out their clothes. It is a small offering, but an important one. The Drop-In Centers, opened by CCNV in 1979, serve many hundreds of people a week in this way. But more is needed: clinics, legal aid, help with paperwork - all offered in a non-demeaning way.

In the Hoover Depression, some people prospered from the suffering of others. Such is the case today. Yet, the 1982 election campaign seems to be whirling by with not a local or national mention that we simply will not tolerate people living and dying on our streets: destitute, alone, and uncared for. One has to ask: is this the Dickens City of Magnificent Intentions or of Magnificent Distances?

Footnotes

[1] *Williams* v. *Barry*, Civil Action No. 80-1104, U.S. District Court for the District of Columbia.

Excerpts from the Neil Henry series in *The Washington Post* are reprinted with the permission of *The Washington Post*.

ross

Life on the Streets

On September 16, 1982, nationally-syndicated columnist Jimmy Breslin set up housekeeping (a makeshift bed, a table, and chairs) on the east side of First Avenue, between 35th and 36th Streets. Breslin wrote:

> *The Plaza will pass as home for me for a couple of days, a couple of nights, and columns will be written and dispatched to this newspaper. The people who will be written about are not orderly, perhaps not so rational. But many of them find that living on the streets is better than being in the dank, crawling rooms to which the city directs them... Perhaps another presence on the streets will cause the public to request housing that is more attractive to the homeless, the wanderers, the wounded, than an empty sidewalk.*
>
> *As their presence at our feet each day indicts us all, some time spent living with these people on the streets, while it will be neither comfortable nor cheerful, seems important.*

It was well past midnight, quiet except for an occasional police cruiser, ambulance, or tourist driving by. Two members of the Community for Creative Non-Violence, Mitch Snyder and Harold Moss, had been living on the streets for about a week. Both were asleep on the heat grate at the corner of 19th and C Streets, Northwest, one block from the Daughters of the American Revolution (DAR) Constitution Hall. Beyond the grate was a sign which identified the building behind it as the "Office of Personnel Management." The OPM fills one square block, as does the Department of the Interior across the street. Completing the scene, a homeless man slept on another grate in front of the Bureau of Mines, on the adjacent corner.

The silence of the night was shattered as a beer bottle, thrown from a passing car, smashed onto the sidewalk inches from Snyder's face. Had he been hit by the jagged fragments, the effects would have been similar to that of a shotgun blast. The people in the car could be heard laughing as they drove away.

During the fall of 1980, we reached the same conclusion as Breslin would two years later: "Some time spent living with these people on the streets... seems important." Two CCNV members moved to the street on December 3 and remained there until the first day of spring - March 21, 1981.

Moss and Snyder had, up until that time, been living at the Community's Drop-In Center. There the homeless could shower, shave, launder or change their clothes, or simply relax. Seven days a week, from 7 A.M. to 4 P.M., hundreds of homeless people made use of the center, and 300 to 500 people a day were served a hot meal between 5:00 and 6:00 in the evening. (This is in addition to CCNV's other soup kitchen which serves an equal number of people a morning meal, and a free food store which provides a bag of groceries to between 200 and 300 people a day.) Both men had also spent a few years organizing and staffing emergency shelters. They were personally familiar with many of Washington's street people.

Meaningful advocacy stems from authenticity and proximity. We had been speaking for the homeless, and we realized that the time had come for us to reduce further the distance that still lay between us. It was necessary that we share, for an extended period of time, the experience and the life of people who call the street their home. In so doing, it was hoped that we would add depth and legitimacy to our advocacy, and we would also help to focus attention on the existence and plight of the homeless.

Following dinner on December 3, Moss and Snyder walked off into the night. Each man carried a plastic trash bag, containing the necessities that would sustain him over the next 3½ months: toilet paper, a blanket, some toothpaste, a bar of soap, a couple of books, a Bible, and a water-bottle. This is their story.

> *We knew that the winter would be as difficult for those who remained in the Drop-In Center as it would be for us. Two people were left to staff the Center and maintain some semblance of order. They would be working all day, every day. Despite these concerns, our thoughts turned toward our own immediate survival. Where would we spend the night? We went in search of a heat grate.*

Government buildings within the Federal Triangle are warmed by massive heating systems located in a labyrinth of underground tunnels. On Constitution and Independence Avenues, around the Mall and the Ellipse, near the State Department, White House, Smithsonian, Washington Monument, and the various court buildings, grates or vents release the heat that builds up underground. A heat grate may be as small as a sewer cover, or it may be large enough to accommodate six or eight or even ten people. Some grates are in the middle of the sidewalk, others are set back a few feet in a grassy area. A few are raised two or three feet off the ground. Most blow dry heat, although a few vent wet steam. In the winter months, the latter are a refuge of last resort. A person lying on a wet steam grate will get soaked within a matter of minutes. On a really cold morning, clothing, hair, and clammy skin freezes solid within minutes after leaving the grate. Still, while it is extremely uncomfortable and unhealthy, it is better than running the risk of frostbite or hypothermia.

It was dark when we left the Center. By the time we walked the half mile or so to the grates, they were already taken. After a couple of hours of walking and searching, we found two small ones on the fringe of the Ellipse. The air coming out of the grates was hot and reeked of sewage. No doubt this was why they were still vacant. After a couple of hours of tossing and turning, we finally fell asleep.

We awoke at dawn - as we would nearly every day we were on the streets. Our plastic tote bags had served as pillows during the night; we hoisted them and walked slowly off.

Our first stop was the public bathroom in Lafayette Park, across from the White House. We waited for an hour or more for it to be opened. At least a dozen of us had gathered by the time the doors were unlocked. After washing up and relieving ourselves, we went across the street to St. John's Episcopal Church. There we spent another hour or two in silence, prayer, and warmth. By then, it was almost time for the soup kitchen to open, so we began walking the 15 or so blocks to get there.

By the time the kitchen began serving at 9:30 A.M., 100 or 200 people were already on line. Many of the men who were turned out of the city shelters by 5:30 or 6 o'clock each morning went straight to the kitchen. There was little else to do at that hour. Hot soup or stew, tea, and bread awaited us. It was basic, but good. What was most important was that it was hot.

Above: Two men, on a heat grate opposite the State Department, during a snowstorm.

When you're on the street, virtually every act involves a wait in line. First come, first served is the rule at shelters, missions, soup kitchens, clothing rooms, and drop-in centers. Among the homeless, a place in line is often worth fighting for. It is the inevitable outcome of too many people competing for too few resources and services. "Hurry up and wait" is heard on the street as often as it is in prison. The line is a constant source of tension, frustration, and anger. This is not at all surprising when one's place on that line could determine whether one gets a bed, or a meal, or a change of clothes. It is also a relentless reminder of one's station in life.

George Orwell, well-known author of *Animal Farm* and *Nineteen Eighty-Four*, also wrote the less familiar *Down and Out in Paris and London*, a semi-autobiographical narrative about poverty and life on the streets. In *Down and Out*, Orwell remarked, with the insight gained of experience, that the "great evil of a tramp's life is enforced idleness."

Time, the greatest of healers, can also be an unmitigated curse. Passing time on the street and "doing" time in prison are very similar experiences, although time spent on the street is more empty and moves more slowly. The question that daily confronts every homeless person is what to do with the day, which seems to stretch out infinitely and inexorably before you. A police officer in the District of Columbia recently described his work as utter boredom punctuated by moments of sheer terror. For the homeless, life could be described as endless tedium broken only by periods of physical and emotional suffering.

For a homeless person in Washington, D.C., the possibilities are limited for keeping warm, or dry, or simply passing the time between bowls of soup at 9 in the morning and 5 in the evening. This is particularly true during the winter months. Libraries, labor pools, churches, hospital emergency rooms, and bus and train stations are the most commonly chosen places of rest and refuge.

In many cities, public transportation systems provide shelter for many destitute people. There are literally thousands of homeless New Yorkers, for instance, who live - day and night - in the subway, riding from one end of the line to the other. There are many others who, particularly at night, ride the buses, transferring from one route to another.

These are not possibilities for Washington's homeless, however. The District's fledgling subway system has very limited hours of operation, and guards are quick to spot and dislodge homeless passengers whose only real destination is the day's end. Because the District of Columbia is a small city, it is nearly impossible to remain invisible and ride the buses for any length of time. This is particularly true late at night, when service is severely limited. Nor can one transfer or ride indefinitely from one end of the line to the other, without being ordered off, or made to pay another fare.

So many homeless people use the Library of Congress that staff members there were offered a 19-week course in how to deal with them. The city libraries, especially the downtown main branch

CCNV member Mitch Snyder on the heat grate where he lived for 4 months.

(Martin Luther King, Jr.), are also well used, although many of the homeless cannot read or concentrate well enough to allow use of the libraries as anything but temporary sanctuaries.

Whether the night is spent at a shelter, on the grates, or in an abandoned building, sleep is invariably fitful or brief or both. Exhaustion becomes the day's constant companion. Sleeping in the library, as in most other places that offer refuge, is forbidden. To remain awake, hour after hour, when the body and the mind are crying out for rest, is sheer torture. But to succumb invariably results in expulsion.

D.C.'s two bus stations - Trailways and Greyhound - serve as refuge only in the absence of other options. Station guards are constantly on the lookout for vagrants, quick to demand that they produce a ticket. In the absence of a ticket, they are just as quick to issue a not-so-polite invitation to depart. Bus and train stations are accessible to the homeless, especially at times and on days when other facilities are not available. Brutality and the law are thus employed to discourage such use. The beating of homeless men and women by station guards is a common occurrence. Horror stories abound. Arrests and prosecutions for trespassing are also a deterrent. Despite these factors, scores of homeless people can be found there on Sunday and at night.

There are only a few churches in Washington that remain open and accessible; most are tightly shut except at times of worship. With the exception of one or two, no church actively encourages the presence of the homeless. Most do just the opposite. At St. Matthew's Cathedral, in spite of the many tourists who daily visit the Roman Catholic landmark, bathrooms are constantly kept locked to discourage their use by homeless men and women.

While street people suffer harassment, threats, and abuse at the hands of bus station guards, many of them are more willing to run that risk than they are to subject themselves to rejection at the hands of men and women of God. Perhaps disdain, disgust, and "excommunication" are easier to accept from a Trailways security officer than from a pastor. Possibly the inconsistency and hypocrisy of the church hurts more and is harder to swallow than rejection at the hands of a commercial establishment. Whatever the reasons may be, it is to the discredit of the local religious community that very few homeless people are to be found within their buildings.

Hospital emergency rooms also provide protection from the elements and a place to pass the time. D.C. General and Howard University Hospital are both well used, as is George Washington University Hospital, although the latter is much smaller and can

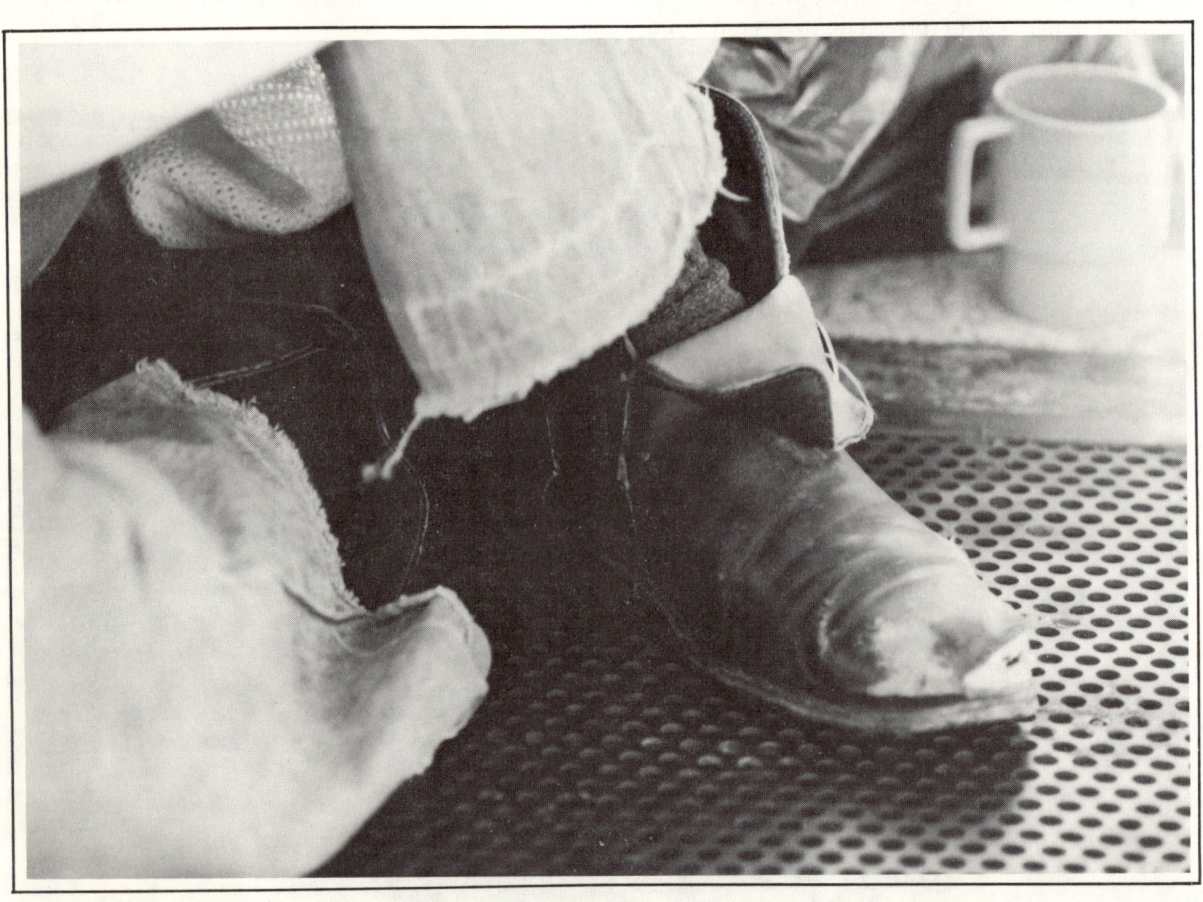

accommodate far fewer people. Homeless men and women spend days at a time in these emergency rooms. The personnel are usually sympathetic, although if too many homeless people begin to gather they will, at some point, be asked to leave.

The handful of labor pools left in the District provide at least a few hours of rest and warmth for some of the men of the street.

D.C.'s many museums are, for the most part, off limits to the street population. The absence of any opportunity to sit and rest, and the constant and close scrutiny by security guards who are quick to expel the homeless make the museums uninviting except under the most adverse weather conditions.

The more destitute and streetworn a person looks, the greater the likelihood of being insulted or told to move on. That is why so many street people work so hard at looking "normal." Those that can't or don't almost never make it inside, regardless of how bad the weather or great the need.

Our daily lives quickly settled into a pattern. When it was very cold, we remained on the grate until we were certain that the bathroom in the park would be open. Life on the street dictates that a disproportionate amount of one's energies and activities will be centered around bathrooms. One quickly learns to predict and control bodily functions and food intake in an effort to avoid late-night emergencies. There are no public bathrooms that remain open around-the-clock, with the exception of the bus stations, but they were a mile or more from where we slept. How easy it is to take for granted the luxury of the availability of a bathroom in the middle of the night. Nothing more assaults and destroys one's dignity, or more quickly reduces one to the level of a wild animal, than having to defecate in an alley, or behind a bush or tree, while praying not to be seen.

The stop at Lafayette Park was followed by some time at St. John's, and then a walk to the soup kitchen. Our visit to the kitchen took a half-hour to an hour, and it was usually uneventful, although an occasional scuffle might erupt. While nothing serious occurred there during our time on the street, people had been badly hurt at the soup kitchen in the past. For that reason, many of the homeless, particularly the more gentle and less aggressive ones, prefer to beg or eat out of trash bins.

After the morning meal, we usually spent a couple of hours at either St. Matthew's Cathedral or the public library. Then it was back to St John's. On most afternoons, we could listen to the organist practice for Sunday's services. Our day usually ended where it began, in Lafayette Park, visiting and talking with the homeless men and women who live there. Called the President's Park because of its proximity to the White House, it is popular among Washington's homeless. There is a public bathroom, it is relatively safe, and the area offers excellent panhandling.

Usually we would set out around sundown on our search for a vacant grate. We spent most of Sunday on the heat grates, because it was warm, because government workers were off, and because there were few tourists in the area during the winter. It was very quiet and very peaceful.

There were a few reasons why we chose to remain on the heat grates rather than use the shelters. First of all, shelter space is always in short supply. It would have been unconscionable for those of us on the street by choice to force out others who need and want to get in from the cold. You can always squeeze another person on the grate, but that is not the attitude at the shelters. Also, we wanted to be visible and accessible.

Not that our decision represented a sacrifice. We much preferred our heat grate to any of the available shelters, either city-run or privately operated. We were very familiar with all of them, well aware of the conditions and the regimen: the brutal guards, the disinterested or hostile staff, the theft, the filth and the vermin, and the thoroughly degrading and dehumanizing environment. For example, ammonia would occasionally be poured in the middle of the dormitory floor; the men, awakened by fumes and gasping for breath, would rush from the room. This was simply a form of insurance so that the guests would not take too long in rising, dressing, and getting back on the street, even though there was nowhere to go for at least two or three hours. On the grates, one could remain until a more reasonable hour. With only occasional harassment or the threat of violence, life on a steam vent was far superior to life in the shelters.

The year before our move to the street, Washington Post *reporter Neil Henry had also tried the life of the homeless. His seven-week sojourn on the streets of Baltimore and Washington resulted in a 12-part series. Henry wrote of his experience in one of D.C.'s municipal shelters:*

> . . . Norton, Blair's security guard, came outside with his nightstick to look for fun. Norton, a chubby man with thick sideburns, knew that nothing panicked Washington bums more than losing their places in line. . .
>
> Norton seemed to understand this very well, when he swaggered outside and declared, "All right, single up, single up! Whoever ain't in line don't sleep here tonight." He stood back with a delighted grin on his face. Most of the men scrambled back against the base of the four-story brick school house, but several - to Norton's irritation - stayed where they were, preferring instead to share smokes and rap.

"Didn't I tell you to move, man?" Norton hollered at one scarlet-eyed old drunk who appeared too wasted to budge. "When I say jump, you jump!"...

The old man stood his ground, peering at Norton with perplexed eyes...

When Norton grabbed him by the collar and prepared to rap him with the stick, another bum zig-zagged his way down the line to get a closer look. Norton, still holding the other man, said to this bum, "Did I invite you, nigger? Get back in your own damn category."

So this onlooker was drawn into the ring, and began talking his own brand of dignity. Norton grabbed him first and levelled his nightstick twice - rap, rap - against the man's ribs. He cried out once - a sustained, pained, pathetic howl - before Norton dragged him by the back of the collar out in the middle of I Street and told him to find somewhere else to sleep that night. Then Norton came back and told the other old drunk to leave unless he, too, wanted the stick. The drunk mumbled and turned his back and slowly walked toward the street, but Norton hit him twice more for good measure across the top of his hunched back and the bum fell into the street cursing and shaking his fists...

... We registered our names with an apathetic young woman who yawned behind a desk in the lobby, which once smelled of chalk erasers and school books but now smelled of whiskey and sweat. We then trooped downstairs to the school's damp basement, where the tensions of the line returned once again. Nowhere in down and out Washington are places in line protected with more ferocity than in the basement of Blair. For here, we all had to strip naked and place our clothes in green garbage bags and stand in line to shower. The quicker we stripped the sooner we got out of there. There were 80 of us struggling to disrobe in a cool smelly room only twice the size of a Dupont Circle efficiency. Afterward, we stood in file, body crammed against body amid odors of liquor, fungus and rot, to wait to shower.

... Several men had open sores festering on their backs and legs. And the scars! One only had to look long enough at a body to find an old knife wound or two...

This wait in line could last as long as 30 minutes, so the men pushed and shoved for space. The shower room contained only four faucets, each of which released only a single rivulet of water to be shared by four or five men. At

the head of the line a worker directed traffic and offered foot powder and Cuprex delouser, which was supposed to be washed off in the shower. Most of the men declined to use it. To them, it was again a matter of pride.

After showering, we entered another small tiled room where a man threw out towels and pajamas. When the towels ran out - the shelter offered only about 20 each night - he handed out old cotton rags that didn't absorb the water so much as spread it around. Our pajamas were cutoffs and torn cotton shirts that we returned the next morning along with the rubber disposable slippers we received.

From there we headed upstairs to another line outside the cafeteria, where we ate string beans, rice, bologna sandwiches and fruit juice...

After dinner we were shepherded upstairs to one of the school's classrooms where 40 army cots were laid out in three rows. Grammar lessons were still chalked to the blackboard here, along with black pride posters and wall hangings - all reminders that this flophouse was once a school filled with children...

At 5 o'clock the next morning, we were herded downstairs to retrieve our clothing. We were supposed to get breakfast then, but, amid complaints that the workers hoarded food and drink, we were sent out into the cold without so much as a cup of hot water. Getting booted out of shelters at such an early hour seemed to be universal.[2]

In January, a little more than a month after the move to the street, the situation at the Drop-In Center became critical: it was much more than Carol and Justin could handle. Harold began spending his days at the Center and continued to spend his nights on the grate. Mitch, who had begun fasting when he moved to the street, had become too weak to make the daily three-to-five mile trek. For the rest of the winter, Mitch remained on the same grate at 19th and C Streets, in front of the Office of Personnel Management, four blocks from the White House, two blocks from the State Department, and one block from D.A.R. Constitution Hall.

As we sat on the grate, day after day, thousands of people walked or drove by. They looked through or beyond us, or away, when we caught them furtively glancing in our direction. It was a frightening and amazing experience. What was more incredible was the discovery of just how quickly one's sense of substance and self-worth melts away under these conditions. Regular contact was maintained with other community members during the course of the winter, but, in less than one week on the streets, we were unable to make or maintain eye contact, even with members of our own community. We were constantly looking down or away. There is a sign prominently hung in the dining room of Danbury Federal Prison that says, "Treat a man as he is, and he will remain as he is. Treat a man as he should be, and that is what he will become." We, who were homeless by choice, had been turned into "bums" by other people's perceptions of us.

It is as though two separate, parallel, and unequal realities exist. For those who are homeless, the rest of the world is alien and irrelevant. The "housed" ones shared none of our concerns or priorities; their hopes and fears, their expectations and their frustrations bore little or no resemblance to our own.

We were constantly preoccupied with the weather. Would it rain or snow? Would it be windy, or would the temperature suddenly drop tonight? At a minimum, our well-being would depend on the answers to those questions; at the extreme, our lives might hang in the balance. Winter is a difficult and painful time of the year for the homeless. Attitudes reflect that reality; during the fall, they become sullen and somber. When rain, snow, or extreme cold was predicted, that was all we thought or talked about.

We are often queried by people who have been panhandled by street people and suspect that any money they give will be spent on alcohol.

What should they do, they ask. We answer that, if they are unwilling to offer the person shelter, they should give him or her some money. Life on the streets is made up of sharp edges and jagged experiences: the long marches, the constant cold and discomfort, the feelings of inferiority and exclusion, and the near-impossibility of an undisturbed night's sleep. Alcohol makes it more possible to survive another day, or get through another night, by rounding off and softening some of those rough edges.

A stiff drink makes it possible to absorb a little more cold and harassment and abuse. It makes more feasible a night's sleep in an abandoned building, where, under a blanket of old newspapers, the stillness is broken by the sound of scurrying rats and your own chattering teeth. You are constantly aware of how exposed and how vulnerable you are to attack. Sleep is possible in doorways, alcoves, and vestibules, once you have deadened that sense of exposure. Washington's homeless, like the destitute of other cities, are often assaulted: beaten and robbed, and slashed or set on fire for no apparent reason. It is a fact of life well-known to the people of the street. It is alcohol that enables you to nod off on a heat grate, parboiled on one side, chilled on the other, as uncomfortable as you would expect to be on a steel and concrete mattress.

A relatively small percentage of the homeless are alcoholics, but many drink. One would have to endure the personal experience of life on the street to understand just how necessary a drink can be. But alcohol is simultaneously a two-edged sword. Many of those who freeze to death during the winter succumb to the false sense of warmth and security that the liquor produces. You are damned if you don't, and, quite possibly, dead if you do. But that is the nature and the essence of life on the streets: impossible conditions and choices.

Monday through Friday, we awoke at dawn with the arrival of the custodial and janitorial workers. Not surprisingly, most of these people were black, unlike the office workers who later passed by. The office personnel began to appear at 7:30 or 8 o'clock, most rushing by just before 9. When we awoke, we folded and bagged the night's paraphernalia - a carpet remnant with which we covered the grate, and a woman's old and torn overcoat that we used as a blanket. Both had been found during our first weeks on the street. Harold would usually leave for the center before 8. Most of the people who passed us seemed oblivious to our existence, but there were a few who greeted us. They will never understand how deeply we appreciated this small sign of recognition.

The next flurry of activity was at lunch time, although most of the workers ate inside. Between 4 and 5 o'clock in the afternoon, the morning's pattern was reversed. One after another and in rapid succession, cars would pull away from the curb, homeward bound. Bundled up against the cold, the government workers - there were nothing but federal office buildings in the area - hurried home.

By 5:30 or 6 o'clock, the area would quiet down considerably, although there was a steady flow of traffic until 10 or 11. On the two or three nights a week when something was happening at Constitution Hall, parked cars would once again fill up the empty streets during the early evening hours. When the hall emptied, thousands of people poured out in a matter of minutes. Not more than four or five times, during the course of the entire winter, did anyone entering or leaving Constitution Hall even acknowledge our existence. One person gave us a dollar, and another gave us a sandwich.

The Presidential motorcade was an occasional diversion. Whenever the President paid an evening visit to the State Department, we knew he was coming before he and his entourage even left 1600 Pennsylvania Avenue. Ten or 15 minutes before the sound of sirens announced his approach, a helicopter would scan the surrounding rooftops - and our grate - with a powerful searchlight. His route never brought him by our corner. We did, however, become accustomed to seeing Interior Secretary James Watt leave the Interior Department each day in a chauffeur-driven limousine. He was invariably engrossed in a newspaper when he passed us by.

The change of Administrations did not go unnoticed on Washington's heat grates. Early on the morning of January 20, 1981, the police stopped by to tell us that we must move on or we would be arrested. Later in the day, we were stopped and searched. The presence of homeless people, in the midst of the luminaries and the day's festivities, would have been incongruous.

Most of our time was spent reading a book or a scavenged newspaper or in thought. Occasionally, another street person would stop by and pay us a visit. Time slowly passed.

The worst periods were the days and nights of bad weather. Inexplicably, whenever it was windy, the grate would shut off. It was as though the wind was blowing through the tunnels, pushing the hot air before it, not allowing it to rise and pass out of the vents. Now and then, the heat would come back on for a few minutes, only to be snuffed out once again, like a candle in a breeze. During those times, there was nothing to do but bundle up with whatever was available and try - usually unsuccessfully - to keep warm.

When it rained or snowed, we kept dry by covering ourselves with a sheet of clear plastic. While the plastic did keep the precipitation at bay, it also kept all of the hot air underneath it. Within seconds, it became unbearable. Every few minutes, we would have to position and reposition ourselves in order to try and keep a constant flow of fresh, cold air circulating under our "umbrella." But, as troublesome and cumbersome as our unwieldy sheet of plastic was, it was far better than nothing. On nights when it rained or snowed, we would look at the grate across the street and see Ross, completely exposed and at the mercy of the elements. At those moments, we would rightly feel steeped in luxury and privilege.

It is at night that the existence of two parallel realities - that of the housed and that of the homeless - is most clear. When the workers, tourists, joggers, theater-goers, and drivers have all called it a day, the streets become the province of the vast army of the homeless. Scores of street dwellers would file past our corner every night. There were bag ladies: gentle and generous Edith, and crazy Jean, who spent her days on downtown street corners yelling at passersby and her nights curled up on the White House sidewalk. Besides the President, Jean's nearest neighbor was Mary, whose usual place of residence was the fence surrounding the White House. There she would sleep sitting up beside the guard tower. There were also men, who carried bags, pushed shopping carts, or toted their worldy possessions on their backs. Silent and alone, they shambled by all night long, shoulders hunched against the cold. There was Willie, who spent his days and nights on a grate by the State Department, eating out of garbage cans. From time to time, he would pass by, usually shirtless and shoeless in his quest for food on the coldest of nights.

We could watch the bent and broken - mostly elderly - people, wandering, marching to and from nowhere. They trembled in the cold, surrounded by heated, lighted, guarded, and empty government buildings. To see this is to witness true lunacy. On bitterly cold nights, and when the rain or snow falls, those buildings are a taunt and a jeer, a constant reminder to the homeless of their insignificance and some implied evil about them. It is nearly impossible, for those who suffer the pain of homelessness, to understand the arbitrary and capricious nature of their circumstances.

Ross was one of those who pushed a shopping cart filled with all the little objects of survival and wonder that he had accumulated during his years on the street. He said that he had served many years in a Maryland prison on a murder charge, and that he was invited to participate in a medical experiment in exchange for his release. As a result of those experiments, his mind has never been the same. Ross believes that the government operates machinery - computers, as he calls them - in the underground tunnels beneath the grates. These absorb his life force and his energy, leaving him too weak to get off the streets. He is well aware that he traded his sanity for his "freedom."

Early one morning, a couple of hours before dawn, we were abruptly awakened by the howling of what we first thought was a badly injured animal. A rage-filled wailing, the sound of pain and grief, tore through the night, searing our minds. But it was not an animal; it was Ross. Standing on his grate across the street from ours, he was screaming, railing against the injustice of his condition, and the insensitivity of a world that allowed him to live as he did. It was a sight and sound never to be forgotten.

Human beings are highly social creatures. We depend, far more than we care to acknowledge, on the acceptance of others and on their perceptions of us. To a large extent, precisely who we are is reflected in the attitudes and reactions other people exhibit toward us. Inclusion in the institutions and the fabric of our society is integral to our sense of substance, significance, well-being, self-worth. To be ignored, cast out, or excommunicated is, in some very real way, to cease to be: I am not acknowledged, therefore, I do not exist. No experience was more powerful or more immediately destructive than the exclusion and the invisibility that accompany homelessness.

There were a few people who tried to reach out to us. On Sunday afternoons, a man visited the grates and left a small bag of food and the reminder that "Jesus loves us." Another person came by on Sunday mornings after church and left each of us a few doughnuts. On occasion, we were given a dollar or two by a passing pedestrian or motorist. Members of a local church brought hot soup and a sandwich to the grates most evenings. A handful of people regularly greeted us or stopped to see how we were doing. But, for every person who expressed some interest in us, or showed concern, or acknowledged our existence, there were many thousands of others who simply looked away. At times, they stepped over or around our prostrate bodies.

We could have done without one of our visitors, Marion Barry, the Mayor of the District of Columbia. He toured the grates one evening, media representatives in tow, inviting the homeless to accompany him to the city shelter. The insensitivity and absurdity of the mayor's performance was not lost on the grate dwellers, although the press dutifully touted his message: these people are homeless by choice; thus there is nothing we can do for them. In more than 3½ months of living on D.C.'s streets, the mayor's action was the most obscene, callous, and perverted that we encountered.

Poverty cannot be chosen, for then it is not poverty but simplicity. That choice makes all the difference. We were not destitute, nor were we alone or powerless. We were in control of our lives; we were mentally competent. Most luxurious and comforting of all, we had friends who loved us and were concerned about us. We were well aware of our privileges and prerogatives. Yet, we have tasted the bitterness of homelessness in our own flesh, and for us, life will never be the same.

We conclude this chapter as we began it, with the words of Jimmy Breslin:

> *As their presence at our feet each day indicts us all, some time spent living with these people on the streets, while it will be neither comfortable nor cheerful, seems important.*

Footnotes

[1]"In the Slow Lane: Money is Mute on the Street," by Jimmy Breslin, *New York Daily News*, September 17, 1982.

[2]"In D.C., Raw and Threatening Things," ("Down and Out," Part 8), by Neil Henry, *Washington Post*, May 4, 1980. This and all other excerpts from Henry's series reprinted with the permission of *The Washington Post*.

"Spaceman" chained to a lamppost while his arresting officer went into Trailways bus station restaurant to eat breakfast.

Memorial service for Jesse Moore.

Thanksgiving Dinner at Lafayette Park.

*You will find that charity
 is a heavy burden
 to carry, heavier than
 the kettle of soup and
 the basket of bread.
But you must your
 gentleness and your
 smile keep.
Giving soup and bread
 isn't all -
 that the rich can do.*

*They are your masters -
 terribly sensitive and
 exacting as you will see -
 but the uglier and dirtier
 they are - the more unjust
 and bitter - the more you must
 give them your love.
It is only because of your
 love - only your love -
 that the poor will
 forgive you the bread
 you give them.*

St. Vincent de Paul

> *The rising Reagan tide was supposed to start lifting all the boats first by April 1981, then by July. Now it's a year after that, and the only thing that's rising is the number of people who have sunk.*
>
> New York Times Editorial
> July 26, 1982

Signs and Symptoms: A Look at 29 Cities

These are indeed the worst of times for the poor of our nation. For those who are but one step from life in the streets, they are desperation-filled days. A reading of the signs - from the unemployment lines to the budget and tax cuts, portends many more seasons of pain. In such a setting, the work of feeding the hungry and sheltering the homeless keeps alive the flickering light of hope. These efforts are, of course, shamefully modest. But to initiate such assistance in the face of great odds is to offer an answer of sorts. It is neither an answer nor an affirmation to those who would have us believe the world will be saved by voluntarism or supply-side economics. Instead it is a response to the meanness and perversion of our national priorities, to the cries of misery we hear, and to what is good and decent within each of us.

What follows are examples of these kinds of efforts. Most of them have started since 1980. In many cases, the programs began with little in the way of money or resources - doors were simply opened, sandwiches made, pots put on the stove - because there were neighbors in need. Most have continued for the same reason.

*

A new 40-bed shelter opened in **Detroit** in July 1982 as the effort of COTS - Coalition on Temporary Shelter, a consortium of religious and civic groups, social service organizations, and business leaders. Such additional facilities are desperately needed in Detroit, one of the big industrial cities devastated by Reaganomics, and economic trends. Unemployment here has been running at about 16 percent. Massive layoffs in the auto industry and the flight of many businesses to the Sun Belt have contributed to this situation.

The prognosis for the winter of 1982-83 is not good. The area experiences harsh weather, the homeless population is on the rise, and, as in virtually every other city in the United States, existing shelter space is totally inadequate. COTS' estimate of 8,000 homeless people in Detroit is supported by documentation of recent winter deaths: in just one weekend during the winter of 1981-82, six homeless men froze to death and a total of 22 cases of hypothermia were reported. The group is making plans for an additional shelter of 100 beds.

More than 1,300 people line up each day at Detroit's several soup kitchens. Two of the oldest of these are the Capuchin Kitchen, which has served more than 10 million meals since its start in 1929, and the Manna Kitchen, feeding more than 300 people daily.

*

Lulu Wilson comes to St. Mary's Church in **Norfolk, Virginia**, every day to make soup, "real soup, not stuff out of a can." Since the end of March 1982, 30 to 50 people a day have come to the church to enjoy a much-needed hot meal, served to them by volunteers. Says Reverend Thomas Quinlan, the church's pastor, "It's a sad, sad indicator of the times when we have to open a soup kitchen. This is a depression, as far as I can tell, and maybe we should admit it."

Six volunteers serve the meal Monday through Friday, offering food and friendship to older people, the unemployed, and, occasionally, a chronically homeless person. Those who come to eat do not have to wait in line to be served, but are brought their meals.

"Going through a line isn't very Christian, I think," says Reverend Quinlan.

*

"I am here because I'm hungry," said a man in line at **Jackson, Mississippi**'s Stewpot Soup Kitchen. In a town where both black and white are poor, the newly-opened facility offers some hope for those who must search for their next meal. Each day at noon, people line up for something hot to eat; their most common sources of difficulty are unemployment and a reduction in benefits. Stewpot is supported by area churches and community groups.

*

The sight of men pulling edible food out of trash cans prompted a parishioner of **Greenville, South Carolina**'s Christ Episcopal Church to look for an answer. The result was Project HOST, which opened January 5, 1981. Twenty people were fed that first day, beneath a sign that reads "No singing, no sermon, just hot, homemade soup."

Project HOST serves 100 meals a day, relying on donated food for its continued existence. The cupboard is literally bare on some days, when a collection of canned goods arrives to meet the immediate need.

*

In 1981, the unemployment rate in **Anderson, South Carolina**, was already nearly 10 percent. That winter, the first of three soup kitchens was opened by Grace Episcopal Church.

*

The Shepherd's Table Soup Kitchen in **Raleigh, North Carolina** now serves 1,000 meals per month to a wide variety of newly-needy people.

*

In **Middletown, New York**, Grace Episcopal Church has opened a daily drop-in center for homeless people with medical needs. The 45 volunteers daily serve 100 sandwiches, free soup, and coffee. Grace Church is attempting to open an overnight shelter in an abandoned local railroad depot as well.

*

Since 1970, **Seattle, Washington**'s Blessed Sacrament Church has been offering a weekly Sunday dinner. They now serve 40,000 to 50,000 meals each year. Parishioners organized the program in response to the severity of Boeing Corporation layoffs. Blessed Sacrament receives $30,000 annually from the St. Vincent de Paul Society. About one-quarter of the food is donated; there are no limits on servings, and leftovers are distributed at the end of the meal. Said one guest, "They understand if you don't have a job. They still treat you like you're somebody."

*

In the Puget Sound city of **Bremerton, Washington**, the Bread and Justice Catholic Worker Community conducted a "Lenten Campaign for the Homeless." For 45 days, beginning Ash Wednesday, February 24, 1982, members and friends of the community took turns sleeping on the steps of the Bremerton Post Office each night to dramatize the plight of those without shelter.

*

Salt Lake City, Utah Mayor Ted Wilson announced the formation of a jobs and housing task force in early 1982. Commenting on the burgeoning number of those in need, he said, "I firmly believe the great majority of these people are honest, decent, individuals unlucky in finding jobs, and Salt Lake City has a responsibility to help them, although I don't want the word out that we are creating a mecca." Mayor Wilson also appealed to mayors in Colorado and Wyoming to do their part to help those in need.

Salt Lake City, the "Crossroads of the West," has attracted many people with its low unemployment rate, but those in search of work far outnumber the jobs available. Officials estimate that 800 people are homeless, about a 400 percent increase over 1981, they claim.

*

In **Washington, D.C.**, McKenna's Wagon makes a half-dozen stops during the evening rush hour. Most of these good-will points are at small "parks" formed at major downtown intersections. At each one, a number of men receive two sandwiches, dessert, and something to quench their thirst. About 100 people are served each evening. The wagon, a converted ice cream truck, is named for Reverend Horace McKenna, a Jesuit priest who died in June 1982, at age 83, after years of service to the poor. A similar undertaking will be initiated, during the 1982-83 winter, by St. Paul's Episcopal Church in conjunction with the Salvation Army. (It was St. Paul's parishioners who brought sandwiches and soup to the heat grates beginning in 1980.)

*

In **Camden, New Jersey**, Leavenhouse daily serves a "free and unconditional" hot meal to anyone who comes. Begun in January 1982, over 40,000 meals were served in the first 10 months of operation. Between 100 and 300 people are served daily. The kitchen relies on community donations; the meal is prepared by volunteers from the black and Hispanic neighborhood.

*

In affluent **Fairfax County, Virginia**, just outside Washington, D.C., a new 24-bed emergency family shelter for county residents is under construction. Mondloch House II will be situated next to its predecessor, a 10-bed shelter opened in 1978. According to United Community Ministries (UCM) director Eleanor Kennedy, requests for emergency assistance in the area have doubled in the last 12 months. UCM served 12,000 people in 1981. That number is expected to double in 1982. The $290,000 shelter is being jointly sponsored by the Fairfax County government and the Episcopal Diocese of Virginia.

"Let's keep the church open tonight for the people who need a place to sleep," said **Denver**'s Father "Woody" Woodrich of Holy Ghost Church. Between 30 and 40 people were expected to make use of the shelter offer, but about 200 actually came. That was in February 1982, and by March, nearly 500 homeless people were sleeping in the church pews each night. Parishioners also began serving their guests three meals a day.

"It's the simplest thing I ever did," said Father Woodrich. "The church just opened its doors and said, 'You are welcome here.' " Not only has the Sunday offering tripled as a result of the congregation's support, but the guests have erased anxieties about their own conduct. There have been not problems but assistance from them, including cleaning the church each morning.

Denver has few other resources. The Denver Rescue Mission's 43 beds are filled each night, and the director says he could use 50 more; requests have nearly doubled since 1981. According to the Denver Catholic Worker, only about 350 beds exist in private agencies such as the mission, and these are always full. About an equal number are turned away as are housed each month, and volunteers cite cases of people sleeping in dumpsters, stairwells, and on sofas in alleys.

As a result of the increased pressure for space, a variety of community and religious organizations has formed the Coalition for Shelter. Although estimates of the size of Denver's homeless population range up to 5,000, a mayoral spokesperson commented, "We don't see any legal charter requirement to provide [shelter]."

*

In the summer of 1981, the Franciscans of St. Anthony's Shrine in **Boston** began a sandwich and coffee line. By January 1982, they were serving 120 people per day. Six months later, the number had risen to 200. The church provides the major support for the program and also receives donations from others who have known hard times. St. Anthony's took its sandwiches outdoors after the priests doing "parlor duty" each day found they were spending much of their time shuttling between hungry visitors and the kitchen.

On February 27, 1982, the Massachusetts Coalition for the Homeless sponsored a public memorial service for local homeless people who had died in recent months. More than 100 people marched to Boston Common to plant small wooden crosses.

*

Prior to the winter of 1981-82, **Columbus, Ohio** had virtually no emergency shelters to meet the growing needs of its poor and unemployed residents. Now the Open Shelter provides assistance to 150 men and women nightly, though a survey showed that many of the guests were using it as permanent housing, for lack of alternatives. The survey also found that 75 percent of those using the shelter were Ohio residents. A community housing task force opened a small family shelter in February 1982, and an additional 25-unit building for families is planned.

*

The Catholic Worker and the Salvation Army in **Sacramento, California** have each opened soup kitchens to feed the area's growing number of hungry and homeless people. The Salvation Army serves about 350 at its weekend meals. This is part of the Salvation Army's growing move to provide emergency services for those in need. An organizational task force reported: "[We] should be prepared . . . for either a national or a territorial campaign program for the poor . . . on the basis of a national emergency."

*

Minneapolis-St. Paul, Minnesota saw an expansion of shelters and soup kitchens in 1981-82. In November 1981, that was but a hope of the Inner Urban Catholic Coalition (IUCC), which represents 25 parishes and agencies. All of those involved were already flooded with requests for aid, and they foresaw further increases. Hundreds of people had been losing assistance payments every month, and it was only a matter of time before the community experienced more drastic consequences. About 60 percent of state General Assistance cases were terminated in July 1981, and while the $200 payments were not large, they represented a sole source of income for many.

By November. the IUCC had located 12 churches and private homes to offer temporary shelter for up to 135 people. The way was cleared for many of these sites to open when the city council lifted local zoning and housing ordinances that would have interfered with the provision of shelter.

Three of the shelters housed men, nine others took in families and single women. One, the Christ Child Center, opened for 40 women, but then sheltered men when only a few women appeared.

Food programs have also proliferated in the Twin Cities area. St. Paul's Loaves and Fishes program at the Dorothy Day Drop-In Center is one of the largest, serving about 125 people three days a week since January 1982. At Minneapolis' St. Stephen's Church, the Loaves and Fishes attendance has swelled from 107 to 260 at the end of the month. During the winter, mothers with children often comprised half the guests at month's end. Again, as thousands are dropped from public assistance and other benefits are cut or eliminated, those affected have nowhere to turn. While volunteers and food have been found to run these meal programs, inadequate resources prohibit daily operation.

*

In **Santa Rosa, California**, the Catholic Worker community opened a new storefront soup kitchen in June 1982. Only 41 people showed up that first day. Until that time, the Worker van would visit a local park and dispense sandwiches to between 50 and 100 people a day.

In line was a 38-year-old former counselor from New Mexico. In search of work and food, he had seen most of the West Coast, slept under the Golden Gate Bridge, and summed it up: "If you would have told me six months ago I'd be in this position, I'd have laughed."

The community also provides the poor of Santa Rosa and Sonoma County with other services. A twice-weekly mobile breakfast program for children serves 30 to 75; produce is also distributed to the children's families. A weekend dinner is served to older people, couples, and families, and it too is supplemented by produce and clothing distribution. Emergency shelter is offered to people over age 55.

These are testimonies to human decency, to common caring and concern. There are, unfortunately, cities and communities where the tide is running the other way, where the example set lies at the other end of the spectrum of human response. There, either fear or self-interest is the operating principle underlying policy; disregard and neglect meet the torrent of unaddressed need.

*

For two nights each month, the homeless in **Orlando, Florida**, can stay for free at the Union Rescue Mission. Officials there believe as many as 500 may be in need of the services they offer. Yet, only about 45 people each night can claim one of the blue tickets that entitle them to a bed, a shower, two meals, and clean clothes. "A fresh start to nowhere," some have called it. The suggestion that additional shelter space is needed is met with official silence.

*

Several members of the **Santa Monica, California** City Council were careful to point out that their September 1982 approval of a plan to study the housing needs of the homeless did not bind them to take any publicly-funded steps to follow up on their findings. Reverend Charles Elswick is pastor of the First Christian Church of Santa Monica, and he believes he has seen more than 1,000 homeless people there in the last five years. They "run the gamut," he says.

Santa Monica City Attorney Robert Myers claims the city has realized a substantial savings by not arresting the homeless for any but the most intolerable offenses. Using a special vagrancy detail, the city picks up people for panhandling, sleeping in parks, and urinating in public. Critics have called for harder-line measures, though, to discourage the homeless from staying; one says that fountains in public parks should be turned on at night to impede sleeping and expresses concern about any program that would attract "the deranged."

*

Hostility toward the "Joad" families of 1982 is reported to have entered the language in the form of a rather ugly term: "Black Tag People." According to news accounts in the summer of 1982, Michigan's black license plates with white letters are used to designate those coming into **Texas** in search of work. The use of "Yankees" applied to these job-seekers is not a term of endearment. A Texas union leader went so far as to announce publicly that union members should not come into the state without a job in hand. Those who do come and are disappointed find the going very hard. Welfare requirements are strict, and only Mississippi offers lower AFDC payments.

*

The National Coalition for the Homeless called trends in **Phoenix, Arizona** "an extermination program." In a July 1982 report, the Coalition recited the series of steps that led to that conclusion:

*

- *Two-thirds of the city's shelter capacity, in the form of a 100-bed men's shelter, was closed in early 1982;*

- *Two soup kitchens have been shut down;*

- *The remaining men's shelter and the Salvation Army food program were scheduled to close in August 1982;*

- *Lying down or sleeping on public property became a misdemeanor in July 1981;*

- *Soup kitchens, missions, and emergency shelters will be kept out of the downtown renewal area by a new November 1981 ordinance;*

- *After 28 years of operation, the Lighthouse Rescue Mission was condemned in early 1982 to clear the way for further development; the Helping Hand Mission almost immediately met the same fate, after 34 years of service;*

- *A local newspaper editor supported these moves with the following comment: "We didn't tolerate prostitutes - why tolerate bums?"*

The only remaining service provider for the homeless will be the St. Vincent de Paul Society, which has declared its intention to stay.

*

In **Alexandria, Virginia**, where the poor and homeless are both black and white, a local newspaper somewhat brightly reported on the presence of the needy: "They have no jobs and no real place to live." Some of the homeless interviewed for the story reported that they had lived in the area for 40 to 50 years, but their presence is displeasing to the gallery owners, craft shop operators, and bistro proprietors who have moved into the strip of vacant buildings and parking lots.

*

In **Fort Lauderdale, Florida**, in the fall of 1981, a city commissioner suggested spraying the garbage with insecticide or kerosene to discourage foraging. The way you get rid of vermin he explained, is to cut off their food supply.

*

In **St. Louis, Missouri**, the homeless live in all the customary spots, as well as in abandoned trains, near the riverfront, and in the shadow of the Gateway Arch. Inevitably they seek to be invisible, but they are unusually hard to find since St. Louis' Skid Row was bulldozed for the new Civic Center. A city-funded agency estimates there are 1,000 homeless men and women served by the fourteen overflowing shelters. Others believe the number is much higher. One of those who isn't satisfied with the city's figures is Reverend Larry Rice. At night he roams through the trains, tunnels, and vacant buildings with a flashlight and a bag of sandwiches. While he stops and prays for protection before stepping off into the dark, Rice said people don't bother him: "They're not used to preachers making house calls."

*

In **Cleveland, Ohio**, a classic case of a neighborhood in transition is presented by Ohio City. where the Ukrainian Orthodox St. Herman's House of Hospitality offers meals and beds for men. The Little Brothers of the Divine Compassion have operated the facility for five years, serving 65,000 meals in 1981 and offering 14,500 nights of shelter.

But their open-door policy has brought them up against those who would change the area. The shelter took in 71 people on a bitter night, even though municipal codes allow only 22. Inspections and harassment have followed, but the shelter's abbot was firm: ". . . there is no place for these men to go. . . I am not going to let them freeze under the Detroit-Superior Bridge."

*   *   *

There are still other cities - major ones among them - where the demands of homelessness have neither come to a boil nor intruded into official consciousness. A few bubbles may have risen to the surface, the private sector strains day after day against impossible odds, and perhaps the local government has even made a winter gesture. But of this last there is no assurance that - meaningless as it might have been - it will be repeated or continued.

*

Philadelphia is such a city. Some label the estimate of 8,000 homeless as "conservative," and there is a desperate housing crisis. More than 22,000 dwelling units are believed to be abandoned; 20,000 to 25,000 others are classified as substandard. More than 12,000 people are on the waiting list for public housing. Fire stations threw open their doors in the 1981-82 winter, and the city held a day-long conference on homelessness. But an official of the medical examiner's office warily states: at least a dozen homeless people die in the winter - and don't use my name. An intensive local newspaper series examined the plight of the forgotten mental patient, but the needed strides have not been made. Whither the "City of Brotherly Love"?

*

The story in **Baltimore, Maryland**, is very similar. A network of small private shelters offers a variety of services. In September 1981, a group of providers met with Mayor William Schaefer, which resulted in the opening of an old public school building for that winter. A long-needed study of homeless women in the city was released about the same time. But the school was not accessible or congenial, and the report addressed but one half of the problem, for shelter for the thousands of men on Baltimore's streets is still provided by the traditional sources, the handful of local missions. Nor is there daytime drop-in space for men. Baltimore, which has waged the gentrification and renovation campaign for longer than many other cities, needs the flame of advocacy renewed. A city so proud of its working-class roots should not be so far removed from those in need.

*

Finally, **Los Angeles**. The private sector is well-grounded there; its Union Rescue Mission is the largest in the world, and the third oldest in the country. But, before celebrating its ninetieth birthday in 1981, the Mission began turning people away for the first time. Its 350 beds and 350 chairs were filled and overflowing. Along with many Western cities, Los Angeles is feeling the strain as an avalanche of young job-seekers hits town from points east. Housing is the number one problem. The Missionaries of Charity and the Catholic Worker community offer a variety of services from shelter to food to a bakery where a few of the jobless can work, but the struggle is uphill; this mountain of need is at odds with prevailing resources.

For some people the American dream has gone as sour as month-old milk. To the few hundred men who spend their nights at the Union Rescue Mission in downtown Los Angeles, the ambitious, aggressive, goal-oriented world of mainstream America is a faraway illusion. These men are the leftovers, the refuse, the ones who lost their way on the road to Dale Carnegie success...

... Somehow you can sympathize with the plight of these men and the pleasure they must feel in little things, like finally being able to take a shower or get a pair of shoes. It is comfortable to believe in the myth that these people are different fundamentally than you or me. That way you don't have to take the trouble of discovering how, in fact, a little of them is inside each of us. One small detour in the road of life and any of us could have passed through the Mission, despite the college education, the good job, and the supportive family. That is a scary proposition. They don't look any differently at this out-of-place guy taking notes than they do at each other. They know what I did not when I walked in - that indeed we are a family and all must come to the desperate realization that time and life are constantly running out.[1]

Footnotes

[1] "Mission: Impoverished," by Sal Manna, *LA Reader*, April 3, 1981.

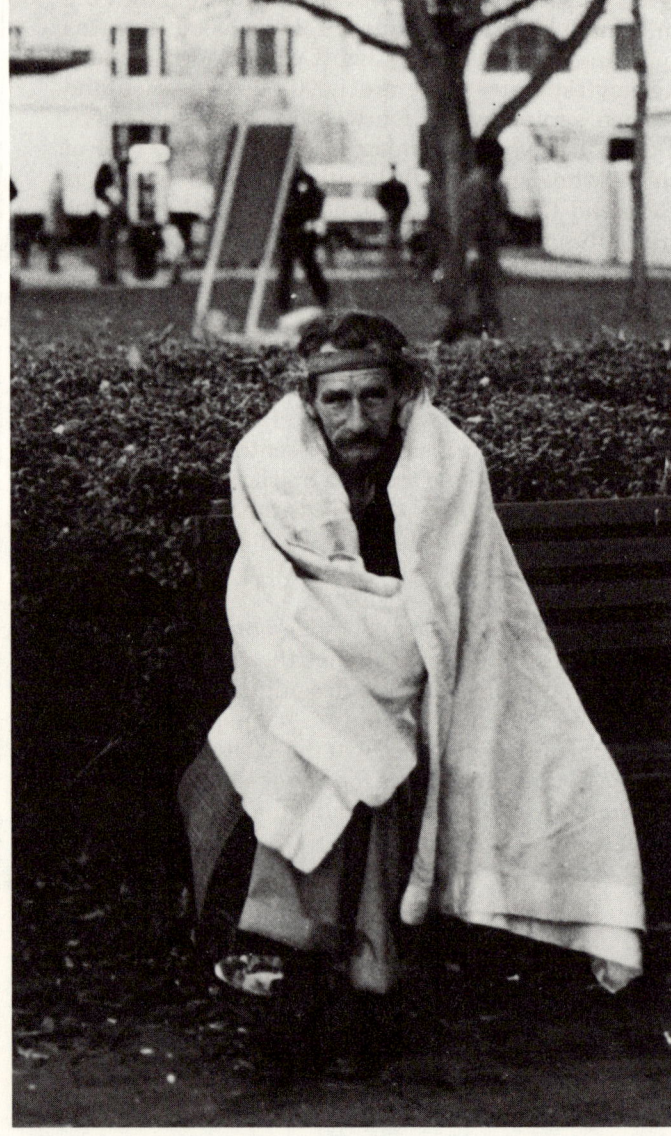

Oral Testimony

On September 30, 1980, Community for Creative Non-Violence members Mary Ellen Hombs and Mitch Snyder appeared before the House District Committee, accompanied by the cremated remains of "John Doe," the first homeless person to freeze to death during the previous winter. Snyder was specially released, for a few hours, from a 60-day jail term that he was serving for an unlawful entry conviction, resulting from accompanying homeless friends to St. Matthew's Cathedral for shelter during a snowstorm on February 9, 1980. Hombs and Snyder made the following comments:

These are the cremated remains of a human being, a man who froze to death last winter, homeless and alone. He was known only as "John Doe."

Over the past five years in the District of Columbia, 29 other people have met the same fate - victims of exposure, indifference, and injustice. Let the bones of this dead man, then, provide the context and the framework within which all that we say is offered.

Envision, if you will, an infinitely long line of people, stretching - five, ten, twenty abreast - as far as the eye can see. There are literally millions of them - men, women, and children. Slowly, painfully, some walking, others shuffling, limping, crawling, they pass before you. These are our nation's untouchables. America's pariah: invisible, disposable, surplus. They are the destitute homeless.

Some are old, all rags and bags, long hair and bushy beards stained yellow with dirt. The pockets of their tattered overcoats and their shopping bags stuffed and bulging with all the little rubbish they collect and live on. Filthy and suffering. Bent and twisted by the downward curve of hunger, desperation, want.

Some are senile. Others alcoholic. There are the autistic, and there are those who talk to God - and to themselves. There are many who cannot even tie their shoelaces without assistance.

There are the amputees and the double amputees. There are the lame, the halt, and the blind. Bodies broken, spirits equally disfigured.

There are the displaced, the disenfranchised, the dispossessed. Madonnas with child, for whom there is no rest and no inn.

Some are children, living alone in a cruel, hard, violent, and selfish world, destined themselves to become cruel, hard, violent, and selfish.

Many are young. Most are black or brown or Latino. Strong. Willing. Able. Unemployed. Unabsorbed. Underdeveloped. Overexposed. Scarred, inside and out, with the jagged wounds of our dirty little war, and our dirty little world. Like fuses, they burn, slowly and surely, fueled by hate, bitterness, and fury.

This is the vast army of America's homeless: the progeny of our ignorance, our indifference, our insulation, and our pathological demand for conformity and productivity. They are a reflection of our unwillingness to confront difficult problems. We point with pride to our forefathers and mothers who fled religious persecution and, in so doing, founded this nation. Yet rarely does it occur to anyone that running from injustice or oppression is not a virtue. But run they did, and we have been chasing our own tails ever since.

Driven by they know not what, the homeless are always on the move: looking for food, clothing, shelter, work; searching, endlessly, for all the prerequisites and necessities of life. They are constantly running, hiding from the voice on high which decrees: "You don't belong here. You-don't-belong. You there! Don't be long! Move on! Move on!"

Hungry, haggard, cold, lonely, frightened, confused, helpless, hopeless, restless, ragged, empty, defeated. Begging, thieving, hawking, selling; silent - transparent - innocent - innocent? In utter and abject misery, they continue to file by.

Row after row, wave after wave passes, assaulting your mind until it grows numb. Each is unique, yet all share a point of commonality: there is no one, not church, nor state, not you, nor I, there is absolutely nobody who cares enough to reach out and bring them back.

How many people in the District of Columbia are homeless? Thousands. How many nationally? Millions. Of that much we are certain.

Precisely how many? Who knows? Certainly not the government. Nor the professionals. Not the religious community. Not even those who work with the homeless know for sure.

We have been told that, in Chicago, there are approximately 1,000 homeless people. We have also been told that, in Chicago, there are nearly 250,000 homeless people. What do the experts say? Those *are* the experts.

In Manhattan, some claim there are less than 10,000 on the streets, while others estimate more than 75,000.

In Baltimore? Take your choice: 320 or 8,000, depending on who you ask.

Those most directly serving D.C.'s street people were asked, "How many?" Their estimates range from 300 to 15,000. There is, however, some agreement in one area: the number of people on the streets of this country has increased dramatically.

Do you get the picture? The picture is: there is no picture. We will discover how many people are on the streets only after they have come inside.

District of Columbia officials acknowledge the existence of a few hundred hard-core street people. "Hundreds," they say. "What's all this nonsense about thousands?" they say. "Exaggeration! Rhetoric! Hyperbole!" they say. But they also say in hushed tones, and only when talking to each other, that more than 12,000 homeless men have passed through the city-operated and city-funded shelters in 26 months.

Why the reluctance on the part of government to acknowledge the dimensions or, in some cases, the very existence of the problem? Simple: who is going to pay for the solution? Besides, as a local judge once commented, the issue lacks "sex appeal." Who cares? Once we've watched a war on television, who is shocked by this? Incensed? Where's the advocacy? The outcry? Then, too, the homeless themselves lack any semblance of power: they don't vote, or consume, and they aren't organized. Statistically, they don't even exist.

Where do the homeless come from? Why are their numbers growing? To those questions, we can provide more definitive answers.

Despite lingering images of street people as "dirty, lazy, drunken bums," those stereotypes bear little, if any, resemblance to the reality of 1980. Nor are the labels "wino" or "tramp" just or accurate in describing today's chronically homeless individual.

Some of the conditions contributing to the increase in homelessness are: 1) **double-digit inflation**, especially as it impacts on fixed incomes; 2) **unemployment**, particularly among minority youth where the rate is running between 40 and 60 percent; 3) the abysmal failure of the **deinstitutionalization** of the nation's mental health system; 4) the wide-spread **shortage of affordable housing**; 5) the **breakdown of traditional social structures, relationships, and responsibilities**; and, 6) the effects of **inflation/recession/depression**, coupled with an increasingly conservative mood in the country and a corresponding decline in social spending.

The situation is simple and dangerous: we continue to cut back on basic services that are necessary for survival, while simultaneously and rapidly adding to the body of people who must rely on these services for their very existence. We would not be exaggerating in describing the situation as critical and explosive. We must constantly and forcefully remind one another, before it is too late, that those who have nothing, have nothing to lose.

We must also bear in mind that the problem of homelessness cannot be effectively resolved in isolation, for it is merely symptomatic of a deeper, systemic ill: an inevitable contradiction that is inherent in a society based on the fallacy that, through isolation, competition, and self-interest, we build a better world.

In December 1976, when we opened our home to those in need of shelter, there were three existing facilities with a total of 174 beds, including ten for women. Currently, there are 500 beds for men, and there is space for 122 women, with two additional 30-bed shelters for women scheduled to open within six weeks.

That's the good news. The not-so-good news is that more than $20 million, in local and federal funds, is spent on overinstitutionalization and the District's emergency shelter program. The waste, human and financial, is staggering. We have, with no success, consistently reminded the mayor, the city council, and appropriate DHS officials that, within 60 to 90 days, that figure could be cut by 75 to 80 percent, with an improvement in the quality and delivery of services.

The bad news is that, by any rational and humane standards, the conditions prevailing within the two municipal shelters for men are completely intolerable and unacceptable. Despite the waste, the filth, the mismanagement, the theft, the dehumanization, and the brutality, we fight to keep them open. Why? Because for those who are willing to use the shelters, in spite of the conditions, the alternative is so much worse.

Obviously, something is very wrong. What is wrong is that the chronically destitute homeless are missing persons, absent from our consciousness, our deliberations, and our lives. Their suffering, which should be most concrete and visible, has become abstract and unseen. Therefore, the homeless find themselves, transparent and alone, standing outside the range of institutional possibilities.

We have built a wall between ourselves and those who have no place to lay their heads. That wall must come down, and it must come down now. The homeless demand shelter, not excuses. They demand dignity and not the demeaning that comes from sleeping on the street. They demand that the insulation of our lives be broken by the payment of the debt of our neglect. They demand that, here and now, in the wealthiest nation on the face of the earth, basic shelter be recognized politically, philosophically, and programmatically as an absolute and inalienable human right. Since these are times of modest expectations, our goal is simple: the creation of adequate, accessible space, offered in an atmosphere of reasonable dignity, for every man, woman, and child who needs and wants to get off the street.

It has been our experience that neither commitment, nor creativity, nor energy, nor any of the other resources necessary to facilitate the realization of that goal appear unless and until people take it all very seriously and very personally.

We have come here to educate, to incite, to beg, to plead, to do anything within our power to encourage you to do everything within *your* power to rid this nation, now and for all time, of this horrible human tragedy. For, if you act intelligently, compassionately, responsibly, humanely, and quickly, you *will* make a difference. That is the hope, the prayer, the expectation, and the demand that we have brought with us this morning.

Since Asheville, North Carolina is one of the cities we looked at in preparing the report which we have put together for this committee, we thought it appropriate to conclude our testimony with a passage written by one of Asheville's native sons, Thomas Wolfe, from "You Can't Go Home Again."

On his nocturnal ramblings about New York, he would observe the homeless men who prowled in the vicinity of restaurants, lifting the lids of garbage cans and searching around inside for morsels of rotten food. He saw them everywhere, and noticed how their numbers increased.... He found out the various places all over the city where such men slept at night.

It was his custom almost every night, at one o'clock or later, to walk across the Brooklyn Bridge, and night after night, with a horrible fascination, he used to go to the public latrine, or "comfort station" which was directly in front of the New York City Hall. One descended to this place down a steep flight of stairs from the street, and on bitter nights he would find the place crowded with homeless men who had sought refuge there.... Most of them were just flotsam of the general ruin of the time — honest, decent, middle-aged men with their faces seamed by toil and want, and young men, many of them mere boys in their teens, with thick, unkempt hair. These were the wanderers, ... [who] drifted across the land and gathered in the big cities when winter came.... Here in New York, in this obscene meeting place, these derelicts came, drawn into a common stew of rest and warmth and a little surcease from their desperation.

George had never before witnessed anything to equal the indignity and sheer animal horror of the scene. There was even a kind of devil's comedy in the sight of all these filthy men squatting upon those open, doorless stools. Arguments ... would sometimes break out among them over the possession of these stools, which all of them wanted more for rest than for necessity. The sight was revolting, disgusting, enough to render a man forever speechless with very pity.

He would talk to the men and find out all he could about them, and when he could stand it no more he would come out of this hole of filth and suffering, and there, twenty feet above it, he would see the giant hackles of Manhattan shining coldly in the cruel brightness of the winter night. The Woolworth Building was not fifty yards away, and a little further down were the silvery spires and needles of Wall Street, great fortresses of stone and steel that housed enormous banks. The blind injustice of this contrast seemed the most brutal part of the whole experience, for there, all around him in the cold moonlight, only a few blocks away from this abyss of human wretchedness and misery, blazed the pinnacles of power where a large portion of the entire world's wealth was locked in mighty vaults.... I think the life we have fashioned in America, and which has fashioned us — the forms we made, the cells that grew, the honeycomb that was created — was self-destructive in nature, and must be destroyed. I think these forms are dying and must die, just as I know that America and the people in it are deathless, undiscovered, and immortal, and must live.

I think the true discovery of America is before us. I think the true fulfillment of our spirit, of our people ... is yet to come. I think the true discovery of our own democracy is still before us. ...

I think the enemy is here before us, too. . . . I think the enemy is here before us with a thousand faces, but I think we know that all his faces wear one mask. I think the enemy is single selfishness and compulsive greed. I think the enemy is blind, but has the brutal power of his blind grab. I do not think the enemy was born yesterday, or that he grew to manhood forty years ago, or that we began without the enemy, and that our vision faltered, that we lost the way, and suddenly were in his camp. I think the enemy is old as Time, and evil as Hell, and that he has been here with us from the beginning. I think he stole our earth from us, destroyed our wealth, and ravaged and despoiled our land. I think he took our people and enslaved them, that he polluted the fountains of our life, took unto himself the rarest treasures of our own possession, took our bread and left us with a crust, and, not content, for the nature of the enemy is insatiate, tries finally to take from us the crust.

I think the enemy comes to us with the face of innocence and says to us:

"I am your friend."

I think the enemy deceives us with false words and lying phrases, saying:

"See, I am one of you — I am one of your children, your son, your brother, and your friend. Behold how sleek and fat I have become — and all because I am just one of you, and your friend. Behold how rich and powerful I am — and all because I am one of you, your humble brother and your friend. Behold," cries Enemy, "the man I am, the man I have become, the thing I have accomplished — and reflect. Will you destroy this thing? I assure you that it is the most precious thing you have. It is yourselves, the projection of each of you, the triumph of your individual lives, the thing that is rooted in your blood, and native to your stock, and inherent in the traditions of America. It is the thing that all of you may hope to be," says Enemy, "for —" humbly — "am I not just one of you? Am I not just your brother and your son? Am I not the living image of what each of you may hope to be, would wish to be, would desire for his own son? Would you destroy this glorious incarnation of your own heroic self? If you do, then," says Enemy, "you destroy yourselves — you kill the thing that is most gloriously American, and in so killing, kill yourselves."

He lies! And now we know he lies! He is not gloriously, or in any other way ourselves. He is not our friend, our son, our brother. And he is not American! For, although he has a thousand familiar and convenient faces, his own true face is as old as Hell.

Look about you and see what he has done.

Reprinted with permission of Harper & Row, Publishers.

Appendices

Some Important Resources

A Proposed Policy Toward
the Elimination of Homelessness
in the District of Columbia

Directory

A Proposed Policy Toward the Elimination of Homelessness in the District of Columbia

The following is a model for the provision of shelter involving all sectors of the community. It is offered in the hope that it may be of value to those who, in government or in the private sector, want to initiate an emergency shelter program that is both cost-efficient and humane. It was adopted by D.C. Mayor Marion Barry on February 14, 1979.

* * *

Something is very wrong. What is wrong is that the walking homeless, the street people, have become missing persons: missing from our consciousness and our deliberations. Therefore, they stand outside the range of institutional possibilities; they have become America's untouchables.

As a result, human beings, God's children all, freeze to death for lack of shelter, or, more accurately they are killed by lack of concern. Some die quickly in abandoned buildings, during snowstorms; some die by degrees, slowly tortured on the rack of poverty. Human suffering, which should be concrete and visible, has become abstract and unseen.

We have built a wall between ourselves and those who have no place to lay their heads. That wall must come down, and it must come down now. The homeless demand shelter, not excuses. They demand dignity and not the demeaning that comes from sleeping on the street. They demand that the insulation of our lives be broken by paying the debt of our neglect. They demand that here and now, in the capital of the wealthiest nation on earth, basic shelter and adequate nutrition be recognized politically, philosophically, and programmatically as an absolute and inalienable human right.

GOALS

The creation of adequate, accessible space, offered in an atmosphere of reasonable dignity, for every man, woman, and child in the District of Columbia who needs and wants shelter, leading to the rapid elimination of homelessness.

The proposed policy is, in part, a response to the diminishing nature of government resources, and the growing recognition that government should not be entrusted with the solution of all problems. The model of cooperation that this policy sets forward will serve as an example for other municipalities faced with the same problems and the same opportunities. In undertaking this effort, the District of Columbia will set the example and lead the way to the eventual elimination of homelessness throughout the country.

DEFINITION OF HOMELESSNESS

The only judge of an individual's need for shelter should be that individual. While it might appear that someone has viable alternatives available, those options cannot be assessed by a third party who has little or no knowledge of their adequacy, emotional ramifications, or other limiting factors. Given the nature of basic shelter, which will never pose a serious challenge to a room or a home of one's own, anyone who requests or is in apparent need of shelter is entitled to it. Yet, every effort must be made commensurate with the development of personal relationships, to aid in the creation of viable alternatives for the homeless.

NEED

During the past two years, 24 people have died of exposure in the District of Columbia.

On any given night, when available shelter space is occupied, it is still possible to count hundreds of people who are homeless and must remain on the street. While the need for additional shelter space is clearly demonstrable and apparent, it is also, at the present time, undetermined. The homeless refuse to stand still and be counted. Nor will they register for the census.

There is no city in the United States that has either accurately determined or met the need for shelter. In part, this is a result of a traditional, but, in this situation, faulty approach. We must reverse this process, realizing that it will only be possible to gain an accurate understanding of the need after it has been met. Consequently, only through the creation of adequate, accessible space, offered in an environment that insures human dignity, will we be able to bring the homeless inside, and finally be able to count them.

While we must proceed with a proportionate sense of urgency, we must also understand that many street people have been deeply hurt and alienated over the years. Many will come to the shelters slowly, and then only if our efforts are sincere and our approach one of justice and right, rather than charity.

RESOURCES

The government has a primary responsibility to respond to the needs of the homeless, as well as having access to the resources necessary to meet that need. Yet, we live in a participatory democracy, where each of us has a direct responsibility for the maintenance of our environment, and the care of the neediest members of our society. The private sector must assume its role in augmenting the efforts of the government, to provide the financial, physical, and human resources required to meet the needs of the homeless.

The business and religious communities must couple their involvement with the participation of concerned citizens in the effort to provide shelter.

Most importantly, the homeless must have the opportunity to become a part of that process, allowing for the self-help contribution to equal participation. Each segment of the community must be encouraged to contribute to that effort in the most cost-efficient manner, but in such a way as to create the quality services to which all are entitled.

Government, at the highest levels, must take the lead in calling forth these resources by initiating a highly public and aggressive campaign to elicit participation. That is, we believe, a realistic approach to responding to the needs of the homeless, as well as establishing a viable, new, creative, and dynamic approach that combines the efforts of the entire community to address common concerns.

It is within that framework that a Mayor's Advisory Commission on the Homeless will be formed. The Commission will be composed of representatives of the religious and business community, government, and the homeless. The role of the Commission will be:

A. To report directly to the Mayor, on the quality and development of shelter.
B. To serve as liaison between the public and private sectors.
C. To actively participate in the ongoing development of resources.
D. To insure the quality and quantity of service in the emergency shelters.
E. To approve all contracts for providing shelter which DHR might choose to negotiate.
F. To improve and develop present policies and programs to better serve these groups within the population receiving shelter according to their unique needs: the elderly, the psychologically and physically disabled, alcoholics, and others

SUMMARY

To expedite the implementation of the proposed policy regarding the creation of adequate, accessible shelter space, leading to the elimination of homelessness in the District of Columbia, and recognizing that winter weather is an immediate peril to life and health, the following must occur with suitable speed:
1. A meeting of representatives of the committee drafting this statement and the Community for Creative Non-Violence with the Mayor and appropriate government officials, and
2. The creation of the Mayor's Advisory Commission on the Homeless.

PROGRAM

I. . . . . . . ACCESSIBILITY
II . . . . . . SERVICE
III. . . . . ENVIRONMENT

I. ACCESSIBILITY

A. *Location*   The location of shelter should be decentralized and based upon the needs of the population they are serving. That is, as much as possible shelters should be within walking distance of the people to be served rather than a distance which would require extensive outreach in order to transport them to shelter.
B. *Neighborhood Support*   Neighborhood support for locating and maintaining shelters will be aggressively sought.
C. *Hospitality Centers*   Where it is not possible to locate a facility so that all in need of shelter in a particular quadrant of the city are within walking distance of that facility, Hospitality Centers would serve as gathering areas where street people could rest and wait to be picked up and brought to the nearest shelter.
D. *Transportation*   Where shelters are located some distance from the areas where street people spend their days, free transportation will be provided from the Hospitality Center to the shelters, and back again the following morning.
E. *Hours of Opening/Closing*   In the establishment of hours of opening of particular shelters, seasonal weather conditions will be a primary governing factor outside of the basic expectation of providing guests with at least eight hours of rest. Every effort will be made to allow guests to remain at the shelter or to provide access to alternative shelters during inclement weather.
F. *Shelter Operation*   The shelters will operate on a year-round basis.

II. SERVICE

A. *Bathrooms*   All shelters must have adequate and operable toilet facilities.
B. *Showers*   All shelters must have adequate and operable shower facilities.
C. *Toilet Articles*   All shelters will provide needed toiletry articles.
D. *Bedding*   All shelters will provide adequate and comfortable sleeping facilities.
E. *Clothing*   All shelters will provide guests with pajamas and slippers. Shelters will also be able to distribute other articles of clothing donated by the community at large.
F. *Food*   All shelters will provide their guests with a hot evening meal and with breakfast in the morning. Where possible the food will be prepared at the shelter itself. The purpose for this is twofold. It is less expensive to buy bulk food and have volunteers prepare it, and it affords an opportunity to include the guests in the work of running and maintaining the shelters.
G. *Recreation*   Each shelter will have a common area where guests will be able to socialize with staff, volunteers, and amongst themselves. The wherewithal for appropriate recreational and leisure-time activities will be provided.
H. *Medical Facilities*   Every effort will be made to provide on-site medical care and mental health services for persons utilizing the shelters.
I. *Laundry Facilities*   Adequate laundry facilities will be provided.
J. *Storage Facilities*   Adequate storage facilities will be provided to protect valuables of the guests.

III. ENVIRONMENT

A. *Intake Procedure*   People will be welcomed to the shelter, informally asked their names, and directed to the various services they might wish to avail themselves of.
B. *Atmosphere*   A pleasant, emotionally inviting, and home-like atmosphere will be created in the shelters.
C. *Level of Equality*   It is very important that there is nothing and no one in the shelters which creates the impression that guests are inferior or second class citzens. Guests must not be herded or ordered but at all times treated courteously and with respect.
D. *Structure for Development*   Each shelter will structure in opportunities for guests to take responsibility by participating in the maintenance and operation of the shelter. Such a program will include several levels of participation leading toward guests becoming members of the staff or toward their referral to outside job opportunities.
E. *Referrals*   Every shelter will have someone capable of referring individuals to outside job opportunities, and other available and appropriate resources.
F. *Staff/Volunteer Levels*   Adequate numbers of staff and volunteers will be present at all times in all shelters and Hospitality Centers.

Directory

- **Alabama**

    Catholic Relief Services
    P.O. Box 759
    Mobile 36601
    (205) 438-1603

- **Arizona**

    Saint Vincent dePaul
    119 South 9th Avenue
    Phoenix 83054
    (602) 258-5619

    Second Harvest
    National Food Bank
    1001 North Central
    Suite 303
    Phoenix 85005
    (602) 252-1777

- **California**

    Catholic Worker Community
    632 Brittania Avenue
    Los Angeles 90033
    (213) 267-8789

    Union Rescue Mission
    226 South Main Street
    Los Angeles 90012
    (213) 628-6103

    Catholic Worker
    619 12th Street
    Sacramento 95814
    (916) 442-5321

    Salvation Army
    2550 Alhambra Boulevard
    Sacramento 95817
    (916) 452-2968

    Martin DePorres House of Hospitality
    2826 23 Street
    San Francisco 94110
    (415) 647-9934

    First Christian Church
    609 Arizona Avenue
    Santa Monica 90401
    (213) 273-3350

    Catholic Worker
    606 Wilson Street
    Santa Rosa 95401
    (707) 573-8342

- **Colorado**

    Citizens Coalition for Shelter
    Ann Presley, Contact
    1134 East Linvale Drive
    Aurora 80014
    (303) 361-4041, 751-2323

    Denver Rescue Mission
    23rd and Lawrence Street
    Denver 80205
    (303) 534-7448

    Holy Ghost Church
    633 19th Street
    Denver 80202
    (303) 571-1556

- **Connecticut**

    New Haven Food Salvage Project
    5241 Yale Station
    New Haven 06520
    (203) 436-1480

    The Soup Kitchen
    79 Beacon Street
    Waterbury 06721
    (203) 753-5676

District of Columbia

Catholic Charities
2800 Otis Street, N.E.
20018
(202) 526-4100

Community for Creative Non-Violence
1345 Euclid Street, N.W.
20009
(202) 332-4332

Food Research and Action Center
1319 F Street, N.W.
20004
(202) 393-5060

Coalition for the Homeless
1419 V Street, N.W.
Room 303
20009
(202) 328-1184

Luther Place Memorial Church
1226 Vermont Avenue, N.W.
20005
(202) 667-1377

Martha's Table/McKenna's Wagon
2437 15th Street, N.W.
20009
(202) 328-6608

Sacred Heart Parish
16th Street and Park Road, N.W.
20010
(202) 234-8000

Saint Elizabeths Hospital
2690 Martin Luther King Avenue, S.E.
20032
(202) 562-4000

Saint Paul's Episcopal Church
2430 K Street, N.W.
20037
(202) 337-2020

Saint Stephen and the Incarnation Episcopal Church
16th and Newton Streets, N.W.
20010
(202) 265-0142

So Others May Eat (SOME)
71 O Street, N.W.
20001
(202) 797-8806

Special Approaches to Juvenile Assistance
SAJA House
745 18th Street, N.W.
20006
(202) 396-1400

Florida

Union Rescue Mission
410 West Central Boulevard
Orlando 32801
(305) 422-4855

Georgia

All Saints Episcopal Church
634 West Peachtree Street, N.W.
Atlanta 30308
(404) 881-0835

Central Presbyterian Church
210 Washington Street, S.W.
Atlanta 30303
(404) 659-0274

Clifton Presbyterian Church
369 Connecticut Avenue, N.E.
Atlanta 30307
(404) 373-3253

Men's Union Mission
54 Ellis Street, N.E.
Atlanta 30303
(404) 659-1708

Open Door Community
910 Ponce de Leon Avenue, N.E.
Atlanta 30306
(404) 377-2110, 874-9652

Saint Luke's Episcopal Church
435 Peachtree Street, N.E.
Atlanta 30308
(404) 837-5427

Trinity United Methodist Church
265 Washington Street, S.W.
Atlanta 30303
(404) 659-6236

Oakhurst Baptist Church
222 Eastlake Drive
Decatur 30030
(404) 378-3677

Diocesan Office for Social Ministry
P.O. Box 14685
Savannah 31406
(912) 352-4992

- **Illinois**

American Indian Center
1630 West Wilson Avenue
Chicago 60640
(312) 275-5871

The Brandecker Lodge
9451 South Hoyne Street
Chicago 60620
(312) 239-2191

Cathedral Shelter
207 South Ashland Avenue
Chicago 60607
(312) 666-3645

Chicago Christian Industrial League
123 South Green
Chicago 60607
(312) 666-2475

Chicago Christian Industrial League
817 West Monroe
Chicago 60607
(312) 666-3474

Chicago Gospel Mission
1125 West Madison
Chicago 60607
(312) 421-8043

8th Day Center For Justice
22 East Van Buren Street
Chicago 60605
(312) 427-4351

Gospel Brothers
933 West Gordon Terrace
Chicago 60613
phone unknown

Gospel League Home
955 West Grand Avenue
Chicago 60622
(312) 243-2480

Hamlin House
1061 West Van Buren Street
Chicago 60607
(312) 666-3333

Helping Hand Mission
111 South Green Street
Chicago 60607
(312) 666-2183

Holy Cross Mission Chapel
126 Des Plaines Avenue
Chicago 60606
(312) 236-5172

The Olive Branch Mission
1047 West Madison Street
Chicago 60607
(312) 243-3373

Pacific Garden Mission
646 South State Street
Chicago 60605
(312) 922-1462

Saint Francis of Assisi House of Hospitality
4652 North Kenmore
Chicago 60640
(312) 561-5073

Saint Pius V Catholic Church
1919 South Ashland Avenue
Chicago 60608
(312) 226-6161

Sarah's Circle
4743 North Kenmore Avenue
Chicago 60640
(312) 561-8842

Covenant Community
1745 Hinman
Evanston 60201
(312) 864-2320

- **Iowa**

Catholic Worker House
713 Indiana
Des Moines 50314
(515) 243-0765

- **Louisiana**

Christian Service Center
505 North Bailey
Abbeyville 70510
(318) 893-6300

Association of Community Organizations for Reform Now (ACORN)
628 Baronne
New Orleans 70113
(504) 525-7110

- **Maryland**

Viva House
26 South Mount Street
Baltimore 21223
(301) 233-2049

- **Massachusetts**

Franciscans of Saint Anthony's Shrine
100 Arch Street
Boston 02110
(617) 542-6440

Haley House
23 Dartmouth Street
Boston 02116
(617) 262-2940, 266-8081

Massachusetts Coalition for the Homeless
34½ Beacon Street
Room 703
Boston 02108
(617) 523-6400 ext. 594

The Pine Street Inn
60 Bristol Street
Boston 02141
(617) 482-4944

Mustard Seed
93 Piedmont Street
Worcester 01609
(617) 752-3905

- **Michigan**

Capuchin Missions Brothers Soup Kitchen
1740 Mount Eliot
Detroit 48207
(313) 579-2100

Coalition on Temporary Shelter (COTS)
1950 Trumbull Avenue
Detroit 48216
(313) 496-0509

Manna Community Meal/Manna Kitchen
1950 Trumbull Avenue
Detroit 48216
(313) 963-8708

- **Minnesota**

Christ Child Center
3801 42nd Avenue, South
Minneapolis 55406
(612) 722-4658

The Salvation Army's Harbour Light
706 1st Avenue, North
Minneapolis 55403
(612) 338-0113

Inner Urban Catholic Coalition
328 West 6th Street
Saint Paul 55102
(612) 291-1815

Saint Paul Loaves and Fishes Program
51 West 9th Street
Saint Paul 55102
(612) 293-0633

- **Mississippi**

Stewpot Soup Kitchen
1103 West Capitol
Jackson 39203
(601) 352-8431

Voice of Calvary
1655 Saint Charles Street
Jackson 39209
(601) 353-1635

• Missouri

Holy Family Catholic Worker
912 East 31 Street
Kansas City 64109
(816) 753-2677

Cass Catholic Worker Community
1849 Cass Avenue
Saint Louis 63106
(314) 621-3085

Nebraska

Catholic Social Service Bureau
P.O. Box 2723
Lincoln 68502
(402) 423-6555

• New Jersey

Leavenhouse
644 State Street
Camden 08108
(609) 966-4596

• New York

Arthur Sheehan House of Hospitality
314 4th Street
Brooklyn 11215
(212) 788-1425

Catholic Charities
191 Joralemon Street
Brooklyn 11201
(212) 596-5500

Grace Episcopal Church
12 Depot
Middleton 10940
(914) 343-6101

Coalition for the Homeless
105 East 22nd Street
New York 10010
(212) 460-8110

Community Service Society
105 East 22nd Street
New York 10010
(212) 254-8900

Manhattan Bowery Project
8 East 3rd Street
New York 10003
(212) 533-8400

Legal Services for the Elderly Poor
132 West 43rd Street
3rd Floor
New York 10036
(212) 391-0120

Rochester Catholic Worker
124 Evergreen Street
Rochester 14605
(716) 232-3656

• North Carolina

Shepherd's Table Soup Kitchen
Church of the Good Shepherd (Episcopal)
215 McDowell Street
Raleigh 27603
(919) 828-0863

• North Dakota

Lutheran Social Services of North Dakota
1325 South 11 Street
Fargo 58107
(701) 235-7341

• Ohio

Saint Herman's Ukranian Orthodox Church
House of Hospitality - Little Brothers of the Divine Compassion
4410 Franklin Boulevard
Cleveland 44107
(216) 631-9860

The Hunger Task Force of Ohio
447 East Broad Street
Columbus 43215
(614) 464-1956

Dayton Free Clinic
1133 Salem Avenue
Dayton 45406
(513) 278-9481

The House of the People
P.O. Box 241
Dayton 45406
(513) 226-1270

- **Oklahoma**

United Methodist Cooperative Ministries
125 West 3rd Street
Room 202
Tulsa 74103
(918) 582-5766

South Carolina

Grace Episcopal Church
711 McDuffy Street
Anderson 29624
(803) 225-8011

Christ Episcopal Church Project HOST
10 North Church Street
Greenville 29601
(803) 271-8773

- **Tennessee**

Memphis Catholic Worker
4385 Given
Memphis 38122
(901) 685-1579

- **Texas**

Casa Juan Diego
P.O. Box 70113
Houston 77007
(713) 869-7376

- **Virginia**

Mondloch House II
c/o Eleanor Kennedy, Director
United Community Ministries
6206 North Kings Highway
Alexandria 22303
(703) 768-7106

Saint Mary's Church
921 Holt Street
Norfolk 23504
(804) 622-4487

Emergency Shelter, Inc.
2 East Main Street
Richmond 23219
(804) 782-9276

Grace House
1116 Floyd Avenue
Richmond 23220
(804) 358-4939

Salvation Army
2010 Farnham Road
Richmond 23236
(804) 270-5461

- **Washington**

Blessed Sacrament Church
5041 9th Avenue, N.E.
Seattle 98105
(206) 632-4390

- **West Virginia**

Romero House of Hospitality
P.O. Box 942
Morgantown 26505
(304) 291-1418

- **Wisconsin**

Casa Maria
1113 North 21st Street
Milwaukee 53233
(414) 344-5743

Some Important Resources

Baxter, Ellen, and Hopper, Kim. *Homeless Adults on the Streets of New York City*. New York: Community Service Society (Institute for Social Welfare Research), February, 1981.

Hopper, Kim; Baxter, E.; Cox, S.; and Klein, L. *One Year Later: The Homeless Poor in New York City, 1982*. New York: Community Service Society (Institute for Social Welfare Research), May 1982.

Mayor's Emergency Shelter Task Force, *Report and Recommendations of the Mayor's Emergency Shelter Task Force*. Richmond, Virginia, June 1981.

Walsh, Brendan, and Davenport, D. *The Long Loneliness in Baltimore: A Study of Homeless Women*. Baltimore, September 1981.

About This Book

This book was written by members of the Community for Creative Non-Violence (except where indicated). CCNV also handled all aspects of production up to the point of offset printing, and the Community will distribute the completed book on a not-for-profit basis.

For information on purchasing copies, please contact:

Homelessness in America
Community for Creative Non-Violence
1345 Euclid Street, N.W.
Washington, D.C. 20009
(202) 332-4332

The Community for Creative Non-Violence

4261-4
5-42